Indian Superfood

Superfood + Superspices = Indian Superfood

A.

Gurpareet Bains

For anyone who dares to dream.
Keep reaching for your star.
Never give up. Never give in.

First published in Great Britain
in 2010 by

Absolute Press
Scarborough House
29 James Street West
Bath BA1 2BT
Phone 44 (0) 1225 316013
Fax 44 (0) 1225 445836
E-mail info@absolutepress.co.uk
Website www.absolutepress.co.uk

Reprinted 2011 (twice)

Text copyright
Gurpareet Bains
Photography copyright
Lara Holmes

Publisher Jon Croft
Commissioning Editor Meg Avent
First Editor Muzaffar Shafi
Book Editor Anne Sheasby
Art Direction and Design
Matt Inwood and Claire Siggery
Publishing Assistant Andrea O'Connor
Photographer Lara Holmes
Food Stylist Aya Nishimura

A catalogue record of this book is
available from the British Library.

ISBN 9781906650292

Printed and bound in Spain
by Graphy Cems

A note about the text
This book is set in Helvetica Neue.
Helvetica was designed in 1957 by
Max Miedinger of the Swiss-based
Haas foundry. In the early 1980s,
Linotype redrew the entire Helvetica
family. The result was Helvetica Neue

Contents

Foreword

For as far back as I can remember, I have always liked to cook. My Mum often reminds me, with great nostalgia, that as a toddler I could be found playing in the kitchen with pots and pans. Nowadays, I am planning meals weeks in advance; doing laps in the swimming pool, with my mouth 'salivating' at the very thought of new menu options. And quite possibly the most obsessive behaviour of all, is waking in the dead of night to text myself a new recipe idea. Food is my passion. I live for it.

I come from a long line of proud Punjabi farmers. They were real 'salt of the earth' people, who harnessed the power of nature to grow food, and created wholesome and delicious meals, fresh from the land. Present day Punjab is India's bread basket – home to a food culture which has been the single biggest regional influence on Indian cuisine as a whole. From the remote and mountainous regions of India to the restaurant kitchens of Britain, the Punjab shapes how we eat Indian food today.

I grew up in England into a large family, surrounded by aunts, uncles, grandparents and a virtual army of brown children (my cousins). Mum would always be cooking up a storm of crispy samosas, spicy pakoras and melt-in-the-mouth gulab jamuns in sweet sugar syrup. And on Sunday, she would make us parathas – freshly rolled pastry, stuffed with a scrumptiously-spiced mashed potato filling, fried lightly on a pan and served crispy and sizzling hot, with lashings of dairy-fresh butter and natural yogurt. Our eyes would remain fixated on our mother. She would masterfully make one paratha at a time, and we would sit wondering who would get the next. At that time, my siblings and I were not unlike baby chicks, waiting to be fed in their nest; proof that even the simplest pleasures in life can turn out to be the most ambrosial.

Approaching my teen years, Mum and Dad bought a grocery store, and this meant they had less time to look after us at home. We had to help much more with household chores. My brother would be in charge of vacuuming and my sister, of dusting. I would be responsible for the bathroom. And it suited me down to the ground. Cleaning, it took minutes, leaving plenty of time to cook. Mum and Dad would often come home to some weird and wonderful concoction that I had cooked up. Dad was always very sweet and ate everything I put in front of him.

Life was good to my parents and their grocery store was a busy one. It was time to expand the 'empire'. The next venture would be the fish and chip shop, where I had been working part-time whilst studying. My brother was given the managerial post, and I would be his apprentice. On the day of opening, I got the main local newspaper to cover our takeover. We featured on the front page, with an opening offer of 'free chips, with fish'. From that day on, the fish and chip shop turned out to be a 'money spinner'. We even turned part of it into a small take-away restaurant. And this is where I served up authentic homemade Indian curries to adoring punters.

As adulthood approached, I felt an urge to 'fly the nest', and left England for sunnier shores. I visited the Middle East, Asia, South East Asia and the Pacific, sampling many culinary delights on the way. From charcoal roasted kebabs in Dubai, to the desert cuisine of Rajasthan, and the fragrant delights of the Thai kitchen; I tried it all.

I stayed for the longest time abroad with my mother's sister, at her home in Byron Bay, the easternmost tip of Australia. The region was blessed with abundant sunlight, sub-tropical rain and cool ocean breezes. True to their Punjabi heritage, my aunt and her family worked the land, farming some of Australia's finest fruit, meat and dairy produce, and exporting it to the world.

My aunt and I would while away for hours, eating food and talking about it. She would often step out of the house and go to the garden, walking carefully, so not to disturb sleeping snakes; returning from the volcanic soil with a huge fistful of the freshest spinach and fenugreek leaves. She would lovingly combine them with fresh onion, aubergine, potato and spices, preparing the most delectable pakoras I have ever eaten. They were crispy, with a light batter, and just enough spice to get the juices flowing. We would dip them into fresh coriander chutney. Eager taste buds would be treated to a luscious medley of savoury spinach, fenugreek and mixed vegetables, and the zing of fresh coriander. It was like biting into a piece of my very own spicy heaven.

It was in Australia where I learned the gastro-delights of multiculturalism; discovering a food culture where a kaleidoscope of ethnic recipes had exploded into a single cuisine, combining the freshest ingredients with every conceivable cooking style known to mankind. It was possible to enjoy by the beachside, fresh salad with poached chicken breast and juicy ripe mango from the tropic of Capricorn, all tossed up in a zesty, Vietnamese-style mint and lemon dressing. And the 'menu of the day' in the cosmopolitan restaurants of Sydney would be tempura-style rock oysters on their shell, with a pungent wasabi dressing; Italian veal and pork meatballs, fragranced gently with cardamom, served on a bed of angel hair spaghetti; and tropical coconut and passion fruit sponge cakes drizzled with raspberry coulis. A food lover's paradise!

Nonetheless, outside of my aunt's kitchen, authentic Indian food in Australia was somewhat lacking. So I often found myself 'persuaded' into cooking for friends. I really got to put my culinary skills to test, making good use of local ingredients and preparing Indian fare with that unique Australian 'twist'. Simple and rustic lamb rogan josh, slow-cooked with sun-dried tomatoes; saag paneer, made with tender baby spinach and soft feta cheese; all served up with a mountain of steaming hot pilau rice. It was great food, washed down with copious amounts of local wine.

After leaving Australia, I headed for Turkey, and opened a restaurant on the Mediterranean coast, finally bringing together my passion for food, with a warm and sunny climate. During the day, I basked in the sun, cooling off in the azure waters of the Aegean Sea. At night I cooked passionately, using the finest Mediterranean produce to create Anglo-Indian restaurant classics such as bhajis, tikka masalas, creamy kormas and Madras curries. Customers from the UK would often show their gratitude with a standing ovation.To this day, I remain uncertain whether they were saluting my food or our mother country. At the end of a long nights work, the sound of gulets rocking gently out at sea would send me to sleep. Life couldn't get any better. But it was all about to change...

During the tourist 'off season', I closed my restaurant and set out to explore Istanbul, the very heart and soul of Turkey. I found myself bedazzled amongst the swarm of humanity, spiralling minarets and the intoxicating sound of muezzins' calls. I headed for a much-needed respite at the Efes Bar, located by the waters of the Bosphorous. Whilst sitting with a glass of lemonade, I gazed around the crowd and my eyes stumbled upon a face which looked familiar. Sitting behind what had to be the largest beer glass I have ever seen, was Lorraine Sinclair, Executive Chef for the Mövenpick Hotel Istanbul. I plucked up enough courage to go over and say, 'Hello'. We hit it off immediately, and she asked me to join her. Lorraine turned out to be quite a loveable rogue, and after a few too many beers she suggested we hold an Indian Food Promotion at the hotel. After a little deliberation, and a few more beers, I took her up on the offer.

Following many months of planning, in 2005, the Mövenpick Hotel Istanbul hosted our Indian Food Promotion. And finally Istanbul's taste buds awoke to the exotic flavours of India. At last, both the Mehmet's and the John's of Turkey, would relish equally in the culinary delights of the Indian kitchen. From regal tandoori salmon, with its crispy outer crust and sweet melt-in-the-mouth interior; to opulent and aromatic flavoured meat curries, soaked up with light, fluffy naans; to majestically rich and creamy kulfis. Spices, in which the Turks had traded for millennia, would finally arouse and conquer their palate, playing it like the strings of a sitar. Turkey surrendered to the delights of Indian cuisine, and by renaming chicken masala to chicken 'mashallah', they had claimed this cuisine as their very own. The media whirled into a frenzy. My mission had been accomplished. I felt the time was right for a new adventure, and I set my sights for the familiar shores of England.

After settling back home, it was time to face some cold hard facts. My love for 'good food' appeared to have got somewhat out of control. It was painstakingly evident that, on my travels, I had gained some excess 'baggage' (a whopping 28 kilos in body weight to be exact!). Feeling great disappointment in myself, I had no stronger desire than the deep yearning to reduce my excess weight. I rejected the conventional and rigid concept of dieting, indulging whole-heartedly on a regime of unlimited fruit and vegetables, and healthy low-fat versions of my favourite foods. I ditched the car, in favour of an active lifestyle, and took up exercise. Over time, I managed to shed a considerable 20 kilos. The new 'healthy me' was born!

It wasn't too long before I began to make culinary observations; concluding that since Madhur Jaffrey, in the 1980's, had undertaken the colossal task of introducing Indian food to the UK and the world, it had moved on tremendously, adapting with zeal to local ingredients and food trends. And eventually metamorphosing into today's low-fat version with 'joie de vivre'. We now had wholesome versions of restaurant classics like chicken tikka masala and lamb rogan josh. All very good, but one question remained, could Indian food be made any healthier? This was to be my new mission.

It has now been over three years since I started developing new and exciting recipes which one day, I hope, will be at the fore-front of healthy food.

Indian Superfood

Introduction

Over recent years, many nutritionists have recognised certain foods for their exceptional health-promoting properties, identifying them as superfoods. Amongst them, berries are celebrated for their antioxidising properties, salmon for its cardiovascular health benefits and soy products for their role in cancer prevention. And, credited with a vast myriad of curative properties, are sea vegetables, widely considered in the East as the 'secret elixir to life'.

It is now more transparent than ever that, in order to enjoy optimal health, our body needs a diet low in fat and calories, and which is also rich in nutrient-dense superfoods. Supermarkets, in particular, have kept up at break-neck speed with recent health trends, stocking exotic pre-packaged superfood products such as sushi rolls made with Japanese seaweed, smoothies bursting with antioxidising fruits from the Amazon, and breakfast cereals scattered full of dried fruits, nuts and seeds from 'four corners' of the earth. All great and excellent news for our well-being, but do superfoods need to be so 'mysterious'?

All we need to do is, for example, look at the distinguished and varied food habits of our Mediterranean neighbours, who are remarkably healthy eating people. They are passionate about fresh fruit, vegetables and food containing low-fat protein, served up with a drizzle of olive oil, a generous helping of tomatoes, and a gulp or two of wine. Science has championed this type of diet as a model diet.

Olive oil is highly regarded for its role in fighting coronary heart disease, whereas wine has been found to contain the antioxidant compound, resveratrol, that promotes cardiovascular health by reducing harmful blood clots and, accordingly, protecting the heart from free radical damage. And, most recently, it has been proven that tomatoes contain lycopene, which is one of nature's most powerful antioxidants. This nutrient has been found to be beneficial in preventing many types of cancer, including that of the prostate and the skin. Surprisingly, cooking and condensing tomatoes increases their lycopene content and, in consequence, even that humble tube of tomato purée, hiding away in your kitchen cupboard, can be considered as a rich source of nutrients.

It is, thus, evident that superfoods are not only the exotic shrink-wrapped foods found schmoozing in the health and chilled sections of our local supermarkets, but are also many of the every-day healthy foods that we take for granted. Some of these include locally-grown fruits that contain vital antioxidants which prevent the oxidation of other molecules, and, therefore, inhibit damage to our body cells. Lean poultry and meat is rich in the trace mineral selenium, which is proven to aid the body's defence mechanism. And, probably, the most astonishing superfood is the modest potato, which also contains phytonutrients that act as antioxidants. All such readily available foods can be included in our diet to enrich it altogether. It is, thereupon, far easier to pursue a diet rich in superfoods than we would commonly believe.

Unsurprisingly, the notion of 'food as medicine' is not a new one, and has been used in practice by ancient civilizations. Early Indian legends contain tales mentioning the sesame seed and its representation of 'immortality'. Babylonian women would eat halva, a mixture of sesame seeds and honey, to prolong their health and beauty. In Islamic tradition, olive oil is recommended in the following terms, "Consume olive oil and anoint it upon your bodies since it is of the blessed tree". It is also stated that olive oil cures seventy diseases. Recent scientific findings have only given credibility to these ancient 'myths', proving that sesame seed contains unique cholesterol-lowering substances, and olive oil has the ability to guard against cardiovascular diseases.

Nevertheless, I can state, with great enthusiasm, that there is a whole lot more that we can do to maximise our health, in addition to feasting on delicious superfoods.

Indian food brazenly employs the use of spices more than any other major world cuisine. Many of these spices have been acknowledged for their medicinal properties and, thus, hereon are coined as 'superspices'. The Indian cuisine mixes a vast array of superspices, utilising them not unlike how an artist would use his paint palette to produce a work of art. Dozens of superspices, including chilli, cardamom and turmeric, are blended together to create the incomparable and multi-layered flavours of the Indian kitchen. Without these superspices, Indian food would be unthinkable.

Astonishingly, the Indian tradition, like no other, has paid great homage to the superspices. Basil (tulsi) is worshipped because of its sanctity to the Hindu god Vishnu, symbolising his wife, Lakshmi. And dried chillies are hung outside homes and businesses, to ward off the 'evil eye' and 'bad spirits'.

To our considerable kismet, the use of superspices is evident not only in faith-related practices but also in India's very own ancient system of alternative health care, known as Ayurveda, which roughly translates in English as 'the science of life' and dates back to 3000 BC. It is believed to be a divine revelation of the Hindu god Brahma, and is among the few traditional forms of medicine to contain a complex system of surgery. This discipline unveils the use of these superspices in full extent, such that they form the backbone of Ayurvedic treatment for the vast majority of ailments and illnesses. Turmeric comprises the base of most remedies and is also used as an antiseptic (being applied directly to wounds); saffron is taken to nurture a long healthy life; and cumin to aid the digestion of food.

Modern day science has corroborated many of the findings made by Ayurveda. And scores of these superspices have been recognised in the West for their medicinal properties, including chilli, as it contains capsaicin, which is known for its ability to reduce skin and muscle pain; ginger for thinning the blood; and saffron for its antioxidising abilities. A recent study carried out by the Cancer Research Unit at the University of Texas even confirmed that phytochemicals derived from spices, such as turmeric, chilli, cloves, ginger, cumin, fennel, basil and garlic, interrupt a variety of diseases, including cancer, atherosclerosis, myocardial infarction, diabetes, allergies, asthma, arthritis, Crohn's disease, osteoporosis, psoriasis, septic shock, and even AIDS. Another research from King's College London certified the traditional Ayurvedic use of nigella in treating rheumatism and other inflammatory diseases, such as Asthma, proving it to be very effective in treating such diseases. [1] [2] With conviction, I can confirm that we are sitting on the tip of a vast and unexplored iceberg – there are hundreds more medical researches that verify the use of superspices to heal the body of, virtually, every ailment.

Unbeknown to many of us, these superspices are also ingredients of over-the-counter medicines. Star anise is used as a key ingredient in the process of manufacturing Tamiflu, a defence for swine or avian flu pandemics, and hence stockpiled by governments across the planet. Upon the recent increased demand in the drug, there has been a shortage in the availability of star anise. Fennel seeds and ginger are contained in gripe water used to treat gastro-intestinal pain in both adults and children. Chilli is an essential ingredient contained in many rubs used for muscle and joint aches. And cloves are popular in soothing the pain common in dental emergencies. But, we don't necessarily need a visit to the pharmacy or laboratory to benefit.

Staggeringly, nearly a quarter of the top antioxidant-rich foods available to us are, in fact, superspices. Comparatively, weight-for-weight, superspices are the most antioxidant-rich foods on the planet. Take, for example, cumin – just under half a teaspoon is equivalent to a standard portion of grapes, based on their antioxidant potential. Or ground cinnamon, where 1 teaspoon contains the equal amount of antioxidants found in two glasses of fresh pomegranate juice.

Now, imagine a cuisine where we could bring together, at mealtimes, both Science and Ayurveda. Wouldn't that be something ground-breaking?

Indian Superfood is the unique synergism between representatives of Science and Ayurveda – superfoods and superspices; the world's most awesome antioxidants, mingling together on a plate. A flawless assimilation of 21st-century East and West. Aromatic and rich masala-style dishes, blending harmoniously with the nutritious properties of sea-vegetables, and crammed full of the antiviral capability of cinnamon; luxurious meat recipes balanced with remarkable digestive enzymes found in fruits, and blessed with the pain-relieving properties of fennel seeds; naans bursting-full of goodness from antibacterial cranberries, and sweets enhanced with the tremendous antioxidising properties of goji berries and saffron... Now, that's food for thought.

Indian Superfood is designed to stimulate both your health and taste buds, making for an altogether original meal-time experience. There are new and exciting recipes such as heavenly-tasting Salmon and Sweet Potato Fishcakes, which can help lower the

risk of heart attack; aromatic, spicy and ever-so-slightly fruity Chicken with Banana and Fenugreek, that will aid the body's muscle-building and digestive processes; Oyster Pakora with Punch and Gusto Fresh Coriander Salsa – a simple canapé designed to stun the most ardent of food critics, and a great source of zinc to support the body's immune function. And, there are naans made with seaweed and roasted pumpkin seeds – a fabulous symphony of ingredients considered to be a 'potion for longevity'; a sublime Black Rice Pudding that will stimulate the metabolism; and many yummy alternatives to classics like chicken tikka masala and lamb rogan josh.

You will find the recipes to be deceptively easy in preparation, many of them requiring only a handful of ingredients, and some taking just minutes to rustle up. For example, the Ginger-Infused Yogurt with Honey and Pomegranate is a combination of only four ingredients and takes merely 3 minutes to prepare.

Rest assured there are no 'fiddly' or 'tricky' recipes. I am far too laid back for any kitchen melodrama – and I expect you're the same! Take, for instance, the meat recipes included in the book. Most of them take a maximum twenty minutes of preparation. And then you can leave them to cook, and get on with enjoying your life. It really is that simple.

To ease off your busy lifestyle, the recipes are split into chapters that reflect the time of day; you will find individual sections for breakfast, lunch and dinner. These are intended to remove any guesswork that has been traditionally associated with combining Indian foods to make a complete meal.

Most of the superfood ingredients can be found on the shelves of your local supermarket, and many of the superspices you will find staring at you, from the spice rack in your kitchen.

We can now enjoy our favourite Indian foods, whilst ensuring a longer and healthier life.

I think it is about time to let the food – the real star – do the talking.

Antioxidants

What is an antioxidant?

Antioxidants are molecules that slow and prevent the oxidation of free radicals, which, if left unhindered, start chain reactions that damage cells. They eliminate these potential chain reactions by removing free radical transmitters and, therefore, inhibiting cell damage. For instance, the cholesterol in our body is not harmful until it is oxidised, and thereby it starts clinging to the blood vessels, which can lead to heart complaints. Antioxidants help to guard against this damage and accordingly make a very positive contribution to our general wellbeing by helping prevent degeneration and disease. They can be found in a vast myriad of superfoods and superspices, and are linked with preventing, and even fighting, diseases such as cancer, heart disease and Alzheimer's, in addition to numerous degenerative conditions.

How do we know which superfoods and superspices are the best source of antioxidants?

The ORAC (Oxygen Radical Absorbance Capacity) value is the scientific measurement of the antioxidant capacity of superfoods and superspices. It has been developed by scientists at the National Institutes of Health in the US. Foods higher on the ORAC scale will more effectively neutralise free radicals. ORAC values of both superfoods and superspices are published by the USDA (United States Department of Agriculture). The average person consumes approximately 1200 ORAC units per day. Research from the USDA suggests that we should consume a minimum of 3,000 ORAC units per day, for significant antioxidant protection and optimal health.

Recommended daily allowance (RDA) of antioxidants

The RDA for antioxidants is derived from the USDA recommendation of 3,000 ORAC units per day.

The amount of antioxidants contained in each of the recipes is calculated by using ORAC value data for raw food ingredients (see page 11), compared to the RDA value. Where ORAC value is unavailable for an ingredient, the amount is estimated using the closest possible alternative ingredient from the same food group.

Cooking increases the antioxidant activity for certain foods, such as tomatoes. Other ingredients that contain vitamin C, including blueberries, lose some of their antioxidant potency in the cooking process. Therefore, cooking times for fruits and other similar ingredients is kept to a minimum.

As an added measure, an amount of 20% has been deducted from each of the RDA percentage figures of the respective recipe, to make up for any potential loss of antioxidants.

By and large, for most of the recipes, dried superspices account for the major part of their antioxidant potential; and these superspices remain impervious to the cooking procedure altogether.

"Phytochemicals derived from spices such as turmeric, chilli, cloves, ginger, cumin, fennel, basil and garlic have been found to interrupt a variety of diseases, including cancer, atherosclerosis, myocardial infarction, diabetes, allergies, asthma, arthritis, Crohn's disease, osteoporosis, psoriasis, septic shock and AIDS. Therefore providing 'reasoning for seasoning'."

The University of Texas, USA[1]

ORAC values

ORAC values of selected superfoods [3]

	ORAC value per 100g		ORAC value per 100g		ORAC value per 100g
Acai berries	102,700	Cranberry juice	865	Peppers, red	791
Almonds	4,454	Cucumbers	214	Pistachio nuts	7,983
Apples	3,082	Dates, dried	3,895	Pomegranate juice	2,341
Apricots, dried	3,234	Goji berries, dried	25,300	Popcorn	1,743
Aubergines	933	Kidney beans, dried	8,459	Potatoes	1,058
Bananas	879	Lemon juice	1,225	Pumpkins	396
Beetroot	1,767	Lentils, dried	7,282	Radishes	1,736
Blueberries	6,552	Lime juice	823	Raisins/Sultanas	3,037
Broccoli	1,362	Limes	82	Red wine	3,873
Cabbage, red	2,252	Mangetout	759	Rocket	1,904
Cabbage, white	508	Mangoes	1,002	Soya beans, dried	5,764
Carrots	666	Navy beans, dried	1,520	Spinach	1,515
Cashew nuts	1,948	Oats	1,708	Strawberries	3,577
Cauliflower	829	Olive oil	1,150	Sweet potatoes	902
Chickpeas, dried	847	Onions, red	1,521	Tea, green, brewed	1,253
Chocolate, dark	20,823	Onions, white	1,034	Tomatoes	367
Cocoa, dry powder	80,933	Orange juice	726	Tomato juice	486
Corn kernels, canned	413	Peas, green	600	Walnuts	13,541
Courgettes	180	Peas, yellow, dried	741		
Cranberries	9,584	Peppers, green	923		

ORAC values of selected superspices [3]

	ORAC value per 100g		ORAC value per 100g
Basil, fresh	4,805	Garlic, dried (flakes)	6,665
Cardamom	2,764		
Chilli, ground (powder)	23,636	Garlic, fresh	5,346
		Ginger, fresh	14,840
Chives	2,094	Ginger, ground	28,811
Cinnamon	267,536	Mint, fresh	13,978
Cloves	314,446	Mustard seeds	29,257
Coriander, fresh	5,141	Pepper, black	27,618
Cumin	76,800	Turmeric	159,277
Curry powder	48,504		

A note for American readers

British and American cookbooks use different measuring systems. In the UK, dry ingredients are measured by weight, with the metric system increasingly replacing the Imperial one, while in the US they are measured by volume.

WEIGHT

7g	$1/4$ ounce	200g	7 ounces
20g	$3/4$ ounce	220–225g	8 ounces
25–30g	1 ounce	250–260g	9 ounces
40g	$1^{1}/_{2}$ ounces	300g	$10^{1}/_{2}$ ounces
50g	$1^{3}/_{4}$ ounces	325g	$11^{1}/_{2}$ ounces
60–65g	$2^{1}/_{4}$ ounces	350g	12 ounces
70–75g	$2^{1}/_{2}$ ounces	400g	14 ounces
80g	$2^{3}/_{4}$ ounces	450g	1 pound
90g	$3^{1}/_{4}$ ounces	500g	1 pound 2 ounces
100g	$3^{1}/_{2}$ ounces	600g	1 pound 5 ounces
110–115g	4 ounces	700g	1 pound 9 ounces
120–130g	$4^{1}/_{2}$ ounces	750g	1 pound 10 ounces
140g	5 ounces	800g	$1^{3}/_{4}$ pounds
150g	$5^{1}/_{2}$ ounces	900g	2 pounds
175–180g	6 ounces	1kg	$2^{1}/_{4}$ pounds

VOLUME

50ml	$1^{3}/_{4}$ fl oz	300ml	10 fl oz
60ml	2 fl oz (4 tbs/$1/4$ cup)	350ml	12 fl oz
75ml	$2^{1}/_{2}$ fl oz (5 tbs)	400ml	14 fl oz
90ml	3 fl oz ($3/8$ cup)	450ml	15 fl oz
100ml	$3^{1}/_{2}$ fl oz	475ml	16 fl oz (2 cups)
125ml	4 fl oz ($1/2$ cup)	500ml	18 fl oz
150ml	5 fl oz ($2/3$ cup)	600ml	20 fl oz
175ml	6 fl oz	800ml	28 fl oz
200ml	7 fl oz	850ml	30 fl oz
250ml	8 fl oz (1 cup)	1 litre	35 fl oz (4 cups)

LENGTH

5mm	$1/4$ inch	8cm	$3^{1}/_{4}$ inches
1cm	$1/2$ inch	9cm	$3^{1}/_{2}$ inches
2cm	$3/4$ inch	10cm	4 inches
2.5cm	1 inch	12cm	$4^{1}/_{2}$ inches
3cm	$1^{1}/_{4}$ inches	14cm	$5^{1}/_{2}$ inches
4cm	$1^{1}/_{2}$ inches	20cm	8 inches
5cm	2 inches	24cm	$9^{1}/_{2}$ inches
6cm	$2^{1}/_{2}$ inches	30cm	12 inches

Before you start

A few pointers to oil your way to great food and health.

Black Rice
Purchase at Chinese or Oriental grocers, or online.

Chillies
I have scaled the amount of chillies used in the recipes.
The range is somewhat flexible, and open to your discretion.
If you like your food hot, use the amount of chillies suggested
towards the higher end of the scale. Remember to increase
gradually, tasting all the time.

Garlic
I tend to use 'fat' cloves.

Mangoes
In the summer months, try using Alphonso mangoes which are
imported from India and Pakistan and can be found in many
Indian and ethnic grocers.

Mango Pulp/Purée
Whenever possible, it's preferable to use mango pulp, which is
made from fragrant Alphonso mangoes. You will find it in most
Indian and ethnic grocers, as well as many larger supermarkets.
It can be substituted with mango purée, which is available in
some larger supermarkets.

Meat
You can exchange beef for lamb, and vice versa, in any of the
recipes. It's recommended to keep the consumption of red
meat to a minimum.

Mushrooms
Try to buy mushrooms which aren't covered in dirt. Wipe them
clean at home. Do not wash, as they soak up fluids like a
sponge, and will discharge excess water into your cooking.

Oven Temperatures
All the recipes in this book have been tested in an electric fan-
assisted oven. We also include the equivalent conventional
electric and gas oven temperatures, but please refer to your
cooker manufacturer's guidelines for more specific information on
adjusting the temperature and time for your cooker, if applicable.

Salt
Better for our well-being, the amount of salt used in the recipes
is quite modest. You may increase it slightly, if you so wish. In
all recipes, we have used level spoon measures for salt only.

Saucepans
Unless the saucepan used in the recipe is specifically stated
as a small or large size, I tend to work with a 20cm saucepan.
If you are using a larger saucepan, the surface area for frying
the spices is increased, and the ingredients are also more prone
to evaporation, therefore you may need to increase the amount
of oil and fluids used in the recipe.

Sea Salad
Buy at health food shops, or online.

Soy Sauce
Be careful when buying soy sauce. Many commercial brands
have sugar added in them, which will clash with the recipe.
Stick with Kikkoman or traditional blends, and always check
their ingredients list.

Suppliers
Most of the ingredients can be found in larger supermarkets.
A few items may need to be sourced from a fishmonger, health
food shop or Indian/speciality grocer. Many of the dry store
ingredients can also be purchased online at
www.indiansuperfood.com

Teaspoon Measures
We have only used level spoon measures for salt in the recipes.
All other ingredients measured using a teaspoon use rounded
spoon measures.

Whole Spices
Indian Superfood recipes use whole spices to impart an
authentic flavour and potent health benefits. If so desired, you
may discard them at the end of cooking

Breakfast

Breakfast, as we have been told for time eternal, is the most important meal of the day. If we kick-start our 'engine' with healthy sustenance, it is more likely that we will continue to eat right for the rest of the day. But many of us never really experience the joys of eating at breakfast time. We accept as true that breakfast consists of ramming toast and shovelling cereal down the proverbial guzzler.

Indian Superfood acknowledges, and whole-heartedly embraces, the necessity for a quick breakfast. For this reason, many recipes are fast to prepare, and some can even be made the night before.

'What? Indian for breakfast?', I hear you asking. Yes, but not quite. This is Indian food with an inspiring twist – it is *Indian Superfood* for breakfast. For example, Spicy Prawn Omelette or mouth-watering Ginger-Infused Yogurt with Honey and Pomegranate, both of which take minutes to rustle up. Who in their right mind could resist such irresistibly healthy temptations?

Breakfast Rice Pudding with Almonds, Honey and Fresh Fruit

Serves 2–3

Inspired by Müller rice pots and a genuine desire for a lighter alternative to hearty oats. I suggest you try starting your day with this chilled breakfast treat, topped with plenty of antioxidising fruits.
The mere mention of almonds, milk and honey conjure up in my mind superfoods that have been recorded for their health and beauty properties for millennia, in both ancient texts and in today's science.

As children, my Mum used to make us drink a fortifying and gut-busting concoction of steaming hot milk enriched with almond meal, ghee and honey.
Even Cleopatra was said to bathe in milk and honey. Oh, how times have moved on. We no longer need a bath full of milk or ghee to reap the benefits. In fact, just consuming a diet that includes low-fat dairy products such as semi-skimmed milk can be linked with successful fat loss. Honey is effective in increasing the population of probiotic bacteria in the gut which help strengthen the immune system and improve digestion, further aiding the body with weight control.

So, why not immerse yourself in this delicious, low-fat breakfast pudding and let your body radiate the goodness from within?

2 tablespoons basmati rice
a small handful of blanched almonds
1 tablespoon honey
1.1 litres semi-skimmed milk
5 cloves
a pinch of salt

fresh fruit and extra blanched almonds and honey, to serve

Place all the ingredients into a deep, heavy-based saucepan and cook over a medium heat until the milk starts to boil. Reduce to a low heat and simmer, uncovered, for 1 hour or until the milk has reduced by half, stirring frequently.

Serve warm or chilled, topped with fresh fruit, a few more almonds and a drizzle of extra honey.

Cook's Note
This recipe can be made one day ahead.

One serving =
55%+ RDA
antioxidants

Antibacterial
cloves

Antifungal
cloves

Antiviral
cloves

Anti-inflammatory
cloves

Analgesic
cloves

" The oils of black pepper, clove and nutmeg were assessed for antibacterial activity against 25 genera of bacteria. These included animal and plant pathogens, food poisoning and spoilage bacteria. The volatile oils exhibited considerable inhibitory effects against all the organisms under test."

Scottish Agricultural College[10]

Curried Baked Beans on Toast

Serves 2

Astonishingly, in Britain, we go through 500,000 cans of Heinz Baked Beans each day. So, coincidentally, and like the great many of us, I grew up eating them too. It's one of the few foods that I can say I have enjoyed from childhood right up to this very day, with conviction. They have comforted me for breakfast, lunch and dinner and everything in-between for the past 30 years or so. From the early 'dinner party' days before my teens, beans were always on the menu. Cousins less adept in the kitchen would look on in awe as I served to them the saucy morsels on hot buttered toast, and at other times with fish fingers or sausages. Mum even tells me baked beans were the first meal I 'cooked' by myself as a child. In fact, to my bemusement, she recounts the story to a great many people.

So, I guess here we have it, Gurpareet's first ever recipe. It's an Indian recipe which is nearly as fast to rustle up as heating the can of beans by itself, and hence is well worth the minute amount of extra effort required that pays so handsomely with oodles more taste and goodness.

Beans are a virtually fat-free alternative to meat protein and contain vitamin B1 and a fountain of minerals including iron, folic acid, zinc and potassium. They lower blood pressure and cholesterol levels and are linked with a reduction in the incidence of heart disease. The mustard seeds add a slightly pungent flavour to the recipe, chipping in a new taste dimension, and all the while protecting like small bullets against cancer cells.

1 tablespoon olive oil
$1/2$ teaspoon each cumin seeds and mustard seeds
1 teaspoon curry powder
400g can baked beans

Pour the olive oil into a deep saucepan, add the cumin and mustard seeds and cook over a low-medium heat until the seeds start to pop – this should take no longer than 1–2 minutes. Sprinkle in the curry powder, mix well and cook for about 20 seconds.

Pour the beans into the saucepan and heat through, stirring occasionally.

Serve with hot toast.

One serving = 120%+ RDA antioxidants

Antibacterial
cumin, mustard

Antifungal
cumin, mustard

Anti-inflammatory
cumin, mustard

Dried Apricots Poached with Lime and Spices

Serves 4

Poaching dried apricots with Indian superspices teases out a mysterious air of exoticism hiding deep within them. The subtle tang and sweetness of the apricots is accentuated by the perfume from the lime leaves, which echoes a bygone era. Each mouthful is reminiscent of being caught up in the sweet hustle and bustle of a royal zenana. They can be made a few days ahead and kept refrigerated until ready to serve.

Dried apricots contain vitamin A, needed for both a healthy heart and eyes – and essential for courting potential suitors. If you're unable to find lime leaves, simply serve with wedges of fresh lime.

200g dried apricots
6 kaffir lime leaves, fresh or frozen
   (available at Oriental grocers)
2 star anise
5 green cardamom pods, lightly
   crushed
3 cloves

Place all of the ingredients in a saucepan with 1 litre cold water. Bring to the boil, then reduce the heat to a simmer and cook, uncovered, for 30 minutes, stirring occasionally.

Remove the pan from the heat and allow the mixture to cool, then refrigerate.

Serve chilled with natural yogurt.

One serving =
70%+ RDA
antioxidants

Antibacterial
cardamom, cloves,
star anise

Antifungal
cardamom, cloves

Antiviral
cloves

Anti-inflammatory
cardamom, cloves

Analgesic
cloves

Eggs Scrambled with Tomatoes, Onion and Pepper

Serves 3

Like many of us, I too love eggs, and I would say this is one of the most glorious ways to enjoy them. The onion and pepper give them an unparalleled 'creamy' lavishness without adding a disproportionate amount of fat and calories; and the tomatoes make them juicy and deliciously rich and tangy-tasting, whilst adding collagen which helps strengthen tendons and slow degenerative diseases.

Eggs are a natural superfood choice, and are very much in vogue these days – they are a complete protein source and contain the supreme nutrient iodine, which is required to produce the thyroid hormone that regulates our metabolism. To boot, the yolk harnesses lutein, which is also found in tomatoes; it is converted by our body into an antioxidant that guards against macular disease. I like to serve these scrambled eggs with a slice or two of fresh bread.

2 tablespoons olive oil
1 small onion, finely diced
1/3 teaspoon salt, or to taste
1 red pepper, deseeded and finely diced
1 green chilli, finely chopped (optional)
2 tomatoes, finely diced
6 eggs, beaten

Place the olive oil, onion and salt in a wide frying pan and cook over a low-medium heat for about 5 minutes or until the onion is light golden brown in colour, stirring frequently.

Add the red pepper and chilli, if using, and continue cooking for about 3–5 minutes or until the pepper is soft. Add the tomatoes and cook for another 5 minutes or until the tomatoes have softened.

Stir in the eggs, mixing them thoroughly into the tomato mixture. When the eggs start bubbling, reduce to a low heat. Cook for 2 minutes and stir. Continue cooking for a further 2 minutes. Stir, then remove from the heat.

Serve with bread of your choice.

One serving = 25%+ RDA antioxidants

Antibacterial
chilli

Antifungal
chilli

Anti-inflammatory
chilli

Analgesic
chilli

Gluten-Free Banana and Walnut Bread

Makes 1 loaf (Serves 6+)

Although cake baking has been introduced to the subcontinent, it has still never quite taken off, most likely, because the ingredients and techniques used previously proved too alien for Indians to embrace fully. My recipe uses only ingredients that are indigenous to the local cuisine, and it also contains no added fat; so, it's about time for India to get busy baking!

Walnuts also contain the highest amount of the polyphenol-rich antioxidant, ellagic acid, which is recognised as a natural cancer preventative, making this gluten-free recipe healthier still. Serve a slice or two to the kids, for breakfast, with some fresh banana and a glass of milk. They will love you for it.

olive oil, for greasing
160g cornmeal
1 teaspoon baking powder
1 teaspoon ground ginger
2 large ripe bananas
2 tablespoons honey
85g sugar
1 egg, beaten
a pinch of salt
a large handful of walnut pieces

Preheat the oven to 180°C/fan 160°C/ Gas Mark 4. Grease a 22 x 11.5 x 6cm loaf tin with some olive oil and set aside.

In a small bowl, mix together the cornmeal, baking powder and ground ginger. Set aside.

Peel and mash the bananas in a large mixing bowl, then add the honey. Add the sugar and mix well to combine. Add the egg, cornmeal mixture and salt and mix through. Fold through the walnuts.

Transfer the mixture to the prepared loaf tin and level the surface. Bake in the centre of the oven for 30 minutes or until the bread is golden brown and firm to the touch.

Leave to cool in the tin for 15 minutes, before turning out on to a wire rack. Serve warm or cold in slices.

One serving =
45%+ RDA
antioxidants

Antibacterial
ginger

Antifungal
ginger

Anti-inflammatory
ginger

Indian Superfood

Ginger-Infused Yogurt with Honey and Pomegranate

We all know that pomegranate is charged with antioxidants that have a similar effect on free radicals as a raging bull has on innocent bystanders, sending them running for cover. But how do we muster this pomegranate bloodbath in a practicable manner? Well, this recipe is my answer, and it achieves for the taste buds what a 'kick in the ass' would do for me.

Each and every mouthful bursts full of sweet and sour pomegranate pearls, combined with ambrosial honey-and-ginger yogurt that bites. A marvellous, antioxidising breakfast treat that's ready to eat at the 'speed of light'; it regulates blood sugar levels, soothes a feisty tummy and will even help you look your best. What more can one ask for? And, if you're a wimp or simply not looking for too much excitement first thing in the morning, you can always replace the pomegranate with blueberries or dried fruit and nuts.

Serves 2

1 pomegranate
300ml natural yogurt
$1/_2$ teaspoon ground ginger
6 teaspoons honey

Cut the pomegranate in quarters. Using your hands or a teaspoon, gently scoop out the seeds and set aside.

In a bowl, mix together the yogurt, ginger and 2 teaspoons of the honey, stirring until smooth.

Pour the mixture into bowls or serving glasses. Top with the pomegranate seeds and remaining honey and serve.

One serving = 45%+ RDA antioxidants

Antibacterial ginger

Antifungal ginger

Anti-inflammatory ginger

"In traditional medical systems, the ability of spices to heal various physical, mental and emotional problems has widely been reported. With this view, analysis was performed on 21 spices. It was found that bishop's weed, black mustard, cardamom, cinnamon, clove, coriander, cumin, curry leaf, dill, fennel, fenugreek, garlic, ginger, onion and saffron contained considerable antibacterial, anti-inflammatory and antifungal properties."

Banaras Hindu University, India[4]

Gluten-Free Savoury Cornmeal Bread with Baby Spinach and Cherry Tomatoes

Makes 1 loaf (Serves 4–6)

This gluten-free recipe is an ingenious remake of the classic North Indian peasant bread, makki di roti, traditionally served with saag. In this contemporary-yet-rustic version, baby spinach leaves, cherry tomatoes and spices are baked inside the bread, adding a bounty of inviting flavour and nutrition. Cherry tomatoes contain lycopene and lutein, two antioxidants that reduce the risk of macular disease and cancer.

For a new deli feel at breakfast or brunch, serve sliced with a light spinach salad and raita.

2 tablespoons olive oil, plus extra for greasing
1 teaspoon cumin seeds
1/4 teaspoon freshly ground black pepper
1/4 teaspoon chilli powder
1 teaspoon salt
1 onion, diced
12 cherry tomatoes, halved
100g baby spinach leaves, coarsely chopped
4 tablespoons chopped fresh coriander
160g cornmeal
1 teaspoon baking powder
340ml semi-skimmed milk
3 eggs, beaten
15g mature Cheddar cheese, grated

extra baby spinach leaves and cherry tomatoes (tossed in a little lemon juice, extra olive oil and rock salt) and raita, to serve

Preheat the oven to 220°C/fan 200°C/ Gas Mark 7.

Grease a 220mm x 84mm x 64mm loaf tin with a little olive oil and set aside.

Place a large frying pan on the stove and heat until it is very hot. Reduce to a low-medium heat, add the cumin seeds and cook until the seeds start to pop – this should take no more than 1–2 minutes.

Add the 2 tablespoons olive oil, the black pepper, chilli powder and salt and cook for just a few seconds. Add the onion and fry until soft, stirring frequently – this should take no more than 5 minutes. Add the tomatoes and cook for approximately 2–3 minutes or until they are soft.

Mix through the spinach and continue cooking until it is wilted – this should take no more than 1–2 minutes. Remove the pan from the heat. Stir in the chopped coriander, mixing well.

In a large mixing bowl, mix together the cornmeal and baking powder, then whisk in the milk until a smooth consistency is acquired. Slowly add the eggs, making sure the mixture is thoroughly combined. Mix through the cheese. Tip the contents of the frying pan into the mixing bowl and stir.

Pour the mixture into the prepared loaf tin. Bake in the centre of the oven for 20–25 minutes or until set.

Leave to cool in the tin for 15 minutes, before turning out onto a wire rack. Serve warm or cold with the baby spinach leaf salad and raita.

One serving = 75%+ RDA antioxidants

Antibacterial
chilli, coriander, cumin, pepper

Antifungal
chilli, coriander, cumin

Anti-inflammatory
chilli, coriander, cumin

Analgesic
chilli

Keema on Toast

Serves 4

Most of us have our own version of keema, or minced meat, that we have a penchant for. North Indian meat eaters, especially those hailing from the Muslim and Sikh communities, are particularly fond of keema in all its 'reincarnations'. Either by itself, or with potatoes or green peas, and usually served with Indian breads, or stuffed in samosas – we love keema.

I remember, as a small child, when visiting our cousins in Birmingham, keema was the peak of the culinary delights to be had. At night, it came served with the obligatory chapattis and, in the morning, stuffed into our breakfast parathas. Spicy keema seemed to hit the 'spot' each time and made the long trip to the Midlands all the more worthwhile. I guess it's the way in which each tiny and soft morsel of meat absorbs the superspices that makes it all the more special.

But it was in Australia where, for me, it came to life as breakfast food. Old worldly Australians would serve it with toast for breakfast. Even now, if you Google 'mince on toast' most links lead to recipes from the antipodes. I have never fathomed why it has never really taken off in Britain as breakfast fare; maybe, it has something to do with our presumption of it being unhealthy. Perhaps, this recipe may turnaround our misconceptions.

Using lean meat, which of course is our best source of animal protein required for fundamental all-round health, and substituting some of it with soy mince, makes it healthier than many of our usual breakfast options. In fact, soy mince contains omega-3 fatty acids essential for optimal cardiovascular health. And if you don't say a word, I am sure nobody will ever guess that you have decreased their meat consumption whilst simultaneously upping their intake of vital soya nutrients.

Grownups and kids alike will love this healthy way to enjoy meat for breakfast. Enjoy keema on toast and, if you like, with a poached egg as well.

2 tablespoons olive oil
1 teaspoon cumin seeds
³/₄ teaspoon salt, or to taste
1 small onion, thinly sliced
1 teaspoon turmeric
400g can tomatoes, blended until smooth
250g minced lamb
100g dried soya mince, soaked in boiling water
1 teaspoon garam masala
1–2 green chillies, chopped (optional)
chopped fresh coriander, to season (optional)

Pour the olive oil into a deep saucepan, add the cumin seeds and cook over a low-medium heat until the seeds start to pop – this should take no longer than 2–3 minutes. Add the salt and onion and fry until the onion is light brown in colour, remembering to stir frequently – this should take no more than 5 minutes.

Sprinkle in the turmeric, mix well and cook for about 20 seconds. Add the tomatoes and cook for about 10 minutes or until the excess juices in the saucepan have dried off, remembering to keep stirring occasionally.

Add the minced lamb to the pan and, mixing well, cook until sealed – this should take no more than 2–3 minutes.

Place the soya mince in a large sieve, pushing it with the back of a spoon to drain out all of the water through the sieve. Add the soya mince to the saucepan and mix through. Bring to a gentle simmer, then cook, covered, for 20 minutes, stirring from time to time.

Season with the garam masala and chillies and chopped coriander, if using, and serve.

One serving = 105%+ RDA antioxidants

Antibacterial
chilli, coriander, cumin, turmeric

Antifungal
chilli, coriander, cumin, turmeric

Antiviral
turmeric

Anti-inflammatory
chilli, coriander, cumin, turmeric

Analgesic
chilli

"Curcumin is a polyphenol present in the spice turmeric, which can directly scavenge free radicals. Thus, curcumin may be a potential antioxidant and anti-inflammatory therapeutic agent against chronic inflammatory lung diseases such as asthma."

University of Rochester, New York, US[19]

Oats with Almonds, Cranberries, Cinnamon and Saffron

Serves 3–4

A warm bowl of oats cooked in milk, cinnamon and saffron, bejewelled splendidly with almonds and cranberries, is reminiscent of my childhood. Mum would give me a steaming bowlful which I would spoon down whilst swinging my legs in gay abandon. With every mouthful, the oats would magically hug my tummy from within and reassure me that everything would be OK. And, since oats help lower bad cholesterol and reduce blood sugar levels, whilst synchronously keeping the tummy feeling full for longer, there is definitely something comforting and dependable about this recipe. When brought together with honey, cinnamon and saffron, each ambrosial mouthful abounds with an Eastern promise of great taste and health.

135g jumbo oats
900ml semi-skimmed milk
2–4 tablespoons honey
a large pinch of ground cinnamon
a pinch of saffron
a pinch of salt
a small handful each of blanched almonds and dried cranberries

extra blanched almonds and dried cranberries, to serve

Add the oats to a deep, heavy-based saucepan and cook over a low-medium heat until the oats change to a slightly darker colour as they roast – this should take about 3–5 minutes. Remember to stir frequently.

Add all the remaining ingredients to the saucepan and mix well. Bring to the boil over a medium heat, then reduce to a gentle simmer and cook, uncovered, for 10 minutes, stirring frequently.

Remove the pan from the heat and serve immediately, sprinkled with the extra almonds and dried cranberries.

One serving =
80%+ RDA
antioxidants

Antibacterial
cinnamon, saffron

Antifungal
cinnamon, saffron

Antiviral
cinnamon

Anti-inflammatory
cinnamon, saffron

Indian Superfood

Red Lentil Kedgeree with Eggs

Serves 4

Red lentils lower the risk of cardiovascular disease and contain antioxidants that are up to fifty times more powerful than vitamin E – not bad for a storecupboard ingredient! Now, if that's not a good enough alibi to encourage you to try out this recipe, what about the taste?... Lentils are simmered in a pampering milk bath with subtle superspices and aromatic basmati rice, and finish off as a velvety-textured kedgeree, topped with eggs.

It is, most assuredly, a satisfying start to the day, especially ideal for the cold, wintry mornings lying in wait for us. And if you feel the cold more than most, you can always add some fresh green chillies and coriander.

1 teaspoon cumin seeds
2 tablespoons olive oil
3/4 teaspoon salt, or to taste
1 onion, diced
1/2 teaspoon turmeric
1 teaspoon paprika
215g red lentils
1 tablespoon basmati rice
900ml semi-skimmed milk
**4 eggs, hardboiled, peeled and sliced
   in quarters (served hot or warm)**
freshly ground black pepper, to taste

Heat a deep saucepan over a very high heat until it is really hot. Reduce to a low-medium heat, add the cumin seeds and cook until the seeds start to pop – this should take no more than 1–2 minutes.

Pour in the olive oil, then add the salt and onion. Cook until the onion is soft, stirring frequently – this will take approximately 5 minutes. Sprinkle the turmeric and paprika into the pan and cook for 1 minute, stirring all the time.

Pour in 450ml boiling water, then add the lentils, rice and milk and bring to the boil. Reduce to a simmer and cook, uncovered, for 40 minutes, stirring occasionally. Make sure the lentil mixture does not boil over.

Serve with the hot or warm egg quarters on top and season with additional salt, if desired, and black pepper.

**One serving =
160%+ RDA
antioxidants**

Antibacterial
cumin, paprika,
turmeric

Antifungal
cumin, paprika,
turmeric

Antiviral
turmeric

Anti-inflammatory
cumin, paprika,
turmeric

Analgesic
paprika

"Under laboratory conditions, 25 plants were tested for their bactericidal activity against Helicobacter pylori which is strongly linked to the development of gastric ulcers and stomach cancer. Among the plants that killed H. Pylori, turmeric was the most efficient followed by cumin, ginger and chilli."

**Royal Free and University College
London Medical School[7]**

Sweet Potato and Mooli Bubble and Squeak

Serves 4

I've always been told that you can put into bubble and squeak whatever you can get your hands on. From leftover veggies to meat, it's all fair-play. So, I really went to town here. Sweet potato and mooli replace the more traditional English preference towards potato and cabbage. Together, with the sugariness of sweet potato and the slight bitterness of mooli, we have a 'mismatch' here that just clicks when the two are brought together with the uplifting superspices.

It's an ultimate breakfast comfort food, and I would recommend it as part of your lazy Sunday therapy when you are close by to the cosiness of your bed – so, if needed, it can be used as a standby stretcher whilst your body takes the intense therapy in its stride. Try it with a blob of ketchup and poached eggs and, if you really want to, as part of a full English breakfast. And, if you have your heart set on something hardcore Indian for breakfast, serve with Chickpeas with Sea Salad and Star Anise and Tamarind Reduction.

Whilst you're lying on your Sunday 'stretcher', it's good to know that just one serving of this recipe will provide you with a full day's requirement of vitamin A.

"Under laboratory conditions, curcumin extracted from turmeric inhibited the herpes simplex virus which can lead to cold sores and genital herpes."

University of Michigan, US[23]

500g sweet potatoes, peeled and cut into large bite-size pieces
200g mooli, peeled and grated
1 small red onion, grated
1 teaspoon salt
1 tablespoon olive oil, plus extra for cooking the patties
2 teaspoons cumin seeds
1 teaspoon turmeric
$\frac{1}{2}$ teaspoon chilli powder (optional)
3 tablespoons gram flour
40g dried breadcrumbs
2 tablespoons grated (peeled) fresh root ginger
20g bunch of fresh coriander, chopped
2 egg yolks

Cook the sweet potatoes in a deep pan of boiling water for approximately 15 minutes or until tender. Drain, then rinse the sweet potatoes under cold running water until cool and drain again. Set aside. (To minimise the loss of nutrients, the sweet potatoes may be steamed or cooked in the microwave, instead of boiling.)

In a large bowl, mix together the mooli, onion and half of the salt and knead for 5 minutes, draining off and discarding the excess juices as you are kneading. Transfer the mixture to a sieve and allow to drain for 5 minutes.

Place 1 tablespoon olive oil and the cumin seeds in a deep saucepan and cook over a medium heat until the seeds begin to pop – this will take no longer than 2–3 minutes.

Remove the pan from the heat and immediately add the turmeric and the chilli powder, if using. Mix well. Add the drained sweet potatoes and the mooli-onion mixture and mash together well. Mix through the remaining salt, the gram flour, breadcrumbs, ginger, chopped coriander and egg yolks, stirring until thoroughly combined. Use the mixture to make 8 patties by forming the mixture into 8 even-sized balls, then flattening each ball a little to form a patty.

Heat some extra olive oil in a frying pan over a medium heat. Cook the bubble and squeak patties in batches until they are golden brown, turning once – this should take about 2–3 minutes for each side. Remove with a spatula and drain well on kitchen paper before serving.

One serving = 175%+ RDA antioxidants

Antibacterial
chilli, coriander, cumin, ginger, turmeric

Antifungal
chilli, coriander, cumin, ginger, turmeric

Antiviral
turmeric

Anti-inflammatory
chilli, coriander, cumin, ginger, turmeric

Analgesic
chilli

Spicy Prawn Omelette

I first had an omelette made with prawns on a sunny day, sitting poolside under a huge frangipani tree which kept dropping its fragrant blooms onto my face. Ever since, the allure of prawn omelette for breakfast has never worn off. If I lived nearer to the Indian Ocean, I would most definitely garnish this recipe with tropical flowers.

Prawns, coriander, ginger and chilli add a wallop of excitement to an ordinary omelette. You can even enliven it a tad more, by adding a sprinkling of chopped fresh green chillies. Prawns up our intake of selenium which helps to regulate a healthy metabolism. However, if you prefer, you can substitute the prawns with baby spinach leaves and a small handful of grated cheese, such as paneer.

2 large eggs
$1/2$ teaspoon curry powder
2 teaspoons sweet chilli sauce, plus extra to serve
a few drops of sesame oil
a small handful of cooked peeled prawns, chopped
a small handful of fresh coriander, chopped
$1/2$ small onion, very finely chopped
1 teaspoon finely grated (peeled) fresh root ginger
salt and freshly ground black pepper, to taste

Preheat the grill to high.

Beat the eggs together in a mixing bowl with the curry powder and 2 teaspoons sweet chilli sauce, then set aside.

Add a few drops of sesame oil to a small frying pan or omelette pan and heat over a medium-high heat.

In the meantime, add the prawns, chopped coriander, onion, ginger and salt and pepper to the egg mixture and combine well.

When the frying pan is hot and the oil is almost smoking, pour in the egg mixture, distributing it evenly over the base of the frying pan. Immediately remove the pan from the stove, place it under the hot grill and cook for 2–3 minutes or until the omelette is set.

Serve with extra sweet chilli sauce and slices of toast or fresh bread.

One serving = 55%+ RDA antioxidants

Antibacterial
chilli, coriander, ginger

Antifungal
chilli, coriander, ginger

Anti-inflammatory
chilli, coriander, ginger

Analgesic
chilli

Lunch

For most of us, lunch – Monday to Friday – is a hurried stop-gap affair in nourishment that breaks the routine monotony of the day. Sitting in front of the PC, hastily demolishing a sandwich, seems to be the order of the day. And there is nothing wrong in doing so. Only perhaps with the help of *Indian Superfood* it can become a somewhat more healthy routine.

There are nutritious lunch box options, such as Sweet Potato Samosa Rolls with Tamarind Reduction or Poached Chicken and Mango Salad with Mustard Seed Dressing. For leisurely weekend and holiday lunches, we have Salmon and Sweet Potato Fishcakes or Mussels Indian Ocean-Style, as well as more traditional tastes of India. Brings a whole new world of meaning to lunch, doesn't it?

Chicken and Green Pepper Jalfrezi

Serves 2–3

Freshness is the very essence of a good jalfrezi, and the Indian Superfood version is no exception. Abounding with antioxidising cumin, ginger, tomato and peppers, this dish's almost floral aromas bloom splendidly, seducing you helplessly to its raptures.

Being cooked for 5 minutes only, the peppers are of an obliging and crunchy texture that contrasts magnificently against a backdrop of soft chicken pieces, whilst simultaneously providing us with well over and above our daily vitamin C requirement.

This is lunchtime dining that's nearly as easy to prepare as whipping up a salad, and so much more rewarding.

2 tablespoons olive oil
2 teaspoons cumin seeds
1/2 teaspoon salt, or to taste
1 small onion, sliced
4 garlic cloves, chopped
2 tablespoons grated (peeled) fresh root ginger
2 teaspoons ground coriander
1 teaspoon turmeric
2 tomatoes, thinly sliced
2 tablespoons tomato purée
8 tablespoons low-fat Greek yogurt
250g skinless, boneless chicken breasts, thinly sliced
2 green peppers, deseeded and thinly sliced
2–6 green chillies, finely chopped
plenty of chopped fresh coriander, to season

Pour the olive oil into a deep saucepan, add the cumin seeds and cook over a low-medium heat until the seeds start to pop – this should take no longer than 2–3 minutes. Add the salt and onion and fry until the onion is light brown in colour, remembering to stir frequently – this should take no more than 5 minutes.

Add the garlic and half of the ginger, mix well, then fry for about 1–2 minutes or until the garlic is a light brown colour. Sprinkle in the ground coriander and turmeric and cook for about 20 seconds.

Add the tomatoes and the remaining ginger, mix well and cook for 5 minutes or until the tomatoes are soft. Stir in the tomato purée and heat through. Pour in the yogurt, mixing thoroughly, and allow it to heat through.

Stir in the chicken, mixing well, then simmer, uncovered, for 5 minutes, stirring frequently. Stir in the peppers and continue to cook for a further 5 minutes, stirring frequently.

Season with the chillies and chopped coriander, mix well and heat through before serving.

One serving = 335%+ RDA antioxidants

Antibacterial
chilli, coriander, cumin, garlic, ginger, turmeric

Antifungal
chilli, coriander, cumin, garlic, ginger, turmeric

Antiviral
garlic, turmeric

Anti-inflammatory
chilli, coriander, cumin, garlic, ginger, turmeric

Analgesic
chilli

Keema with Sweet Potatoes and Peppers in a Tomato Sauce

Serves 4

My brother reckons this is the best keema he has ever tasted, and I am guessing he believes so because of his recently-developed penchant for healthier foods. With no fat dripping out of it and with a nutritious twang of antioxidising tomatoes, pepper and 'creamy' sweet potatoes, I know exactly what it is that he likes about it.

Enjoy this Indian Superfood alternative to keema aloo occasionally as part of a balanced lifestyle. It's a fabulously moreish recipe which kids would love too. If you're fortunate enough to have any left over, try it stuffed into a toasted sandwich.

2 tablespoons olive oil
1 teaspoon each fenugreek seeds and
   cumin seeds
$1/2$ teaspoon nigella seeds
$3/4$ teaspoon salt, or to taste
1 small onion, thinly sliced
6 garlic cloves, finely chopped
1 teaspoon turmeric
2 teaspoons garam masala
3 tablespoons grated (peeled) fresh
   root ginger
2–6 green chillies, chopped
2 x 400g cans tomatoes, blended until
   smooth
500g minced lamb
1 small sweet potato, peeled and diced
   into small cubes
1 green pepper, deseeded and diced
chopped fresh coriander, to season

Pour the olive oil into a deep saucepan, add the fenugreek, cumin and nigella seeds and cook over a low-medium heat until the seeds start to pop – this should take no longer than 2–3 minutes. Add the salt and onion and fry until the onion is light brown in colour, remembering to stir frequently – this should take no more than 5 minutes.

Stir in the garlic and fry for about 1–2 minutes, or until a light brown colour. Sprinkle in the turmeric, mix well and cook for about 20 seconds. Add half of the garam masala and mix well. Add the ginger, chillies and half of the tomatoes and mix well.

Cook for about 10 minutes or until the excess juices in the saucepan have dried off, remembering to keep stirring occasionally. Add the minced lamb and cook, mixing continuously, until it is sealed – this should take no more than 5 minutes.

Add the sweet potato, pepper and remaining tomatoes. Bring to a simmer, then cook, uncovered, for 30 minutes – remember to stir occasionally.

Season with the chopped coriander and remaining garam masala. Serve with your choice of sides.

One serving = 220%+ RDA antioxidants

Antibacterial
chilli, coriander, cumin, fenugreek, garlic, ginger, nigella, turmeric

Antifungal
chilli, coriander, cumin, fenugreek, garlic, ginger, nigella, turmeric

Antiviral
garlic, turmeric

Anti-inflammatory
chilli, coriander, cumin, fenugreek, garlic, ginger, nigella, turmeric

Analgesic
chilli, fenugreek, nigella

Roasted Vine Tomato, Vegetable and Cinnamon Soup

Serves 4

Tomatoes are a champion source of potassium, niacin, vitamin B6 and folate, which are identified with lowering high cholesterol levels and the risk of heart disease; and when accompanied with cinnamon, which reduces blood sugar levels, we are talking about some serious heart loving here.

It's a soup that's sure to be an instant hit with those of you who are fortunate enough to have a tomato crush going on. It's a kind of hybrid between tomato soup and the Indian burtha; the superspices giving it a real meatiness – a quality that would even make it good enough to pour over pasta.

Tomatoes and pepper are also equipped with a platoon of lycopene, which is made even easier for our body to absorb by the lengthy cooking process involved in this recipe. It's a stupendously tasty way to get nearly 500g of veggies per serving down the guzzler, without much effort at all!

1 aubergine (about 300g), pricked with a fork
1 large onion (left unpeeled)
1 red pepper
1kg vine-ripened tomatoes
2 tablespoons olive oil
1 tablespoon mustard seeds
1 small onion, sliced
4 garlic cloves, chopped
2 tablespoons grated (peeled) fresh root ginger
1 teaspoon turmeric
1 tablespoon ground coriander
1–2 green chillies, chopped
1¹/₃ teaspoons salt, or to taste
1 cinnamon stick
plenty of chopped fresh coriander

natural yogurt and extra chopped fresh coriander, to garnish

Preheat the oven to 200°C/fan 180°C/Gas Mark 6. Place the whole aubergine, onion, pepper and tomatoes on a baking tray and bake in the centre of the oven for 45 minutes or until they are soft.

Remove the vegetables from the oven and allow them to cool a little. Peel the onion. Remove the stalks from the aubergine and pepper and deseed the pepper. Roughly chop the vegetables and place in a bowl.

Pour the olive oil into a deep saucepan, add the mustard seeds and cook over a high heat until the seeds start to pop – this should take no longer than 1–2 minutes. Reduce the heat to low-medium, then add the onion to the pan. Cook for 5 minutes or until the onion is a light brown colour – this should take no more than about 5 minutes; remember to stir frequently.

Add the garlic and ginger and cook over a medium heat until the garlic is golden brown in colour, making sure that you stir frequently. This process will take no longer than 2–3 minutes. Add the turmeric and ground coriander and cook for 20 seconds, stirring.

Now add the roasted vegetables, chillies, salt, cinnamon stick and 250ml boiling water and bring to a simmer. Cover the pan and simmer gently for 30 minutes, stirring from time to time.

Take the saucepan off the heat and remove the cinnamon stick. Stir in the chopped coriander. Now take a hand-held blender and blitz the soup until it is a velvety smooth texture.

Drizzle the soup with the yogurt and sprinkle with some more chopped coriander. Serve with naan or any bread of your choice.

One serving = 295%+ RDA antioxidants

Antibacterial
chilli, cinnamon, coriander, garlic, ginger, turmeric
Antifungal
chilli, cinnamon, coriander, garlic, ginger, turmeric

Antiviral
cinnamon, garlic, turmeric

Anti-inflammatory
chilli, cinnamon, coriander, garlic, ginger, turmeric

Analgesic
chilli

Indian Superfood

Green Coriander Chicken

Serves 4

In this recipe, lean chicken is bathed blissfully in a rich yogurt sauce with a gargantuan amount of antioxidising coriander. It's an effortless-to-prepare recipe that fills your tummy whilst simultaneously fuelling the immune system and taste buds – all without you even breaking a sweat in the kitchen.

A tremendously aromatic dish, perfumed with the intense and passionate floral bouquet of fresh green coriander; so many exhilarating flavours literally explode on the palate, allowing you a rare opportunity to discover an army of taste buds that you didn't realise you even had. I adore this recipe so much that I wonder, with each mouthful, whether it would taste any better if I was eating it made out of herbs from the overflowing garden-beds that are imagined to exist in Shangri-La? And I doubt it would.

"Curcumin is an orange-yellow component of turmeric, a spice often found in most Indian curries. Traditionally known for its anti-inflammatory effects, curcumin has been shown in the last two decades to be a potent immunomodulatory agent. Curcumin at low doses can enhance antibody responses. This suggests that curcumin's reported beneficial effects in arthritis, allergy, asthma, atherosclerosis, heart disease, Alzheimer's disease, diabetes, and cancer may be due in part to its ability to modulate the immune system. Together, these findings warrant further consideration of curcumin as a therapy for immune disorders."

The University of Texas, US[24]

a large bunch of fresh coriander (about 80g), coarsely chopped
1 large tomato, cut into quarters
6 garlic cloves, finely chopped
3 tablespoons grated (peeled) fresh root ginger
2–4 green chillies, chopped
3/4 teaspoon salt, or to taste
1 teaspoon sugar
500g natural yogurt
1 teaspoon turmeric
1 tablespoon olive oil
500g skinless, boneless chicken breasts, cut into bite-size pieces
freshly ground black pepper, to taste

In a food processor, blend together the coriander, tomato, garlic, ginger, chillies, salt, sugar and yogurt until smooth, then pour the mixture into a bowl and set aside.

Place the turmeric in a deep saucepan and pour in the olive oil. Cook over a low-medium heat until the turmeric starts to sizzle – this should take no more than 1–2 minutes.

Add the chicken and cook until sealed all over, stirring frequently – this should take no more than 5 minutes.

Now slowly pour in the yogurt-and-spice mixture, mixing well, then bring to a gentle simmer. Simmer, uncovered, for 10 minutes, stirring from time to time.

Season to taste with black pepper. Serve with your choice of sides.

One serving = 115%+ RDA antioxidants

Antibacterial
chilli, coriander, garlic, ginger, pepper, turmeric

Antifungal
chilli, coriander, garlic, ginger, turmeric

Antiviral
garlic, turmeric

Anti-inflammatory
chilli, coriander, garlic, ginger, turmeric

Analgesic
chilli

Roasted Cherry Tomato, Aubergine and Potato Subzi

Serves 3–4

Here's a wonderful example of what magic we can weave with a few simple and healthy ingredients and very little seasoning. Even though I'm not a vegetarian, this is still one of my favourite recipes of all time.

The roasted and caramelised vegetables take on a character which fracases with the tangy tomato and ginger sauce; a tug-of-war ensues between the two to win over your taste buds, which emerges in your favour when you gobble them down together. This subzi is light and impossibly rich in taste – both at the same time! Who'd have thought good health could taste so great?

Ginger, tomatoes and aubergines are all effective at reining in bad cholesterol, and the vast quantity of tomatoes 'injects' lycopene into your body. I am sure you will agree this is a brilliant way to help you on the way to getting your 5-a-day. Another perk of this recipe is that it's so easy to make; in fact, it almost feels like cheating. Now, I just need to find someone to cook it for me!

750g cherry tomatoes
1 potato, cut into bite-size pieces
300g aubergine, cut to a similar size as the potato pieces
1 tablespoon olive oil, plus extra for roasting
2 garlic cloves, finely chopped
½ teaspoon turmeric
1 teaspoon salt, or to taste
1 teaspoon sugar
1–2 green chillies, finely chopped
1 tablespoon finely grated (peeled) fresh root ginger
2 tablespoons coconut milk (optional)

chopped fresh coriander, to garnish

Preheat the oven to 200°C/fan 180°C/Gas Mark 6. Rub the cherry tomatoes and the potato and aubergine pieces in the extra olive oil, place in a single layer in a roasting tin and roast in the centre of the oven for approximately 15–20 minutes or until cooked through.

Pour 1 tablespoon olive oil into a deep saucepan, add the garlic and cook over a low-medium heat until the garlic becomes a golden brown colour, stirring all the time – this should take no more than 2–3 minutes. Add the turmeric, salt and sugar, mix well and cook for 20 seconds.

Add the chillies, ginger, coconut milk, if using, and half of the cooked cherry tomatoes to the saucepan and, using a hand-held blender, blitz to a smooth paste.

Bring the mixture in the saucepan to the boil, then reduce to a rapid simmer and cook for 5 minutes. Add the remaining roasted vegetables and mix well, making sure to heat through.

Garnish with the chopped coriander and serve with your choice of sides.

One serving =
125%+ RDA
antioxidants

Antibacterial
chilli, coriander, garlic, ginger

Antifungal
chilli, coriander, garlic, ginger

Antiviral
garlic, turmeric

Anti-inflammatory
chilli, coriander, garlic, ginger, turmeric

Analgesic
chilli

Indian Superfood

Mussels Indian Ocean-Style

Serves 4–6

Mussels are rich in zinc, which is essential for the immune function, wound-healing and stabilising blood sugar levels. In this particular recipe, they are camouflaged in a rich sauce of tomato, which contains some of nature's most powerful antioxidants, well-known in helping to prevent sunburn and cancer. Also, the mustard seeds, dotting the sauce like tiny grenades, are part of the cruciferous family, venerated for their potent and warlike stance towards cancer cells.

Hostility aside, it's very delicious grub. I suggest you crack open a bottle of Chenin Blanc and invite some friends over for a finger-licking seafood lunch. Life's little pleasures are a lot simpler than we are led to believe.

2 tablespoons olive oil
1 teaspoon fennel seeds
1 tablespoon mustard seeds
6 garlic cloves, finely chopped
1 tablespoon grated (peeled) fresh root ginger
1 teaspoon garam masala
2 x 400g cans tomatoes, blended until smooth
1 tablespoon coconut milk
2–4 green chillies, chopped
1/2 teaspoon sugar
3/4 teaspoon salt, or to taste
1kg fresh mussels in their shells, de-bearded and washed
chopped fresh coriander, to season

Pour the olive oil into a deep and wide saucepan, add the fennel and mustard seeds and cook over a high heat until the seeds start to pop – this should take no more than 1–2 minutes. Remove the pan from the heat and allow the oil to cool for a moment or two.

Add the garlic and ginger to the saucepan and fry over a medium heat until golden brown in colour – this should take no more than 2–3 minutes (If the garlic and ginger stick to the pan, add a few drops of cold water). Add the garam masala and cook for 1 minute, making sure to stir frequently to avoid any sticking.

Mix in the tomatoes, coconut milk, chillies, sugar and salt, then bring the mixture to a rapid simmer. Reduce to a low simmer and cook, uncovered, for 10 minutes.

Add the mussels to the saucepan and mix through, making sure they are coated with the sauce. Cover the pan and cook for about 5 minutes or until the mussels have opened, shaking the pan occasionally. Discard any unopened mussels.

Season with the chopped coriander. Serve with naan or a bread of your choice.

One serving = 125%+ RDA antioxidants

Antibacterial
chilli, coriander, fennel, garlic, ginger, mustard

Antifungal
chilli, coriander, fennel, garlic, ginger, mustard

Antiviral
garlic

Anti-inflammatory
chilli, coriander, fennel, garlic, ginger, mustard

Analgesic
chilli, fennel

Salmon and Sweet Potato Fishcakes

Serves 5

Who doesn't like fishcakes? Whether you're from London or Chiang Mai, we can all recount at least one occasion when a comforting fishcake grabbed us by the cuff and threw us into bliss; you tried rejecting its charms, but resistance was futile. I still remember from my days working in the fish and chip shop, where in the heated display cabinet, the lighting used to make the fishcakes shine a succulent amber colour, akin only to Donatella Versace's ethereal glow. It was as if from their resplendence they could almost seduce me there and then.

So, for moments of weakness, here's a healthier version that we can willingly submit to. Sweet potato radiates a tremendous amount of vitamin A, salmon beams omega-3 fatty acids that increase activity of white cells in the body, and coriander acts as a gentle sedative. This hybrid of the Indian aloo tikki has to be amongst the world's most divine-tasting fishcake. The crunchy exterior of the fishcake leads into the warm and velvety melt-in-the-mouth interior of the sweet potato and buttery salmon, which is tempered beautifully with just the right measure of superspices that leave you feeling like a golden Buddha in nirvana.

750g sweet potatoes, peeled and cut into large bite-size pieces
1 tablespoon olive oil, plus extra for cooking the fishcakes
1 tablespoon cumin seeds
1½ teaspoons each caraway seeds, turmeric and chilli powder
2 tablespoons ground coriander
1 egg yolk
200g cooked salmon fillet, flaked (or canned salmon, drained and flaked)
4 tablespoons chopped fresh coriander

3 tablespoons grated (peeled) fresh root ginger
4 tablespoons gram flour
65g dried breadcrumbs
1½ teaspoons salt

mixed salad leaves, lemon wedges and sweet chilli sauce, to serve

Cook the sweet potatoes in a deep pan of boiling water for approximately 15 minutes or until tender. Drain, then rinse the sweet potatoes under cold running water until cool and drain again. Place in a mixing bowl and set aside. (To minimise the loss of nutrients, the sweet potatoes may be steamed or cooked in the microwave, instead of boiling.)

Pour 1 tablespoon olive oil into a frying pan, add the cumin and caraway seeds and cook over a low-medium heat until the seeds turn a golden roasted colour – this should take no more than 2–3 minutes. Remove the frying pan from the heat. Immediately add the turmeric, chilli powder and ground coriander and mix well.

Pour the spice mixture into the bowl of sweet potatoes. Mash the potatoes until

they are quite smooth, then add the egg yolk, mixing it in well. Now add the flaked salmon, chopped coriander, ginger, gram flour, breadcrumbs and salt and mix well.

To make the fishcakes, divide the mixture into 10 equal portions. Roll each portion into a ball in the palms of your hand and squash it down slightly to make a round patty. The fishcakes should each be about 7cm in diameter. To avoid the fishcakes sticking to your palms, you may need to wash your hands with cold water from time to time.

Pour enough extra olive oil into the frying pan to cover the bottom of the pan and heat over a medium-high heat. Add the fish cakes to the pan, a few at a time, and cook for 2–3 minutes on each side until they are a golden brown colour.

Remove with a spatula and drain well on kitchen paper before serving. Serve with mixed salad leaves, lemon wedges and sweet chilli sauce.

One serving = 205%+ RDA antioxidants	Antiviral turmeric
Antibacterial chilli, coriander, cumin, ginger	**Anti-inflammatory** chilli, coriander, cumin, ginger, turmeric
Antifungal chilli, coriander, cumin, ginger, turmeric	**Analgesic** caraway, chilli

Prawn and Coconut Pilau

Serves 3–4

I'm a big fan of prawns. Although I can tire of eating chicken and fish, it seems my love of prawns is infinite. And that's perfectly hunky-dory, because prawns are a fab source of protein which help us to grow big and strong. In this pilau, I use the healthiest white rice, basmati, and stir-fry it in cholesterol- and blood pressure-lowering olive oil.

Crunchy grains of aromatic rice, prawns, coconut and benign Indian superspices, make for a welcome change to the pilau's we are accustomed to. It's a great mid-week recipe that even the kids will adore.

All things considered, if you're one of those miscreants (you would know if you are one) who habitually bastardises perfectly good recipes, please do feel at ease to substitute the prawns with tofu or cooked meat and, if you must, with leftovers. I guess this recipe is as flexible, and as healthy, as you are, so it's not a faux pas to make a few changes. No hard feelings.

2 tablespoons olive oil
125g green peas (fresh or frozen)
1 carrot, coarsely grated
1 onion, thinly sliced
1 tablespoon grated (peeled) fresh root ginger
200g cooked peeled prawns
2 tablespoons desiccated coconut
$1/2$ teaspoon salt, or to taste
1 teaspoon curry powder
1 quantity Foolproof Pilau, chilled (see page 134)

fresh lime wedges, spring onions and chopped fresh coriander, to garnish

In a non-stick wok, heat 1 tablespoon olive oil over a high heat until the oil is very hot and starts to smoke. Now add the green peas, carrot, onion, ginger and prawns and stir-fry for 2–3 minutes or until the vegetables are cooked. Take the contents out of the wok to a warm plate and set aside.

Return the wok back to a high heat, pour in the remaining olive oil and heat until hot. Now add the coconut, salt and curry powder and stir.

Add the cooked pilau and stir through until the rice is coated with the spices. Mix in the stir-fried vegetables and prawns and heat through until hot.

Garnish with the lime wedges, spring onions and coriander and serve.

One serving =
70%+ RDA
antioxidants

Antibacterial
chilli, coriander, ginger

Antifungal
chilli, coriander, ginger

Anti-inflammatory
chilli, coriander, ginger

Analgesic
chilli

Puy Lentil Dahl Soup

Serves 2–3

I cannot recall meeting an Indian kid who doesn't enjoy eating lentils. Sure, we would all have our dislikes, maybe fish or spinach, but notably never lentils. So, I never could quite comprehend why so many of my English buddies were averse to them, as they would be to a mosquito on heat. But then again, 'we' Indians have had centuries of vegetarianism, and have been eating lentils instead of meat to get the recipe for dahl down pat. Consequently, I feel that I can say, boldly and without hesitance, that with this soup I can teach the French a thing or two about what best to do with their brilliant Puy lentils.

Volcanic Puy lentils imbue a wonderfully earthy, fruity and almost sweet flavour into this soup. When the lentils are swept up into the lava of Indian spicing, the aftermath is an unimaginably simple and unadulterated pleasure for the taste buds. I am quite partial to a bowl or two with plenty of fresh bread, spread thinly with butter. Lentils also lower incidence of cardiovascular diseases and reduce cholesterol, whilst improving the flow of blood and oxygen in the body. The addition of a good dose of garlic to this recipe not only adds immeasurable taste but also helps produce more natural 'killer' cells in the blood to fight off infections.

200g Puy lentils
1 tomato, diced
2 tablespoons tomato purée
40ml good-quality soy sauce (make sure there is no added sugar)
1/2 teaspoon each chilli powder and turmeric
2 tablespoons olive oil
8 garlic cloves, chopped
2 tablespoons grated (peeled) fresh root ginger
salt and freshly ground black pepper, to taste

Put the lentils, tomato, tomato purée, soy sauce, chilli powder, turmeric and 2.5 litres boiling water in a large, deep saucepan. Bring to the boil, then reduce the heat and simmer rapidly, uncovered, for 45 minutes, stirring occasionally. The soup should be of a reasonably thick consistency, but still allowing the lentils to move around in the liquid quite easily.

A few minutes before the lentil mixture is cooked, put the olive oil into a frying pan with the garlic and ginger and cook over a low-medium heat until golden brown, stirring frequently – this should take no more than 2–3 minutes (if the garlic and ginger stick to the pan, add a few drops of cold water).

Pour this spice mixture into the soup and mix well, then simmer for 2 minutes. Season with salt and black pepper. Serve with naan or any other bread of your choice.

One serving =
350%+ RDA
antioxidants

Antibacterial
chilli, garlic, ginger, turmeric

Antifungal
chilli, garlic, ginger, turmeric

Antiviral
garlic, turmeric

Anti-inflammatory
chilli, garlic, ginger, turmeric

Analgesic
chilli

Baby Potatoes in a Rich Broccoli, Tomato and Coconut Masala

Serves 4

I have to admit that, for years, I hadn't been a big aficionado of broccoli, finding it bitter in taste and almost a little tough, akin to what I imagine it would be like if I were eating a small tree – a bonsai perhaps? Nevertheless, and jokes aside, broccoli is not to be sniffed at but consumed, as it is linked with a decreased risk of aggressive prostate and bowel cancer. One serving of broccoli also provides us with a mammoth 175% of our daily vitamin K requirements.

Baby Potatoes in a Rich Broccoli, Tomato and Coconut Masala is nothing like how you'd imagine broccoli to taste, it's more like the Punjabi classic aloo gobi, only much more gratifying. Perhaps you can summon to memory the film, 'Bend It Like Beckham', and the scene where the overbearing mother tells her daughter that to be successfully married she would need to learn how to make aloo gobi? Well my take on it is a deliciously rich and 'creamy' one, with lots of melt-in-the-mouth potato and broccoli. Even if you're not a vegetarian, you have to try this at least once. It's so very satisfying, and leaves you wondering why we fuss over meat at all.

I think back to the day when I made it last, and recall my Mum overcome by the distinct aromas, breaking her house-rules and taking a bowl full of it into her lounge room to munch in front of the television. Fennel and nigella seeds add analgesic properties to best help us deal with the daily strains of life.

Try it with naans or chapattis and if, after tasting, you still don't like broccoli – you are lying to yourself. And when you get around to making it one day soon, according to Mrs. Singh, it might somehow 'harvest' that ever-elusive Mr. or Ms. Right.

2 tablespoons olive oil
1/2 teaspoon each cumin seeds, nigella seeds and fennel seeds
1 teaspoon salt, or to taste
1 small onion, thinly sliced
4 garlic cloves, finely chopped
1 teaspoon turmeric
4 tomatoes, finely chopped
2 tablespoons grated (peeled) fresh root ginger
2–4 green chillies, chopped
400ml light coconut milk
1kg baby potatoes, cut in half
300g broccoli florets

chopped fresh coriander, to garnish

Pour the olive oil into a deep saucepan, add the cumin, nigella and fennel seeds and cook over a low-medium heat until the seeds start to pop – this should take no longer than 2–3 minutes. Add the salt and onion and fry until the onion is light brown in colour, remembering to stir frequently – this should take no more than 5 minutes.

Stir in the garlic and fry for about 1–2 minutes or until a light brown colour. Sprinkle in the turmeric, mix well and cook for about 20 seconds. Add the tomatoes, ginger and chillies and cook for about 10 minutes or until the tomatoes are cooked through and any excess juices in the saucepan have dried off, remembering to keep stirring occasionally.

Pour in the coconut milk, mix well and bring to a simmer. Add the potatoes and broccoli florets, mix well, then return to a simmer. Cover and cook gently for about 20–30 minutes, stirring occasionally, until the potatoes and broccoli are tender.

Garnish with the chopped coriander and serve with your choice of sides.

One serving =
145%+ RDA
antioxidants

Antibacterial
chilli, coriander, cumin, fennel, garlic, ginger, nigella, turmeric

Antifungal
chilli, coriander, cumin, fennel, garlic, ginger, nigella, turmeric

Antiviral
garlic, turmeric

Anti-inflammatory
chilli, coriander, cumin, fennel, garlic, ginger, nigella, turmeric

Analgesic
chilli, fennel, nigella

Aubergine and Red Peppers with Crab and Coconut

Serves 4

Sweet and nutty-tasting crab meat, rich in omega-3, works splendidly well with the spicy and savoury vegetables. Canned crab makes the recipe more accessible. It's low in calories and rich in protein. Fennel seeds act to suppress appetite.

So, if you're planning to get into last year's bikini or swim-shorts and strut your booty on the beach like a hot crab, this recipe is ideally suited to your cause.

2 tablespoons olive oil
1 teaspoon cloves
1 teaspoon each cumin seeds and
    fennel seeds
$\frac{1}{2}$ teaspoon nigella seeds
1 teaspoon salt, or to taste
2 small onions, thinly sliced
6 garlic cloves, finely chopped
1 teaspoon turmeric
6 tomatoes, finely chopped
2–6 green chillies, chopped
2 tablespoons grated (peeled) fresh
    root ginger
2 red peppers, deseeded
2 large aubergines, stalks removed
2 x 170g cans crab meat, drained
chopped fresh coriander and
    desiccated coconut, to season

Pour the olive oil into a deep saucepan, add the cloves and cumin, fennel and nigella seeds and cook over a low-medium heat until the seeds start to pop – this should take no longer than 2–3 minutes. Add the salt and half of the onions and fry until the onions are light brown in colour, remembering to stir frequently – this should take no more than 5 minutes.

Stir in the garlic and fry for about 1–2 minutes or until a light brown colour. Sprinkle in the turmeric, mix well and cook for about 20 seconds. Add the tomatoes, chillies, ginger and the remaining onions and cook for about 15 minutes or until the tomatoes are cooked to a pulp – remember to keep stirring occasionally.

In the meantime, cut the peppers and aubergines into large bite-size pieces. Once the tomatoes are cooked, add the peppers and aubergines to the pan. Cover and cook over a gentle heat for about 30 minutes or until the vegetables are cooked through, remembering to stir frequently.

A few minutes before the end of cooking, mix through the crab meat, chopped coriander and coconut and heat through.

Serve with your choice of sides.

"The extracts of 12 plants selected on the basis of the folk-medicine reports were examined for their antibacterial effects against eight pathogenic bacteria. Clove extract proved to be the most effective against the bacteria tested."

University Cadi Ayyad, Marrakech, Morocco[11]

One serving =
265%+ RDA
antioxidants

Antibacterial
chilli, cloves, coriander, cumin, fennel, garlic, ginger, nigella, turmeric

Antifungal
chilli, cloves, coriander, cumin, fennel, garlic, ginger, nigella, turmeric

Antiviral
cloves, garlic, turmeric

Anti-inflammatory
chilli, cloves, coriander, cumin, fennel, garlic, ginger, nigella, turmeric

Analgesic
chilli, cloves, fennel, nigella

Indian Superfood

Exotic Mushroom Subzi

Serves 2–3

Exotic mushrooms, such as shiitake and oyster, contain beta-glucan which stimulates the immune system. To boot, they also have a powerful antiviral and anticancer effect on the body which is proven by science.

For this recipe, I find whole oyster mushrooms work really well, and are readily available at most supermarkets. However, if you're out to impress someone or, like me, to scare Granny, you can always make it with the long, stringy and alien-looking Enoki mushrooms that can be found readily at Chinese grocers and in some supermarkets. I have also made this recipe using Buna Shimeji, Eryngii, Maitake and Shiroshimeji mushrooms. They all add their own unique and almost sweet flavour, as well as being much more tender than regular mushrooms.

This particular recipe is very close to my heart as it tastes just like Mum's cooking. It's astonishingly rich and creamy-tasting, borrowing the typical characteristics of exotic mushrooms, and it is peppered with a good smattering of analgesic nigella seeds. Beyond any doubt, this is one of my all-time favourite recipes – it's far too exotic and satisfying to be just a side. Try it with crispy chapattis. This is a mighty fine way to take some 'medicine'!

2 tablespoons olive oil
1 teaspoon nigella seeds
4 garlic cloves, finely chopped
2 small onions, cut into quarters and
   pulled apart
1 tablespoon grated (peeled) fresh root
   ginger
1 green chilli, finely chopped
1 teaspoon turmeric
$^3/_4$ teaspoon salt, or to taste
2 tomatoes, cut into quarters
250g exotic fresh mushrooms (if very
   large, cut them into bite-size pieces)

Pour the olive oil into a large frying pan, add the nigella seeds and cook over a low-medium heat until the seeds begin to pop – this should take no longer than 2–3 minutes. Remove the pan from the heat and allow the oil to cool for a moment or two.

Add the garlic to the pan and cook over a medium heat until it begins to sizzle. Now add the onions, ginger and chilli and fry until the garlic and ginger are golden brown in colour and the onions are almost transparent, stirring frequently – this should take no more than 5–10 minutes.

Add the turmeric and salt and continue to cook for 20 seconds, stirring all the time. Add the tomatoes and cook until soft, stirring frequently – this should take no longer than 5 minutes.

In the meantime, wipe the mushrooms clean; do not wash.

Once the tomatoes are ready, add the mushrooms, mix well and cook over a low heat, covered, for 10 minutes, stirring occasionally.

Serve with your choice of sides.

One serving =
190%+ RDA
antioxidants

Antibacterial
chilli, garlic, ginger, nigella, turmeric

Antifungal
chilli, garlic, ginger, nigella, turmeric

Antiviral
garlic, turmeric

Anti-inflammatory
chilli, garlic, ginger, nigella, turmeric

Analgesic
chilli, nigella

Hot Summer's Day Potato Salad

Serves 4

In a typically long, hot Indian summer, when the mercury peaks well over 40°C, people sensibly refrain from consuming heavy foods, instead preferring chilled raitas served with tepid chapattis, pilau, Bombay aloo, pickles and salad.

In this contemporary take on the Indian summer lunch, we combine the potatoes and salad into the raita itself. Yogurt and mint strive competitively to cool down your hot body. All you need is some bread and perhaps a tall glass of ice-chilled white beer for a utopian lunch.

Melissa and I used to have this with naans, sitting under huge sun umbrellas overlooking gulets rocking gently out in the azure Mediterranean Sea. It was a life far from the ordinary. But, no matter how hard I tried, Melissa was forever more interested in her beer. Too much beer always leads to trouble in paradise. For, sweet-faced Melissa had an even greater penchant for starting pub brawls, much to the dismay of our Turkish neighbours. Stick to one beer, I say.

2 large potatoes, cut into large cubes
1 tablespoon olive oil
a handful of mangetout, sliced into strips
1 garlic clove, finely chopped
1 teaspoon paprika
1kg low-fat Greek yogurt
a handful of cherry tomatoes, cut in half
1 red onion, thinly sliced
2–4 green chillies, sliced (optional)
$1/2$ teaspoon salt, or to taste
a large handful of mint leaves, coarsely chopped
plenty of chopped fresh coriander, or herbs of your choice
freshly ground black pepper, to taste

Cook the potatoes in a pan of boiling water until tender. Drain, rinse under cold water until cool, then drain well. Set aside.

Pour the olive oil into a deep saucepan and cook over a medium heat until it's almost smoking. Throw in the mangetout and garlic and stir-fry for 30 seconds. Remove the pan from the heat and mix through the paprika. Allow to cool.

In a large bowl, combine the potatoes, mangetout mixture and all the remaining ingredients, seasoning to taste with black pepper.

Serve with your choice of sides.

Cook's Tip
Try this recipe with poached (cold) chicken instead of the potatoes.

One serving = 105%+ RDA antioxidants

Antibacterial
chilli, coriander, garlic, mint, pepper

Antifungal
chilli, coriander, garlic, mint

Antiviral
garlic

Anti-inflammatory
chilli, coriander, garlic

Analgesic
chilli

Red Lentils and Chicken with Cumin and Black Cardamom

Serves 4–6

Some things in life aren't fair, but this one is an exception. It's in fact more than fair. Take a peep down below to see how easy this curry is in its preparation. When you get around to making it, weigh it to the great taste you get in return.

Succulent chicken pieces in the most exquisite red lentil and roasted cumin seed dahl, and that pretty much sums it up. If I were to have died without tasting this, what a terrible shame it would be. Fortunately, eating lentils lowers the incidence of cardiovascular diseases and reduces cholesterol. As a result, my chances of eating this one a few more times are increased.

215g red lentils
500g skinless, boneless chicken breasts, cut in half
3/4 teaspoon salt, or to taste
1/2 teaspoon turmeric
2 tablespoons grated (peeled) fresh root ginger
1 teaspoon ground ginger
3 teaspoons cumin seeds
5 black cardamom pods or 10 green cardamom pods, lightly crushed
2 tablespoons olive oil
1 small onion, thinly sliced
6 garlic cloves, finely chopped
2–6 green chillies, chopped

Place the lentils, chicken, salt, turmeric, fresh ginger, ground ginger, 2 teaspoons of the cumin seeds and the cardamom pods in a deep saucepan. Pour in 900ml boiling water and return the water to a gentle simmer. Cook, uncovered, for 40 minutes, remembering to stir frequently to avoid sticking. If the lentils thicken too much, you may need to add a little more boiling water. At the end of the cooking time, the lentils should resemble a pulp and have a consistency similar to that of a thick pumpkin soup.

In the meantime, pour the olive oil into a frying pan, add the remaining cumin seeds and cook over a low-medium heat until the seeds start to pop – this should take no longer than 2–3 minutes.

Add the onion and fry until light brown in colour, remembering to stir frequently – this should take no more than 5 minutes. Stir in the garlic and chillies and fry for about 2–4 minutes or until the garlic is a golden brown colour.

Once the lentils are ready, stir the spice mixture into the lentil mixture and simmer for just a few minutes.

Serve with your choice of sides.

One serving = 230%+ RDA antioxidants

Antibacterial
cardamom, chilli, cumin, garlic, ginger, turmeric

Antifungal
cardamom, chilli, cumin, garlic, ginger, turmeric

Antiviral
garlic, turmeric

Anti-inflammatory
cardamom, chilli, cumin, garlic, ginger, turmeric

Analgesic
chilli

" Cardamom was tested for its antibacterial effects towards E. Coli, Staphylococcus aureus, Bacillus cereus and Listeria monocytogenes. Essential oil of cardamom could effectively inhibit growth of all the tested bacteria."

King Mongkut's University of Technology Thonburi, Bangkok, Thailand[6]

Poached Chicken and Mango Salad with Mustard Seed Dressing

Serves 2–3

Lean chicken breast is beneficial for building and maintaining muscle tone. It also contains the feel-good amino acid tryptophan. Mango is not only a brilliant source of vitamins A, C and E, and of fibre, iron, minerals, antioxidants and flavonoids, but is also a vibrant wellspring of lutein, which is employed by our body as an antioxidant to protect eyesight. Remarkably, mustard seeds have been exploited medicinally from very early times; both Pythagoras and Hippocrates prescribed a vast number of treatments based on mustard.

The fusion of melt-in-the-mouth chicken, perfumy mango flesh, fresh coriander and basil, tossed up in a punchy mustard seed dressing, is quite breathtaking. Make sure to find yourself a glass of chilled Chardonnay, somewhere to sit and, if at all possible, a slither of sunshine, prior to chowing it down and becoming hopelessly overwhelmed by the 'fabulosity' of it all.

2 skinless, boneless chicken breasts
1/2 teaspoon mustard seeds
2 tablespoons extra-virgin olive oil
1 tablespoon Spicy Chilli Oil
(see page 147)
juice of 2 limes
rock salt, to taste
100g rocket leaves or mixed green
salad leaves of your choice
1 small red onion, thinly sliced
12 cherry tomatoes
1 mango, peeled, stoned and sliced
a small handful each of fresh basil
leaves and fresh coriander leaves

In a deep saucepan, bring plenty of water to the boil. Place the chicken breasts into the water and return to the boil. Once the water begins to boil, take the pan off the heat and cover with a lid. Allow the chicken breasts to sit in the water and poach for 2 1/2 hours (this stage of the process can be done the morning prior to lunch).

Remove the chicken breasts from the water using a slotted spoon, slice the chicken and set aside in the refrigerator. Discard the poaching liquid.

To prepare the dressing, place the mustard seeds in a deep saucepan (this will minimise the amount of seeds that will jump out of the pan and onto your kitchen worktops) and pour both the oils into the pan. Cook over a high heat until the seeds start to pop. Remove the pan from the heat and allow the oil to cool for a moment or two.

Once the oil has cooled, pour in the lime juice and mix in the rock salt to taste – this will be your dressing.

In a deep mixing bowl, using your hands, mix together the chicken, rocket leaves, onion, tomatoes, mango, basil and coriander leaves and the dressing, making sure all of the leaves are well coated with the dressing. Serve immediately with Wholemeal Pumpkin and Caraway Seed Bread (see page 142).

One serving = 110%+ RDA antioxidants

Antibacterial
basil, chilli, coriander, mustard

Antifungal
chilli, coriander, mustard

Anti-inflammatory
basil, chilli, coriander, mustard

Analgesic
chilli

Antiviral
basil

Stir-Fried Tofu with Bean Sprouts and Coconut

Serves 4

It's as if an Indian health spa goddess has gone meticulously through this recipe with a pen in each of her legion of hands and cross-checked so it ticks all the right boxes. Few and far are main meal recipes that can purport to be under 150 calories per portion, whilst simultaneously being low-fat, low carb, high protein, vegan and somehow tasting fit for a Queen, despite the fact of being capable of demolishing even a King-size hunger, and taking only minutes to whizz up. Impossible is nothing in the New India.

1 tablespoon olive oil
1 teaspoon mustard seeds
1/2 teaspoon nigella seeds
a piece of fresh root ginger (no larger than the size of a small matchbox), peeled and cut into small batons
2 garlic cloves, sliced
1/2 teaspoon turmeric
1/3 teaspoon chilli powder
2 tablespoons desiccated coconut
250g firm tofu, drained and cut into strips
400g bean sprouts
3/4 teaspoon salt, or to taste

chopped fresh coriander, to garnish
soy sauce and pilau, to serve

Heat a non-stick wok over a high heat until it is very hot. Pour the olive oil into the wok and heat until the oil is almost smoking – this should take no more than 1 minute.

Add the mustard and nigella seeds and cook until they start to pop – this should take no longer than 1 minute. Stir in the ginger and garlic and stir-fry until aromatic – this should take no longer than 1 minute. Sprinkle in the turmeric and chilli powder and mix well. Stir in the coconut.

Throw the tofu and bean sprouts into the wok and stir-fry until heated through. Mix through the salt.

Garnish with the chopped coriander. Serve with soy sauce and pilau.

One serving = 95%+ RDA antioxidants

Antibacterial
chilli, coriander, garlic, ginger, mustard, nigella, turmeric

Antifungal
chilli, coriander, garlic, ginger, mustard, nigella, turmeric

Antiviral
garlic, turmeric

Anti-inflammatory
chilli, coriander, garlic, ginger, mustard, nigella, turmeric

Analgesic
chilli, nigella

Chicken with Baby Spinach and Coriander

Serves 4

Since the original recipe of chicken palak is already a superfood recipe, I haven't changed much in the way of ingredients in my adaptation, but, I have greatly reduced the amount of fat used and simplified the cooking process.

As I see it, Indian cooking, much like many other classical cuisines (French comes to mind,) often has complex methods which can be compared to a knot tied in a shoelace. Over time, this knot appears to tighten and becomes difficult to untie; and the Indian cuisine has had plenty of time to develop these knots. We can either ignore the problem, throwing it into the 'too-hard basket' and risk losing the shoe. Or we can be patient, give it a real hard look and untie the knot. Afterwards, everything reverts back to being more accessible again.

It's in this methodical manner that I have approached this recipe to make it healthier, and much easier to make at home. With the vegetables equating to well over half the amount of chicken, it certainly is a very balanced recipe. I hope you like it.

2 tablespoons olive oil
15 green cardamom pods, lightly crushed
1 teaspoon cumin seeds
$1/2$ teaspoon nigella seeds
$3/4$ teaspoon salt, or to taste
1 small onion, sliced
6 garlic cloves, finely chopped
1 teaspoon turmeric
500g skinless, boneless chicken breasts, cut into bite-size pieces
200g baby spinach leaves, coarsely chopped
40g bunch of fresh coriander, coarsely chopped

2 large tomatoes, cut into quarters
3 tablespoons grated (peeled) fresh root ginger
2–4 green chillies, chopped
250g low-fat Greek yogurt
1 teaspoon garam masala
freshly ground black pepper, to taste

Pour the olive oil into a deep saucepan, add the cardamom pods and cumin and nigella seeds and cook over a low-medium heat until the seeds start to pop – this should take no longer than 2–3 minutes. Add the salt and onion and fry until the onion is light brown in colour, remembering to stir frequently – this should take no more than 5 minutes.

Stir in the garlic and fry for about 1–2 minutes or until a light brown colour. Mix in the turmeric and cook for 20 seconds. Add the chicken and cook until sealed all over, stirring frequently – this should take no more than 5 minutes.

In the meantime, in a food processor, blend together the baby spinach, chopped coriander, tomatoes, ginger, chillies and yogurt to make a purée. Set aside.

Once the chicken is sealed, pour the blended yogurt-and-spice mixture into the pan, mixing it into the chicken, then bring to a gentle simmer. Simmer gently, uncovered, for 25 minutes, stirring from time to time.

A few minutes before the end of cooking, sprinkle in the garam masala and season to taste with black pepper.

Serve with your choice of sides.

One serving =
175%+ RDA
antioxidants

Antibacterial
cardamom, chilli, coriander, cumin, garlic, ginger, nigella, turmeric

Antifungal
cardamom, chilli, coriander, cumin, garlic, ginger, nigella, turmeric

Antiviral
garlic, turmeric

Anti-inflammatory
cardamom, chilli, coriander, cumin, garlic, ginger, nigella, turmeric

Analgesic
chilli, nigella

Indian Superfood

Sweet Potato Samosa Rolls with Tamarind Reduction

Makes 10 samosa rolls (Serves 4–5)

A virtually non-fat rewrite of the traditional samosa, and, although magnificently light in taste, it's surprisingly filling.

The combination of gooey, lightly spiced sweet potato, crunchy, limey bean sprouts and the nutty-tasting digestive cumin, is a most pleasing and refreshing one indeed.

These samosas are a great-tasting sustenance for either your lunchbox, or whilst sitting at the dining table in the company of friends. Just one serving of sweet potato provides us with over 350% of our minimum daily vitamin A requirements – now, how's that for lunchtime tête-à-tête?

500g sweet potatoes, peeled and cut into large bite-size pieces
1 tablespoon olive oil
1 teaspoon cumin seeds
1/2 teaspoon each turmeric, chilli powder and salt, plus an extra pinch of salt
a handful of green peas (fresh or frozen)
a large handful of bean sprouts
juice of 1/2 lime
5 large rice papers (available from Oriental grocers)

Tamarind Reduction, to serve (see pages 144–145) (see also Cook's Tip)

Cook the sweet potatoes in a deep pan of boiling water for approximately 15 minutes or until tender. Drain, then rinse the sweet potatoes under cold running water until cool and drain again. Place in a mixing bowl and set aside. (To minimise the loss of nutrients, the sweet potatoes may be steamed or cooked in the microwave, instead of boiling.)

Pour the olive oil into a separate saucepan, add the cumin seeds and cook over a low-medium heat until the seeds begin to pop – this will take no longer than 2–3 minutes. Add the turmeric and cook for 20 seconds, stirring all the time. Add the chilli powder and salt and cook for a further 20 seconds, mixing well.

Remove the pan from the heat. Add the cooled sweet potatoes to the spice mixture and mash well, then mix through the peas. Set the mixture aside.

In a separate bowl, mix together the bean sprouts and lime juice and sprinkle over the extra pinch of salt. Set aside.

Pour plenty of warm water into another large bowl and place one rice paper at a time into the water, leaving it to soak for 15 seconds. Remove the rice paper from the bowl, shaking off any excess water. Spread it out on a chopping board. Scoop, in a narrow line (reaching from the top to the bottom of the rice paper), 4 heaped teaspoons of the cooled sweet potato mixture and a generous sprinkle of the bean sprouts, into the centre of the rice paper. Roll the rice paper into a neat spring-roll shape and cut it in half, widthways. Repeat the process of soaking the rice papers in warm water and then filling them individually until finished.

Serve the samosa rolls with the tamarind reduction.

Cook's Tip
If you are short of time, you may substitute the Tamarind Reduction with a shop-bought sweet chilli sauce.

One serving (2 samosa rolls) = 80%+ RDA antioxidants

Antibacterial
chilli, cumin, turmeric

Antifungal
chilli, cumin, turmeric

Antiviral
turmeric

Anti-inflammatory
chilli, cumin, turmeric

Analgesic
chilli

Prawns with Red Cabbage

Serves 4

It's amazing that, even when we don't try too hard with our cooking, how easy it is to impart that authentic Indian flavour to our food. Within minutes, we can stir-fry a crunchy nest of cabbage, and hidden deep within it, are rewarding pockets of deliciously spicy prawns.

Impressively, red cabbage multitasks by containing not only cancer-fighting compounds, but also anthocyanins, found most commonly in deep-coloured berries and grapes, which can prevent degenerative diseases.

A word of warning though – unless you happen to be calling a rabbit, please don't eat this whilst simultaneously using a phone. I happened to be on the end of a crunchy-cabbage-eating call, and it was nothing short of terrifying.

1 tablespoon olive oil
1 teaspoon each cumin seeds and
   mustard seeds
1/2 teaspoon nigella seeds
a piece of fresh root ginger (no larger
   than the size of a small matchbox),
   peeled and cut into small batons
2 garlic cloves, sliced
1/2 teaspoon each turmeric and chilli
   powder
240g cooked peeled king prawns
1 small onion, sliced
1/2 red cabbage, finely shredded
1/3 teaspoon salt, or to taste

chopped fresh coriander, to garnish
lemon wedges and pilau (see pages
   134–136), to serve

Heat a non-stick wok over a high heat until it is very hot. Pour the olive oil into the wok and heat until it's almost smoking – this should take no more than 1 minute.

Add the cumin, mustard and nigella seeds and cook until they start to pop – this should take no longer than 1 minute. Add the ginger and garlic and stir-fry until aromatic – this should take no longer than 1 minute. Sprinkle in the turmeric and chilli powder and mix well.

Throw the prawns, onion and red cabbage into the wok and stir-fry for 4–5 minutes or until the cabbage is cooked through but still crunchy. Mix through the salt.

Garnish with the chopped coriander. Serve with lemon wedges and pilau.

One serving =
165%+ RDA
antioxidants

Antibacterial
chilli, cumin, garlic, ginger, mustard, nigella, turmeric

Antifungal
chilli, cumin, garlic, ginger, mustard, nigella, turmeric

Antiviral
garlic, turmeric

Anti-inflammatory
chilli, cumin, garlic, ginger, mustard, nigella, turmeric

Analgesic
chilli, nigella

Peppers Stuffed with Basmati Rice and Paneer

Serves 4–6

I only have to think of stuffed peppers to be whisked away by my mind's eye to the Mediterranean. Almost every day I'd walk back from the bazaar through the narrow and cobbled, winding streets where more often than not, in the heat of the day, elderly ladies with faces worn by the sun and with the sweetest of smiles, would be sitting under grape vines stuffing all sorts of vegetables with rice and herbs to make dolmades. How fortunate we are to have memories and to be able to dream.

Although my stuffed peppers are Indian at heart, they are also heavily influenced by this mesmerising ethos. Instead of stuffing with just paneer, I combine rice, onions and herbs together with it, transforming them into a complete and healthy meal. Rather than baking, they are steamed. And, ultimately, they are served chilled instead of hot. It's Indian and Mediterranean culinary styles fused effortlessly in the guise of a complete salad meal within a pepper. Serve them chilled and sliced in half with a good guzzle of Spicy Chilli Oil or olive oil and a side salad. Make sure to use small peppers so they cook through properly. If you like, once they are chilled, they can also be grilled just before serving to give them a charcoal flavour.

12 small peppers (use a mixture of colours)
2 tablespoons olive oil
a pinch of saffron
1 teaspoon freshly ground black pepper
2 teaspoons cumin seeds
1 teaspoon mustard seeds
4 garlic cloves, finely chopped
2 tablespoons grated (peeled) fresh root ginger
2 red onions, finely diced
2$\frac{1}{2}$ teaspoons salt

250g paneer, grated or crumbled
75g basmati rice
40g bunch of fresh coriander, finely chopped
25g bunch of fresh mint, leaves finely chopped
25g bunch of fresh dill, finely chopped
2–4 green chillies, finely chopped (optional)
3 firm tomatoes, cut into quarters

Spicy Chilli Oil (see page 147) or olive oil, and a mixed leaf salad, to serve

Slice off the tops from the peppers, trying to keep the stalks intact; reserve the tops. Deseed the peppers, then set aside.

Pour the olive oil into a deep saucepan, add the saffron, black pepper and cumin and mustard seeds and cook over a medium heat until the seeds start to pop – this should take no longer than 2–3 minutes. Remove the pan from the heat and allow the oil to cool for a moment or two.

Stir in the garlic and ginger and fry for about 2–3 minutes or until the garlic is a light brown colour. Remove from the heat and set aside.

Place the onions, together with 1 teaspoon of the salt into a large bowl. Knead the onions until they are almost transparent in colour – this should take no longer than 5 minutes. Add enough cold water to cover the onions, then drain. Once again, add enough cold water to cover the onions, then place them into a sieve to drain.

Place the paneer, rice, drained onions, chopped herbs, chillies and $\frac{1}{2}$ teaspoon salt into the saucepan with the spice mixture, mixing well.

Fill the peppers tightly with the rice mixture, then push a wedge of tomato on top of each one, pushing it into the rice – this will help to keep the mixture inside the peppers whilst cooking. Tidy up the peppers by pushing any rice mixture back into them, then replace their tops.

Place the peppers upright in a deep and wide saucepan (at least 25cm in diameter), making sure to position them so they don't topple over – they will have to fit quite snugly. Pour 450ml boiling water into the saucepan, adding it from the side of the pan, being careful not to pour the water into the peppers. Add the remaining salt to the water and bring to a simmer. Cover and simmer gently for 20 minutes or until the peppers are soft.

Carefully lift the peppers out of the water to a plate using tongs. Leave the peppers to cool, then refrigerate until chilled, before serving.

Serve sliced in half with a generous glug of spicy chilli oil or olive oil and a mixed leaf salad.

One serving = 235%+ RDA antioxidants

Antibacterial
chilli, coriander, cumin, dill, garlic, ginger, mint, mustard, pepper, saffron

Antifungal
chilli, coriander, cumin, dill, garlic, ginger, mint, mustard, saffron

Antiviral
garlic

Anti-inflammatory
chilli, coriander, cumin, dill, garlic, ginger, mustard, saffron

Analgesic
chilli

Chicken Korma with Apple, Mint and Cumin

Serves 4

For me, an Indian curry has never captured the very essence of summer quite as well as this chicken korma. Each mouthful ricochets flavours of fresh mint leaves and baskets full of apples. It's a positively original taste sensation, and one that's moulded each time into something personal by our choice of apples. Fibre-rich apples, combined with lean chicken, make it a very replenishing meal indeed. And, mint cools and soothes the body – perfect for lunching on balmy summer days.

25g bunch of fresh mint, leaves removed
2 eating apples, peeled, cored and cut into quarters
2 tablespoons grated (peeled) fresh root ginger
2 green chillies, chopped
³/₄ teaspoon salt, or to taste
400ml light coconut milk
1 teaspoon cumin seeds
10 green cardamom pods, lightly crushed
4 garlic cloves, finely chopped
1 tablespoon olive oil
1 teaspoon turmeric
500g skinless, boneless chicken breasts, cut into bite-size pieces

chopped fresh coriander and a few extra mint leaves, to garnish

In a food processor, blend together the mint leaves, apple quarters, ginger, chillies and salt with the coconut milk. Set aside.

Place the cumin seeds, cardamom pods and garlic into a deep saucepan with the olive oil and cook over a low-medium heat until the garlic starts to brown – this should take no longer than 1–2 minutes. Add the turmeric, mix well and cook for about 20 seconds.

Add the chicken and cook until sealed all over, stirring frequently – this should take no more than 5 minutes.

Now slowly pour in the coconut milk mixture, mixing with the chicken, then bring to a simmer. Simmer, uncovered, for 10 minutes, stirring from time to time.

Garnish with the chopped coriander and extra mint leaves and serve with your choice of sides.

One serving = 160%+ RDA antioxidants

Antibacterial
cardamom, chilli, coriander, cumin, garlic, ginger, mint, turmeric

Antifungal
cardamom, chilli, coriander, cumin, garlic, ginger, mint, turmeric

Antiviral
garlic, turmeric

Anti-inflammatory
cardamom, chilli, coriander, cumin, garlic, ginger, turmeric

Analgesic
chilli

" The essential oil extracted from cumin seeds has been proven to be very effective against all tested bacteria. Cumin oil is equally or more effective when compared with standard antibiotics."

Gorakhpur University, India[13]

Christmas Venison with Cranberries and Nutmeg

Serves 4

If you're like me, that is, an individual who prefers a trouble-free Christmas, this recipe could be the one for you. Cook some up, then keep it on standby for doting guests over the holiday period.

As can be expected, the use of tender pieces of venison, sweet cranberries, red wine and nutmeg, give it a distinctly festive feel, and antioxidants aplenty, not commonly found in traditional curries. Venison, being a low-fat meat, means you can indulge a little without having to worry about an expanding girth, which would ultimately require curtailment in the New Year.

Everyone, from Grandma, right down to the kids, will love this rich, sweet and fruity curry. For extra special Christmas cheer, wash it down with a toddy of warm Indian Christmas Spicy Mulled Wine (page 178).

2 tablespoons olive oil
1/2 teaspoon cloves
1/2 teaspoon each cumin seeds and
   nigella seeds
3/4 teaspoon salt, or to taste
1 small onion, thinly sliced
6 garlic cloves, finely chopped
1 teaspoon each turmeric, ground
   nutmeg and ground ginger
2 tomatoes, finely chopped
2–6 green chillies, chopped
500g venison steaks, cut into bite-size
   pieces
2 handfuls of dried cranberries
400ml cranberry juice drink
100ml red wine
a knob of butter

Pour the olive oil into a deep saucepan, add the cloves and cumin and nigella seeds and cook over a low-medium heat until the seeds start to pop – this should take no longer than 2–3 minutes. Add the salt and onion and fry until the onion is light brown in colour, remembering to stir frequently – this should take no more than 5 minutes.

Stir in the garlic and fry for about 1–2 minutes or until a light brown colour. Sprinkle in the turmeric, nutmeg and ginger, mix well and cook for about 20 seconds. Add the tomatoes and chillies and cook for about 5 minutes or until the tomatoes are cooked through and any excess juices in the saucepan have dried off – remember to keep stirring occasionally.

Add the venison to the pan, together with the cranberries, mix well and cook until the meat is sealed all over, stirring frequently – this should take about 5 minutes.

Pour in the cranberry juice drink and red wine and bring to a simmer. Leave to simmer over a gentle heat, uncovered, for 40 minutes or until the meat is tender, stirring frequently to avoid sticking.

Mix through the butter. Serve with your choice of sides.

One serving = 195%+ RDA antioxidants

Antibacterial
chilli, cloves, cumin, garlic, ginger, nigella, nutmeg, turmeric

Antifungal
chilli, cloves, cumin, garlic, ginger, nigella, nutmeg, turmeric

Antiviral
cloves, garlic, nutmeg, turmeric

Anti-inflammatory
chilli, cloves, cumin, garlic, ginger, nigella, turmeric

Analgesic
chilli, cloves, nigella

Chicken with Blueberries and Cinnamon

Serves 4

Having so many blueberry anthocyanins, which aid memory power and promote fat loss, jutting around in a chicken curry, is something quite wonderful. A whopping amount of cinnamon, one of the top three of the world's most powerful antioxidising foods, further blasts this recipe into its superfood status. Yogurt and fresh coriander help you to stay in tip-top shape by expediting the body's digestive processes.

You may assume this curry to be sweet in taste, but nothing could be further from the truth. The tart yogurt and superspices negate much of the natural blueberry sweetness and what we are left with is a light, yet traditional and tangy-tasting, chicken curry, ideal for summertime eating.

This recipe was part of the 'world's healthiest meal' that I created in 2009, which became an overnight hit when Chris Evans declared live on-air that it was 'the best curry I've ever tasted.'

200g fresh or frozen blueberries
20g bunch of fresh coriander, coarsely chopped
2 tablespoons grated (peeled) fresh root ginger
3/4 teaspoon salt, or to taste
500g low-fat Greek yogurt
4 garlic cloves, finely chopped
3 tablespoons olive oil
1 teaspoon turmeric
2 tablespoons ground cinnamon
1 teaspoon chilli powder
500g skinless, boneless chicken breasts, cut into bite-size pieces
1 teaspoon garam masala

extra chopped fresh coriander, to garnish

In a food processor, blend together the blueberries, chopped coriander, ginger, salt and yogurt to make a purée. Set aside.

Place the garlic in a deep saucepan with the olive oil and cook over a low-medium heat until the garlic starts to turn a brown colour – this should take no longer than 1–2 minutes. Add the turmeric, mix well and cook for about 20 seconds. Stir in the cinnamon and chilli powder and cook for a further 20 seconds.

Add the chicken and cook until sealed all over, stirring frequently – this should take no more than 5 minutes.

Now slowly pour in the yogurt mixture, mixing it into the chicken, then bring to a simmer over a low heat. Simmer, uncovered, for 10 minutes, stirring from time to time. Mix through the garam masala.

Garnish with the extra chopped coriander and serve with Goji Berry and Green Pea Pilau (see page 136).

One serving = 470%+ RDA antioxidants

Antibacterial
chilli, cinnamon, coriander, garlic, ginger, turmeric

Antifungal
chilli, cinnamon, coriander, garlic, ginger, turmeric

Antiviral
cinnamon, garlic, turmeric

Anti-inflammatory
chilli, cinnamon, coriander, garlic, ginger, turmeric

Analgesic
chilli

" A few essential oils were tested against food poisoning, spoilage fungi, plant and animal pathogens. Cinnamon oil showed the strongest antifungal activity."

University of Belgrade, Serbia and Montenegro[9]

Mackerel with Peppers and Potato

Serves 4

As kids, we grew up eating canned fish. It was always curried pilchards as it was Mum's preference. In Australia, when trying to make Mum's recipe, I couldn't come to find pilchards. So, this is how I conjured up this duly ace recipe. Mackerel doesn't break down into a keema as pilchards do. Instead, the fillets are firm and tend to retain their form; in fact, their texture is more akin to chicken than to fish.

In this recipe, I show you how to transform inexpensive storecupboard ingredients into a fabulous omega-3 fatty acid and lycopene-loaded meal. Because mackerel is quite meat-like, it's also a great fish to tackle for the few amongst us who still blush like schoolgirls when served seafood.

2 tablespoons olive oil
1 teaspoon each fennel seeds and cumin seeds
1/2 teaspoon nigella seeds
1/2 teaspoon salt, or to taste
1 small onion, thinly sliced
6 garlic cloves, finely chopped
1 teaspoon turmeric
2 teaspoons garam masala
1/2 400g can tomatoes, blended until smooth
2 peppers (any colour), deseeded and diced
3 tablespoons grated (peeled) fresh root ginger
2–6 green chillies, chopped
6 x 125g cans mackerel fillets in spicy tomato sauce or tomato sauce
1 potato, diced into cubes no larger than 1.5cm
chopped fresh coriander, to season

a few spring onions, sliced, to garnish

Pour the olive oil into a deep saucepan, add the fennel, cumin and nigella seeds and cook over a low-medium heat until the seeds start to pop – this should take no longer than 2–3 minutes. Add the salt and onion and fry until the onion is light brown in colour, remembering to stir frequently – this should take no more than 5 minutes.

Stir in the garlic and fry for about 1–2 minutes or until a light brown colour. Sprinkle in the turmeric and half of the garam masala, mix well and cook for about 20 seconds.

Add the tomatoes, peppers, ginger and chillies and mix well. Cook for about 5 minutes or until the excess juices in the saucepan have dried off, remembering to keep stirring occasionally.

Add the mackerel (including the tomato sauce) to the pan and heat through, stirring occasionally. Stir in the potato. Bring to a simmer, then cover and simmer over a gentle heat for 20 minutes or until the potato is tender – remember to stir occasionally.

A few minutes prior to the end of cooking, mix through the remaining garam masala and the chopped coriander and heat through.

Garnish with the spring onions. Serve with your choice of sides.

One serving = 225%+ RDA antioxidants

Antibacterial
chilli, coriander, cumin, fennel, garlic, ginger, nigella, turmeric

Antifungal
chilli, coriander, cumin, fennel, garlic, ginger, nigella, turmeric

Antiviral
garlic, turmeric

Anti-inflammatory
chilli, coriander, cumin, fennel, garlic, ginger, nigella, turmeric

Analgesic
chilli, fennel, nigella

Chicken, Banana and Goji Berry Tikka Masala

Serves 4

*I first developed this recipe for the fabulous food editor, Alex Wenman at NOW magazine. Since then, a certain celebrity has written in to me to say "I'm definitely a bit of a curry expert and this dish f***** rocks!!!" – such unconfined joy! So, to cut a long story short, there could be no Indian Superfood book without this star-fangled recipe.*

Fruitilicious and delicious Chicken, Banana and Goji Berry Tikka Masala is an ultimate Indian Superfood recipe. It makes use of bananas aplenty, which means it has a rich and satisfying taste, without being fattening. Goji berries add an absolute whopper amount of vitamin C that you'd never normally find in an Indian chicken curry.

*If you like chicken tikka masala and bananas, you will f***** love this one – see, I said it like a celebrity!*

2 tablespoons olive oil
1 teaspoon each fenugreek seeds and
    mustard seeds
2 garlic cloves, finely chopped
3 tablespoons grated (peeled) fresh
    root ginger
1 teaspoon turmeric
2 bananas, peeled and mashed to a
    pulp
2 green chillies, coarsely chopped
³/₄ teaspoon salt, or to taste
1 tablespoon tomato purée
400ml light coconut milk
500g skinless, boneless chicken
    breasts, cut into bite-size pieces
2 tablespoons dried goji berries

chopped fresh coriander, to garnish

Pour the olive oil into a deep saucepan, add the fenugreek and mustard seeds and cook over a high heat until the mustard seeds start to pop – this should take no more than 1–2 minutes. Remove the pan from the heat and allow the oil to cool for a moment or two.

Add the garlic and ginger to the pan and cook over a low-medium heat until they are a golden brown colour, stirring frequently – this should take no more than 2–3 minutes. Sprinkle in the turmeric, mix well and cook for about 20 seconds.

Now add the banana pulp, chillies, salt, tomato purée and coconut milk, stir to mix, then bring to a rapid simmer. Add the chicken and mix well. Bring to a gentle simmer, then cook, uncovered, for 7 minutes.

Sprinkle in the goji berries and continue to simmer for 3 minutes. If the sauce becomes too 'gluey', pour in some boiling water, little by little, mixing all the time, until it attains a thick, gravy-like consistency.

Garnish with chopped coriander and serve with your choice of sides.

One serving = 165%+ RDA antioxidants

Antibacterial
chilli, coriander, garlic, ginger, fenugreek, mustard, turmeric

Antifungal
chilli, coriander, garlic, ginger, fenugreek, mustard, turmeric

Antiviral
garlic, turmeric

Anti-inflammatory
chilli, coriander, ginger, fenugreek, mustard, turmeric

Analgesic
chilli, fenugreek

Basmati Rice Salad with Tuna, Eggs and Cranberries

Serves 4–6

You may be surprised to learn, but salads are very popular in India and are definitely a part of the traditional culinary culture. Kachumbers of diced or sliced onion, tomato and cucumber with a dash of vinegar or lime juice and fresh coriander are typical of salads eaten all over India for an eternity. However, they are never served as the centrepiece of a meal, instead being used as a healthy side to bolster the nutritional value of main courses. Although they are made delicious by relying on a few good items of garden produce, there's nothing quite as refreshing as making a meal of a salad.

This recipe is heavily inspired by memories of a school trip to France, where we pulled over on a coach journey for lunch in a sunny woodland area to feast on baguette and canned rice salad. I have never quite got over my vestal rendezvous with the silky grains of rice, flaky tuna and squidgy savoury pieces of 'black magic' (which turned out to be my first encounter with black olives) in a tangy vinaigrette. It was assuredly more 'exotic' and better-tasting than any salad I had ever come across back home in late 1980's England. I am still licking my lips to this very day at the thought of it.

My rendition of these memories is combined here in this recipe with a bounty of Indian-inspired superfoods and superspices, which impart that unique flavour we have come to expect of the subcontinent. I have a feeling that India will take to rice salad like a duck to water.

Don't be put off by the longer-than-usual list of ingredients; this salad is, without ado, quite literally just thrown together. It's usually a good idea to make the pilau one day before, as it needs to be chilled before use. You can also try experimenting with any of the other flavours of pilau. Serve by itself or with some fresh bread.

1 quantity Garlic Pilau, chilled
   (see pages 134–136)
2 tablespoons olive oil
1 teaspoon each cumin seeds and
   mustard seeds
1 tablespoon mild curry powder
2 tablespoons sesame oil
4 tablespoons white wine vinegar
2 teaspoons English mustard
salt and freshly ground black
   pepper, to taste
200g can tuna, drained and broken
   down into small chunks
200g can sweetcorn kernels, drained
1/2 400g can chickpeas, rinsed and
   drained
a handful of dried cranberries
50g baby spinach leaves
1/2 cucumber, peeled and sliced
a handful of Kalamata or black olives
20 vine-ripened cherry tomatoes
3 spring onions, thinly sliced
1–2 green chillies, finely chopped
   (optional)
40g bunch of fresh coriander, chopped
3 eggs, hardboiled, cooled, peeled and
   sliced in half

a few extra cherry tomatoes, black
   olives and dried cranberries, to
   garnish
lemon wedges, to serve

In a large bowl, using your hands, massage the garlic pilau gently until the grains separate from one another. Set aside.

Pour the olive oil into a deep saucepan, add the cumin and mustard seeds and cook over a low-medium heat until the seeds start to pop – this should take no longer than 2–3 minutes. Add the curry powder, mix well and fry for 20 seconds. Remove the pan from the heat and allow to cool for a few moments.

Add the sesame oil, vinegar and mustard to the pan, mix well until combined and season to taste with salt and black pepper, then set aside. This will be your salad dressing.

Stir the tuna, sweetcorn, chickpeas, cranberries, baby spinach, cucumber, olives, tomatoes, spring onions, chillies, if using, and chopped coriander into the pilau, then add the salad dressing and stir to mix.

Top with the eggs and garnish with a few extra cherry tomatoes, olives and cranberries. Serve the salad with the lemon wedges.

One serving = 160%+ RDA antioxidants	**Anti-inflammatory** chilli, coriander, cumin, mustard
Antibacterial chilli, coriander, cumin, mustard	**Analgesic** chilli
Antifungal chilli, coriander, cumin, mustard	

Baked Spicy Passion Fruit Chicken

Serves 4

We grew up munching on tandoori-flavoured baked chicken pieces that would be served uniformly to us at nearly every social gathering, lock, stock and barrel, from weddings to Christmas Day lunch. In fact, if we ever caught 'wind' of baked chicken not being on the menu, possibly because the function was being hosted by a vegetarian family, it would be enough for us to try and wean out of the event.

The love affair started out in the 1980's when people served chicken joints. In the 1990's, and well into the new millennium, this preference metamorphosed into tender breast fillets, and recently it has started reverting back to a trend in jointed chicken pieces – thank you, Anjum. The only thing that hasn't changed over all of this time is the basic marinade recipe. And that's until now. This recipe is something that you must try at least once.

Passion fruit not only imparts an exotic flavour but also acts as a souring agent and super meat tenderiser, as well as adding as much potassium as a banana to the already healthy low fat pieces of chicken. Marinate the pieces of chicken overnight so that the superspices and passion fruit enzymes can work their magic and simultaneously flavour and tenderise them right down to the bone. For even more scrumptious pieces of chicken, try using smaller joints which pick up the flavours intensely. Serve with a simple salad, pilau and raita.

700g chicken joints, skinned and pierced randomly with a sharp knife
3 passion fruits, cut in half and pulp and seeds scooped out
6 garlic cloves, chopped

2 tablespoons grated (peeled) fresh root ginger
4–6 green chillies, finely chopped
100ml natural yogurt
1 tablespoon ground coriander
1 teaspoon tandoori masala powder or garam masala
1 teaspoon salt, or to taste
2 tablespoons olive oil, plus extra for greasing
20g bunch of fresh coriander, chopped

salad and raita, to serve

Place the chicken joints in a bowl and set aside.

Place all of the remaining ingredients in a food processor and blend until smooth. Pour the mixture over the chicken joints, mixing well. Cover and leave to marinate in the refrigerator for up to 24 hours.

Remove the chicken from the refrigerator. Preheat the oven to its maximum temperature setting.

Oil a baking tray with some extra olive oil. Place the chicken pieces on the baking tray in a single layer, shaking off any excess marinade. Discard any leftover marinade.

Lower the oven temperature to 200°C/fan 180°C/Gas Mark 6. Bake the chicken in the centre of the oven for 35–45 minutes or until tender and cooked to your liking, remembering to turn over the pieces of chicken once, halfway through cooking.

Serve with salad, raita and pilau.

One serving = 75%+ RDA antioxidants

Antibacterial
chilli, coriander, garlic, ginger

Antifungal
chilli, coriander, garlic, ginger

Antiviral
garlic

Anti-inflammatory
chilli, coriander, garlic, ginger

Analgesic
chilli

" The clinical applications of benzodiazepines, such as diazepam, as anti-anxiety drugs, are limited by their unwanted side effects. Therefore, the development of new pharmacological agents is well justified. Among medical plants, coriander has been recommended for relief of anxiety in traditional Iranian folk medicine. Under laboratory test conditions, coriander extract has proven to have an anti-anxiety effect and may have potential sedative and muscle relaxant effects"

Shiraz University of Medical Sciences, Iran[12]

Dinner

Dinner is almost certainly the most memorable meal of the day. It is that sacrosanct time of the day when one leaves the world outside the front door, and unwinds at home amidst the company of loved ones. It is the time to commune with great food and wine.

I am a firm believer that after a long, hard day at work or play, we should spend less time cooking in the kitchen. Therefore, all of these recipes are swift in preparation. Most of them take a maximum of 20 minutes to prepare and then you can leave them covered to cook, and get on with enjoying your evening.

It is for this special meal of the day, that I have reserved the most time-honoured Indian favourites. And it is here that you will find superfood alternatives to restaurant classics like Chicken Tikka Masala or Lamb Rogan Josh, as well as many newcomers. At long last, we can savour our preferred Indian foods without the 'guilt', knowing that they are actually healing the body whilst satisfying the tummy. Now that's food for thought.

Sweet and Sour Tamarind Beef

Serves 3–4

Darting around the taste buds, just like the way a ping pong ball does mid-flow in a Chinese tournament, this dish is sweet, sour, hot and tangy – all at the same time. It manages the 'impossible' by hitting all the right spots. In fact, Ayurvedic therapists also teach us that we should try and include as many different tastes into our meal, to encourage balance. To boot, tamarind is also effective at lowering cholesterol levels. So, there are at least a few persuasive reasons to give this one a go.

2 tablespoons olive oil
1 teaspoon each nigella seeds and
    fennel seeds
3/4 teaspoon salt, or to taste
1 small onion, thinly sliced
6 garlic cloves, finely chopped
1 teaspoon turmeric
2 teaspoons garam masala
2 teaspoons ground ginger
1/2 400g can tomatoes, blended until
    smooth
2–6 green chillies, chopped
3 tablespoons grated (peeled) fresh
    root ginger
1 teaspoon sugar
6 tablespoons Tamarind Reduction
    (see pagse 144–145)
500g lean beef, diced
chopped fresh coriander, to season

Pour the olive oil into a deep saucepan, add the nigella and fennel seeds and cook over a low-medium heat until the seeds start to pop – this should take no more than 2–3 minutes. Add the salt and onion and fry until the onion is light brown in colour, remembering to stir frequently – this should take no more than 5 minutes.

Add the garlic and cook until it is a golden brown colour, stirring frequently – this should take no more than 2–3 minutes. Add the turmeric and 1 teaspoon of the garam masala, mix well and cook for about 20 seconds. Mix through the ground ginger, then add the tomatoes, chillies, fresh ginger, sugar and half of the tamarind reduction. Cook for about 5 minutes or until the excess juices in the saucepan have dried off, remembering to keep stirring occasionally.

Add the beef to the pan, mix well and cook until sealed all over, stirring constantly – this should take no more than 5 minutes.

Pour in enough boiling water to cover the meat. Return the water to a simmer, then leave to simmer, uncovered, for 1 hour or until the meat is tender, stirring occasionally. Add a little extra boiling water, if the sauce dries out too much.

Season with the remaining garam masala and tamarind reduction and the chopped coriander. Serve with your choice of pilau.

One serving = 230%+ RDA antioxidants

Antibacterial
chilli, coriander, fennel, garlic, ginger, nigella, tamarind, turmeric

Antifungal
chilli, coriander, fennel, garlic, ginger, nigella, turmeric

Antiviral
garlic, turmeric

Anti-inflammatory
chilli, coriander, fennel, garlic, ginger, nigella, turmeric

Analgesic
chilli, fennel, nigella

Lamb with Red Kidney Beans

Serves 4–6

Mami ji in Crawley always used to cook with kidney beans. At times, it seemed she was the only person in the entire world, or at least in our family, cooking them. For me, kidney beans became synonymous with visiting her. Knowing what would be served for dinner would make the 'long' drive down to Crawley even more worthwhile. As if her bubbly personality and laughter, which could launch corks from bottles of champagne, wasn't enough.

My recipe is a true peasant style of cooking, influenced heavily by the homely flavours of the Kashmir province in India. If you like your food simple, this recipe is for you. The natural flavours of lamb and kidney beans are brought to life by the mellow charcoal smokiness of the black cardamom. Kidney beans also add a low fat protein and fibre source to our diet. And, just like lamb, they are a powerhouse of the feel-good amino acid tryptophan, and when combined with the aphrodisiac properties of black cardamom, we have here comfort food which sets a new benchmark.

2 tablespoons olive oil
10 black cardamom pods, lightly crushed
$3/4$ teaspoon salt, or to taste
1 small onion, thinly sliced
6 garlic cloves, finely chopped
1 teaspoon turmeric
2 teaspoons garam masala
1 teaspoon ground ginger
400g can tomatoes, blended until smooth
2–6 green chillies, chopped
3 tablespoons grated (peeled) fresh root ginger
1 teaspoon sugar
500g lean lamb (preferably leg), diced
400g can red kidney beans, rinsed and drained

Pour the olive oil into a deep saucepan, add the cardamom pods and cook over a low-medium heat until the oil is hot and the cardamom pods start to release their aroma – this should take no more than 2–3 minutes. Add the salt and onion and fry until the onion is light brown in colour, remembering to stir frequently – this should take no more than 5 minutes.

Add the garlic and cook until it is a golden brown colour, stirring frequently – this should take no more than 2–3 minutes. Add the turmeric and 1 teaspoon of the garam masala, mix well and cook for about 20 seconds. Mix through the ground ginger, then add the tomatoes, chillies, fresh ginger and sugar. Cook for about 10 minutes or until the excess juices in the saucepan have dried off, remembering to keep stirring occasionally.

Add the lamb to the pan, mix well and cook until sealed all over, stirring constantly – this should take no more than 5 minutes.

Add the kidney beans to the pan, together with enough boiling water to cover the meat. Return the water to a simmer, then leave to simmer, uncovered, for 1 hour or until the meat is tender, stirring occasionally. Add a little extra boiling water if the sauce dries out too much.

Season with the remaining garam masala. Serve with your choice of sides.

One serving =
195%+ RDA
antioxidants

Antibacterial
cardamom, chilli, coriander, garlic, ginger, turmeric

Antifungal
cardamom, chilli, coriander, garlic, ginger, turmeric

Antiviral
garlic, turmeric

Anti-inflammatory
cardamom, chilli, coriander, garlic, ginger, turmeric

Analgesic
chilli

Summer Evening Chilled Yogurt Soup with Black Rice and Potato

Serves 4

'Wow!' is the word that resounded from my mouth upon first tasting this summer soup. I was in total shock and awe at how something so very simple, could taste, well, so out of this world.

The blending of yogurt, coloured neon yellow by turmeric, with crunchy and aromatic cumin seeds, al dente black rice and melt-in-the-mouth potato, is an experience you won't be forgetting in a hurry. It is, definitely, one of the most opulent chilled soups you can serve to your dinner guests.

What's even more astounding is that this soup, which has all the attributes of fine dining, has its foundations in rural India and is something my Mum grew up eating in her village, albeit without the black rice and potato. Biji, my grandmother, used to give a tarka to the yogurt and serve it with chapattis as a substitute for curry. If only she could have seen how her 'stand-in curry' would one day make the gazpacho look so 1980's.

The active agent in turmeric which gives it its bright colour, and to this soup, its brilliant neon lustre, is a polyphenol known as curcumin. Polyphenols are also found in bright-coloured fruits. So, turmeric is a fast and easy way to eat in colour – naturally.

2 tablespoons black rice (can be substituted with red or brown rice)
1 small potato, diced
salt and freshly ground black pepper
2 tablespoons olive oil
1 teaspoon cumin seeds
1 small onion, chopped
2 garlic cloves, finely chopped
2–4 green chillies, finely chopped (optional)
1/2 teaspoon turmeric
1kg chilled natural yogurt (not Greek or thick yogurt)
2 spring onions, finely sliced

fresh coriander leaves, to garnish

Put the black rice into a deep saucepan, cover with plenty of boiling water, return to the boil and simmer for 25 minutes. Meanwhile, cook the potato in a separate pan of boiling salted water until tender. Drain the rice and potato, rinse in plenty of cold water, drain again and set aside.

Pour the olive oil into the deep saucepan, add the cumin seeds and cook over a low-medium heat until the seeds start to pop – this should take no longer than 2–3 minutes. Add the onion and fry until light brown in colour, remembering to stir frequently – this should take no more than 5 minutes.

Add the garlic and chillies and mix well. Fry for about 1–2 minutes or until lightly browned. Sprinkle in the turmeric, stir to mix and cook for about 20 seconds.

Remove the pan from the heat and cool slightly, then slowly pour in the yogurt, stirring all the time. Mix through the rice, potato and spring onions. If necessary, stir in a little chilled water to achieve the desired consistency.

Season to taste with salt and black pepper. Garnish with the coriander leaves and serve immediately.

One serving =
70%+ RDA
antioxidants

Antibacterial
chilli, coriander, cumin, garlic, pepper, turmeric

Antifungal
chilli, coriander, cumin, garlic, ginger, turmeric

Antiviral
garlic, turmeric

Anti-inflammatory
chilli, coriander, cumin, garlic, ginger, turmeric

Analgesic
chilli

Chicken with Banana and Fenugreek

Serves 4

This superfood alternative to Chicken Madras is a spicy and ever-so-slightly fruity dish that will go down well with lovers of the traditional Indian curry. It's high in protein, and is further supplemented with banana, which keeps the tummy feeling fuller for longer and is rich in carbohydrate that helps prevent radical swings in blood sugar levels.

The fenugreek imbues a warm, earthy flavour that almost seems to amplify the sweetness of the banana. Interestingly, fenugreek is also an anti-pyretic, which means it reduces the high body temperature occurring during a fever – this curry could well be the Indian Superfood answer to the Jewish Penicillin, chicken soup!

Accordingly, fenugreek leaves are revered in the Indian kitchen. My aunt is a fine example of this veneration. She grows it in her volcanic soil garden in Byron Bay, Australia, whilst dodging wild kangaroos and some of the world's most deadly King Brown snakes. After harvesting it, she carefully dries it out, packs it and, as a prime example of 'coal to Newcastle', takes it to India, where it's distributed amongst her ageing siblings. Finally, it's taken by a multitude of aunts and uncles to the four corners of the Earth.

At home, in England, it's kept at the back of Mum's kitchen cupboard above the stove. I am fortunate enough that she allows me to use it; others are not so lucky. But for the most she doesn't even know that I've had my hand in the jar!

So is it worth making a special trip to an Indian grocery store? The answer is, most definitely, a yes; and at least you won't be toying with venomous snakes, aeroplanes and kangaroos to get your hands on some.

2 tablespoons olive oil
1/2 teaspoon each fennel seeds, fenugreek seeds and nigella seeds
4 garlic cloves, finely chopped
2 tablespoons grated (peeled) fresh root ginger
1 teaspoon turmeric
1 teaspoon ground ginger
1 teaspoon chilli powder
500g skinless, boneless chicken breasts, cut into bite-size pieces
1 ripe banana
4–6 green chillies, chopped
1 tablespoon dried fenugreek leaves (available from Indian grocers)
50ml good-quality soy sauce (make sure there is no added sugar)
2 tablespoons tomato purée
1 teaspoon garam masala
chopped fresh coriander, to season

desiccated coconut, to garnish (optional)

Pour the olive oil into a deep saucepan, add the fennel, fenugreek and nigella seeds and cook over a medium heat until the fennel seeds are a roasted colour – this should take no more than 2–3 minutes. Remove the pan from the heat and allow the oil to cool.

Once the oil-and-spice mixture has cooled, add the garlic and fresh ginger to the pan and cook over a low-medium heat until the garlic is a golden brown colour, stirring frequently – this should take no more than 2–3 minutes (if the garlic and ginger stick to the pan, add a few drops of cold water). Add the turmeric, ground ginger and chilli powder, mix well and cook for about 20 seconds.

Add the chicken to the pan, mix well and cook until sealed all over, stirring all the time – this should take no more than 5 minutes.

Peel and mash the banana, then add it to the pan, along with the chillies, fenugreek leaves, soy sauce and tomato purée. Stir and heat through.

Add 500ml boiling water and bring back to the boil. Reduce to a low simmer and cook, uncovered, for 30 minutes, stirring from time to time.

Season with the garam masala and chopped coriander, and garnish with the coconut, if using. Serve with your choice of sides.

One serving = 145%+ RDA antioxidants

Antibacterial
chilli, coriander, fennel, fenugreek, garlic, ginger, nigella, turmeric

Antifungal
chilli, coriander, fenugreek, garlic, ginger, nigella, turmeric

Antiviral
garlic, turmeric

Anti-inflammatory
chilli, coriander, fenugreek, garlic, ginger, nigella, turmeric

Analgesic
chilli, fennel, fenugreek, nigella

Lamb with Sweet Potato and Almonds

Serves 4

North Indian and Mughlai at heart, reflected by the use of almonds and lamb; even so, this recipe also pays homage to the style of cooking you would normally associate with Mumbai, where locals fortify meat curries with potato.

An additional superfood blast is given to it by replacing the regular potato with anti-inflammatory and antioxidant-rich sweet potato, which better equips our body to deal with its day-to-day functions. Cardamom adds a clearly traditional lambaste and, when used in cooking and ingested, helps prohibit the growth of bacteria in the body.

Garnishing with almonds not only gives the finished dish an added texture, but also blesses it with natural vitamin E and the amino acid arginine which boosts all-round immunity.

2 tablespoons olive oil
$1/2$ teaspoon cloves
$1/2$ teaspoon each fennel seeds and nigella seeds
10 green cardamom pods, lightly crushed
10 garlic cloves, finely chopped
3 tablespoons grated (peeled) fresh root ginger
1 teaspoon turmeric
1 tablespoon ground coriander
$1^1/2$ teaspoons garam masala
400g lean lamb (preferably leg), cut into bite-size pieces
3 tablespoons tomato purée
50ml good-quality soy sauce (make sure there is no added sugar)
2 onions, diced
$3/4$–1 teaspoon chilli powder
1 teaspoon ground ginger

1 sweet potato, peeled and cut into large bite-size pieces

chopped fresh coriander and flaked almonds, to garnish

Pour the olive oil into a deep saucepan, add the cloves, fennel and nigella seeds and cardamom pods and cook over a medium heat until the seeds start to pop – this should take no more than 2–3 minutes. Remove the pan from the heat and allow the oil to cool a bit.

Add the garlic and fresh ginger to the pan and cook over a low-medium heat until the garlic is a golden brown colour, stirring frequently – this should take no more than 5 minutes (if the garlic and ginger stick to the pan, add a few drops of cold water).

Add the turmeric, mix well and cook for about 20 seconds. Sprinkle in the ground coriander and $1/2$ teaspoon of the garam masala, mix well and continue to heat for a further 20 seconds.

Add the lamb, tomato purée, soy sauce, onions, chilli powder, ground ginger and 600ml boiling water. Return to the boil, then reduce to a simmer. Cook over a gentle heat, uncovered, for 30 minutes, stirring occasionally.

Add the sweet potato and mix well. Continue cooking, uncovered, for a further 30 minutes or until the meat is tender. To avoid sticking, stir more frequently towards the end of the cooking time.

Season with the remaining garam masala and garnish with the chopped coriander and flaked almonds. Serve with your choice of sides.

One serving = 250%+ RDA antioxidants

Antibacterial
cardamom, chilli, cloves, coriander, fennel, garlic, ginger, nigella, turmeric

Antifungal
cardamom, chilli, cloves, coriander, garlic, ginger, nigella, turmeric

Antiviral
cloves, garlic, turmeric

Anti-inflammatory
cardamom, chilli, cloves, coriander, garlic, ginger, nigella, turmeric

Analgesic
chilli, cloves, fennel, nigella

Indian Superfood

Tandoori-Spiced Salmon Fillet with Sweet Potato and Green Pea Masala Mash

Serves as many as you wish (see recipe)

Wildfire is one word that comes to mind when I think of this recipe. Ever since I first created it, it has spread through my friends and beyond, even into Pakistan, setting everyone alight with ecstasy. It meant that, Asian mums who wouldn't eat salmon, finding the omega-3 rich fish overwhelming in taste, could finally indulge themselves. Consequently, they also found it to be awesomely easy in preparation, almost too easy considering the great-tasting end product – and that's the 'secret' success story behind this recipe. I guess my friends have never really given me a fair chance to put across to them the health benefits, so here goes.

Research has shown that by eating at least one portion of salmon per week, we can decrease the likelihood of a heart attack, and sweet potato lowers insulin-resistance in individuals who suffer from diabetes. You can make the salmon with or without the masala mash. I quite often have it with just a salad. With the masala mash, it's a darn fine successor to Friday night fish and chips, and easier on the waistline too.

For the mash

Per person you will need:
300g sweet potatoes, peeled and cut into large bite-size pieces
1 tablespoon olive oil
$1/2$ teaspoon cumin seeds
$1/3$ teaspoon turmeric
$1/3$ teaspoon each chilli powder and salt (both optional)
a handful of green peas (fresh or frozen)

For the salmon

Per person you will need:
1 tablespoon tandoori masala powder
1 tablespoon cold water
150g salmon fillet, skinned
2 tablespoons low-salt steak seasoning
1 tablespoon olive oil

green salad and lemon wedges, to serve

Before you start, turn the oven on to heat at its maximum temperature setting with a baking tray placed inside.

Make the mash. Fill a deep saucepan with water and bring to the boil. Add the sweet potato pieces to the pan, return to the boil, cover and cook for about 15 minutes or until the sweet potatoes are tender. Drain well and set aside. (To minimise the loss of nutrients, the sweet potatoes may be steamed or cooked in the microwave, instead of boiling.)

Pour the olive oil into a separate deep saucepan, add the cumin seeds and cook over a low-medium heat until the seeds begin to pop – this will take no longer than 2–3 minutes. Add the turmeric and cook for 20 seconds, stirring all the time. Add the chilli powder and salt, if using, and cook for a further 20 seconds, mixing well.

Remove the pan from the heat. Add the cooked sweet potatoes to the spice mixture and mash well. Mix through the green peas, then cover, set aside and keep warm.

Prepare and cook the salmon. Mix the tandoori masala powder with the cold water and coat the salmon with this mixture. Sprinkle the steak seasoning on each side of the salmon (use more or less steak seasoning, to suit your taste).

Pour the olive oil into a frying pan and heat over a medium heat. When the oil is hot, place the salmon fillet into the frying pan and cook for 1–2 minutes on each side or until you have a golden crust both sides. Transfer the salmon to the hot baking tray. Bake at the top of the hot oven for 5 minutes.

Serve the salmon fillet and sweet potato mash immediately with a green salad and lemon wedges.

One serving = 325%+ RDA antioxidants

Antibacterial
chilli, cumin, turmeric

Antifungal
chilli, cumin, turmeric

Antiviral
turmeric

Anti-inflammatory
chilli, cumin, turmeric

Analgesic
chilli

Baby Spinach with Tofu

Serves 2–3

Saag paneer has been one of my favourite foods from a very young age. My fondest memory of it is from a trip to Uttar Pradesh, the Wild West of India; Bhuajee served us steaming bowlfuls laden with ghee.

In this recipe, I rehabilitate saag paneer by taking it far away from its love relationship with saturated fats, and bringing it back as something, as yummy as ever, whilst packing into it a potent trilogy of low-fat superfoods. Garlic and spinach help guard against heart disease, and tofu is a soy product, which the American Heart Association has found to be beneficial for cardiovascular health. Who'd have thought that one of our Indian classics could turn out to be so angelic?

"Curcumin is a predominant compound derived from turmeric; it shows antibacterial and anti-inflammatory activity and is an antineoplastic that inhibits and combats the development of abnormal mass growth in cells."

Chang Gung University, Taiwan[20]

2 tablespoons olive oil
5 garlic cloves, finely chopped
2 tablespoons grated (peeled) fresh root ginger
2–6 green chillies, finely chopped
$^3/_4$ teaspoon salt, or to taste
$^1/_2$ teaspoon turmeric
500g baby spinach, washed, drained and coarsely chopped
200ml light coconut milk
250g firm tofu, drained and cut into bite-size pieces

Place the olive oil in a deep saucepan with the garlic, ginger and chillies and cook over a low-medium heat until golden brown in colour, stirring frequently – this will take no more than 5 minutes (if the garlic and ginger stick to the pan, add a few drops of cold water).

Sprinkle in the salt and turmeric, stirring well, and cook for 20 seconds. Add the spinach in two batches, one batch first and the second when the first batch has wilted, stirring frequently. Cover and cook over a medium heat for 15 minutes, stirring regularly to allow the mixture to cook evenly.

Pour in the coconut milk. Using a hand-held blender, blitz the mixture to a purée (to do this, you may need to transfer the spinach to a smaller dish, then return it to the saucepan). Stir in the tofu and heat through.

Serve with raita and naan or a bread of your choice.

One serving =
220%+ RDA
antioxidants

Antibacterial
chilli, garlic, ginger, turmeric

Antifungal
chilli, garlic, ginger, turmeric

Antiviral
garlic, turmeric

Anti-inflammatory
chilli, garlic, ginger, turmeric

Analgesic
chilli

Salmon with Tamarind

Serves 4

My brother has been bugging me for this recipe ever since I first cooked it; I told him he would have to wait for Indian Superfood to be published. Bless; you can't blame him for asking though.

The rich salmon flesh works wonderfully with the sweet and sour tamarind. The very thought of it makes my lips smack with anticipation. Tamarind is, in fact, also used in India to treat the common cold. It has a flushing effect and, when taken, causes the nose and eyes to water, thus, clearing nasal blockage. So if called for, feel free to add a little extra.

When the tamarind is partnered with salmon, which is awash with omega-3 fatty acids that increase activity of white blood cells in the body to eliminate bacteria and, therefore, fight off infection, we have quite a duo here.

2 tablespoons olive oil
1 teaspoon each cumin seeds and coriander seeds
1/2 teaspoon mustard seeds
4 garlic cloves, finely chopped
2 tablespoons grated (peeled) fresh root ginger
1/2 teaspoon turmeric
1 tablespoon Tamarind Reduction (see pages 144–145)
1 tablespoon tomato purée
400ml light coconut milk
2 green chillies, finely chopped
3/4 teaspoon salt, or to taste
1/2 teaspoon sugar
500g salmon fillets, skinned and cut into large bite-size pieces

chopped fresh coriander and lemon wedges, to garnish

Pour the olive oil into a deep, wide saucepan, add the cumin, coriander and mustard seeds and cook over a high heat until the seeds start to pop – this should take no longer than 1–2 minutes. Remove the pan from the heat and allow to cool.

Add the garlic and ginger to the pan and fry over a low-medium heat until golden brown – this should take no more than 2-3 minutes (if the garlic and ginger stick to the pan, add a few drops of cold water). Sprinkle in the turmeric and cook for about 20 seconds, stirring all the time.

Add the tamarind reduction, tomato purée, coconut milk, chillies, salt and sugar and mix well, making sure the tomato purée dissolves. Bring the sauce to a rapid simmer. Stir in the salmon, then reduce to a gentle simmer and cook, uncovered, for 4–5 minutes or until the salmon is cooked through.

Garnish with the chopped coriander and lemon wedges and serve. Best eaten with pilau and salad.

One serving = 100%+ RDA antioxidants

Antibacterial
chilli, coriander, cumin, garlic, ginger, mustard, tamarind, turmeric

Antifungal
chilli, coriander, cumin, garlic, ginger, mustard, turmeric

Antiviral
garlic, turmeric

Anti-inflammatory
chilli, coriander, cumin, garlic, ginger, mustard, turmeric

Analgesic
chilli

Beef with Papaya and Cloves

Serves 3–4

This superfood alternative to beef masala combines the pain-relieving properties of cloves and fennel seeds, with the powerful enzymes found in papaya that aid the body's digestive process by breaking down the meat proteins and, thereby, making our affair with beef a whole lot more harmonious for our body. The melding of papaya and cloves with beef imparts a distinctly exotic and sultry feel to this dish.

It is nosh that is wonderfully rich, as well as aromatic, and is reminiscent of the classical-style curries found on Indian restaurant menus the world over.

2 tablespoons olive oil
10 cloves
1 teaspoon fennel seeds
1/2 teaspoon nigella seeds
10 garlic cloves, finely chopped
3 tablespoons grated (peeled) fresh root ginger
1 teaspoon turmeric
500g lean beef, cut into bite-size pieces
2 onions, diced
3 tablespoons tomato purée
50ml good-quality soy sauce (make sure there is no added sugar)
1 teaspoon ground ginger
1/2–1 teaspoon chilli powder
1 1/2 teaspoons garam masala
2/3 of a small papaya (about 320g when whole), peeled, seeded and diced (you need about 180g prepared papaya flesh)
chopped fresh coriander, to season

Pour the olive oil into a deep saucepan, add the cloves and fennel and nigella seeds and cook over a medium heat until the seeds start to pop – this should take no more than 2–3 minutes. Remove the pan from the heat and allow the oil to cool for a moment or two.

Add the garlic and fresh ginger to the pan and cook over a low-medium heat until they are a golden brown colour, stirring frequently – this should take no more than 5 minutes (if the garlic and ginger stick to the pan, add a few drops of cold water). Add the turmeric, mix well and cook for a further 20 seconds.

Add the beef, onions, tomato purée, soy sauce, ground ginger, chilli powder, 1/2 teaspoon of the garam masala and 600ml boiling water, mix well, then bring to the boil.

Reduce the heat to a gentle simmer and cook, uncovered, for 45 minutes, making sure to stir occasionally to avoid any sticking. Add a little more boiling water, if necessary.

Mix in the papaya and continue cooking for a further 15 minutes or until the meat is tender, stirring occasionally. Season with the remaining garam masala and some chopped coriander. Best eaten with naan or pilau.

One serving = 255%+ RDA antioxidants

Antibacterial
chilli, cloves, coriander, fennel, garlic, ginger, nigella, turmeric

Antifungal
chilli, cloves, coriander, garlic, ginger, nigella, turmeric

Antiviral
cloves, garlic, turmeric

Anti-inflammatory
chilli, cloves, coriander, garlic, ginger, nigella, turmeric

Analgesic
chilli, cloves, fennel, nigella

Lamb with Roasted Vegetables

Serves 4–6

Although lamb is higher in fat than many other meats, this recipe could still be a dieter's best friend. Lamb and fennel seeds muscle-in collectively to suppress appetite and the tryptophan from the lamb works at elevating one's frame of mind. To make it better still, a plethora of cholesterol-lowering vegetables from the Mediterranean are employed to counteract some of the saturated fats found in lamb.

Best of all, roasting the aubergine, onions, tomatoes and pepper adds a caramelised barbecue twang to this classical rogan josh-style dish. It is well worth the extra preparation time required.

1 aubergine (about 300g) pricked with a fork
3 onions (left unpeeled)
1 red pepper
6 tomatoes
2 tablespoons olive oil
1 cinnamon stick
1 teaspoon fennel seeds
$1/2$ teaspoon nigella seeds
10 garlic cloves, finely chopped
2 tablespoons grated (peeled) fresh root ginger
1 teaspoon turmeric
$1^{1}/2$ teaspoons garam masala
400g lean lamb (preferably leg), cut into bite-size pieces
50ml good-quality soy sauce (make sure there is no added sugar)
$1/2$–1 teaspoon chilli powder
1 teaspoon ground ginger
chopped fresh coriander, to season

Preheat the oven to 200°C/fan 180°C/Gas Mark 6. Place the whole aubergine, onions, pepper and tomatoes on a baking tray and bake in the centre of the oven for 45 minutes or until they are soft. Remove the vegetables from the oven and allow them to cool a little. Peel the onions, remove the stalks from the aubergine and pepper, and deseed the pepper. Roughly chop the vegetables and place in a bowl. Set aside.

Pour the olive oil into a deep saucepan, add the cinnamon stick and fennel and nigella seeds and cook over a low-medium heat until the seeds start to pop – this should take no more than 2–3 minutes. Remove the pan from the heat and allow the oil to cool a little.

Add the garlic and fresh ginger to the pan and cook over a medium heat until they are a golden brown colour, stirring frequently – this should take no more than 5 minutes (if the garlic and ginger stick to the pan, add a few drops of cold water). Add the turmeric, mix well and cook for about 20 seconds. Sprinkle in $1/2$ teaspoon of the garam masala, mix well and continue cooking for a further 20 seconds, stirring frequently.

Stir in the lamb, oven-roasted vegetables, soy sauce, chilli powder, ground ginger and 300ml boiling water, return to the boil, then reduce to a simmer. Cook over a gentle heat, uncovered, for 1 hour or until the meat is tender, stirring occasionally; to avoid sticking, stir more frequently towards the end of the cooking time.

Season with the remaining garam masala and the chopped coriander. Serve with your choice of sides.

One serving = 285%+ RDA antioxidants

Antibacterial
chilli, cinnamon, coriander, fennel, garlic, ginger, nigella, turmeric

Antifungal
chilli, cinnamon, coriander, fennel, garlic, ginger, nigella, turmeric

Antiviral
cinnamon, garlic, turmeric

Anti-inflammatory
chilli, cinnamon, coriander, fennel, garlic, ginger, nigella, turmeric

Analgesic
chilli, fennel, nigella

Indian Superfood

Mango Chicken

Serves 4

This mouthwatering and deliciously rich and fruity mango chicken is a super-duper evolved version of our naughty-but-national dish – chicken tikka masala. I think there is something magical about this recipe and am betting Mango Chicken will be an overnight success and challenge chicken tikka masala as a potential heir to our national dish.

From a nutritional point of view, I can boast of a little wizardry in the recipe. Both mustard seeds and mango pulp are containerised with antioxidants and flavonoids that aid the immune system function and reduce the incidence of cancer – this one's a multitasker alright.

2 tablespoons olive oil
1 teaspoon mustard seeds
$1/2$ teaspoon fenugreek seeds
2 garlic cloves, finely chopped
3 tablespoons grated (peeled) fresh root ginger
1 teaspoon turmeric
2 green chillies, chopped
$3/4$ teaspoon salt, or to taste
1 tablespoon tomato purée
300ml mango pulp/purée
300ml light coconut milk
500g skinless, boneless chicken breasts, cut into small bite-size pieces

chopped fresh coriander, to garnish

Pour the olive oil into a deep saucepan, add the mustard and fenugreek seeds and cook over a high heat until the mustard seeds start to pop – this should take no more than 1–2 minutes. Remove the pan from the heat and allow the oil to cool for a moment or two.

Add the garlic and ginger to the pan and cook over a low-medium heat until they are a golden brown colour, stirring frequently – this should take no more than 2–3 minutes (if the garlic and ginger stick to the pan, add a few drops of cold water). Add the turmeric, mix well and cook for about 20 seconds.

Add the chillies, salt, tomato purée, mango pulp and coconut milk, mix well and bring to a rapid simmer. Add the chicken and mix well, return to a gentle simmer, then cook, uncovered, for 10 minutes or until the chicken is cooked and tender.

Garnish with the chopped coriander. Serve with your choice of sides.

One serving = 130%+ RDA antioxidants

Antibacterial
chilli, coriander, fenugreek, garlic, ginger, mustard, turmeric

Antifungal
chilli, coriander, garlic, fenugreek, ginger, mustard, turmeric

Antiviral
garlic, turmeric

Anti-inflammatory
chilli, coriander, fenugreek, garlic, ginger, mustard, turmeric

Analgesic
chilli, fenugreek

Indian Superfood

Koftas in Tomato Sauce with Indian Vermicelli

Serves 4–6

Traditional Indian recipes for koftas in sauce don't tend to use as much tomato as mine, which naturally borrows the practice from Italy, giving the recipe that distinctive superfood twist by adding loads of lycopene, which is beneficial in preventing cancer. Cashews and olive oil introduce healthy fats into the recipe. As you first taste the sauce, you'd be forgiven if you thought it was Italian, but that's only until you bite into the koftas. Flavoured decadently with Indian superspices, they release a heady and pleasant aroma into your mouth, which gently overpowers one's senses; and there is no mistaking this is an Indian dish. Served on a bed of vermicelli, your mind once again wanders back to Italy; but these are seviyan – Indian vermicelli. Rather like Sonia Gandhi, this recipe is impossibly, yet possibly, Indian and Italian, both at the same time – a perplexity which could only be an Indian one.

For an occasional indulgence, finely grate over some paneer – it won't melt like an Italian cheese; it will, however, add its own creamy Indian originality.

For the meatballs
25g unsalted cashews
1 small onion, cut into quarters
2 garlic cloves, peeled
2 tablespoons garam masala
1 teaspoon ground ginger
1 teaspoon fennel seeds
$1/2$ teaspoon salt
20g bunch of fresh coriander, coarsely chopped
2–4 green chillies, chopped
1 large egg
250g minced lamb

For the sauce
2 tablespoons olive oil
10 green cardamom pods, lightly crushed
2 teaspoons cumin seeds
$3/4$ teaspoon salt, or to taste
1 small onion, thinly sliced
6 garlic cloves, finely chopped
1 teaspoon turmeric
1 teaspoon garam masala
4 x 400g cans tomatoes, blended until smooth
3 tablespoons grated (peeled) fresh root ginger
2–6 green chillies, chopped

chopped fresh coriander, to garnish
cooked seviyan (Indian vermicelli) or pasta, to serve

For the meatballs, put the cashews into a food processor and process until they resemble breadcrumbs. Add the onion, garlic, garam masala, ground ginger, fennel seeds, salt, chopped coriander, chillies and egg and blitz. Add the minced lamb and blitz so that the meat passes completely through the blade three times and is thoroughly combined.

Divide the meat mixture into 16 equal portions and shape each one into a small round ball. (If you find the mixture to be too moist to handle, add some dried breadcrumbs into it and mix well.) Set aside.

For the sauce, pour the olive oil into a deep saucepan, add the cardamom pods and cumin seeds and cook over a low-medium heat until the seeds start to pop – this should take no longer than 2–3 minutes. Add the salt and onion and fry until the onion is light brown in colour,

remembering to stir frequently – this should take no more than 5 minutes.

Stir in the garlic and fry for about 1–2 minutes or until a light brown colour. Sprinkle in the turmeric, mix well and cook for about 20 seconds. Add the garam masala and mix well.

Add a quarter of the tomatoes, together with the fresh ginger and chillies, and cook for about 10 minutes or until the excess juices in the saucepan have dried off, remembering to keep stirring occasionally. Add the remaining tomatoes, mix and bring to a gentle simmer.

Carefully place the meatballs into the tomato sauce (do not mix for the first 10 minutes). Simmer over a gentle heat, uncovered, for 45 minutes, stirring occasionally.

Garnish with the chopped coriander. Serve with cooked seviyan (Indian vermicelli) or pasta of your choice.

One serving = 285%+ RDA antioxidants

Antibacterial
cardamom, chilli, coriander, cumin, fennel, garlic, ginger, turmeric

Antifungal
cardamom, chilli, coriander, cumin, fennel, garlic, ginger, turmeric

Antiviral
garlic, turmeric

Anti-inflammatory
cardamom, chilli, coriander, cumin, fennel, garlic, ginger, turmeric

Analgesic
chilli, fennel

Beef with Sea Salad and Mustard

Serves 3–4

A classical combination of 'reef and beef' in an aromatic and rich masala-style curry that's destined to make a regular appearance at mealtimes. It contains sea vegetables that are nature's richest source of iodine which helps regulate our metabolism, cinnamon that suppresses appetite by lowering blood sugar levels, and protein aplenty so you most definitely won't go hungry.

This recipe could be a rare hit with both the Friday night lager crowd and diet gang alike!

2 tablespoons olive oil
1 teaspoon mustard seeds
1 cinnamon stick
10 garlic cloves, finely chopped
2 tablespoons grated (peeled) fresh root ginger
1 teaspoon turmeric
1¹/₂ teaspoons garam masala
500g lean beef, cut into bite-size pieces
2 tablespoons tomato purée
50ml good-quality soy sauce (make sure there is no added sugar)
2 onions, diced
1 teaspoon ground ginger
¹/₂ teaspoon chilli powder
2 tablespoons sea salad (available from health-food shops)
chopped fresh coriander, to season

Pour the olive oil into a deep saucepan, add the mustard seeds and cinnamon stick and cook over a high heat until the mustard seeds start to pop – this should take no more than 1–2 minutes. Remove the pan from the heat and allow the oil to cool for a moment or two.

Add the garlic and fresh ginger to the pan and cook over a low-medium heat, and they are a golden brown colour, stirring frequently – this should take no more than 5 minutes (if the garlic and ginger stick to the pan, add a few drops of cold water). Add the turmeric, mix well and cook for about 20 seconds. Sprinkle in ¹/₂ teaspoon of the garam masala, mix well and continue cooking for a further 20 seconds.

Add the beef, tomato purée, soy sauce, onions, ground ginger, chilli powder and 500ml boiling water and return to the boil. Reduce to a simmer, then cook over a gentle heat, uncovered, for 1 hour or until the meat is tender, stirring occasionally. To avoid sticking, stir more frequently towards the end of the cooking time. Add a little more boiling water, if required – the sauce should be very thick in consistency.

About 10 minutes prior to the end of cooking, sprinkle in the sea salad and mix well.

Season with the remaining garam masala and the chopped coriander. Serve with your choice of sides.

One serving = 310%+ RDA antioxidants

Antibacterial
chilli, cinnamon, coriander, garlic, ginger, mustard, turmeric

Antifungal
chilli, cinnamon, coriander, garlic, ginger, mustard, turmeric

Antiviral
cinnamon, garlic, turmeric

Anti-inflammatory
chilli, cinnamon, coriander, garlic, ginger, mustard, turmeric

Analgesic
chilli

Chicken Thighs and Chickpeas in a Rich Jalfrezi-Style Stew

Serves 4

There is reassuring comfort to be had in losing oneself in a hot, steaming bowlful of this stew. I find the combination of melt-in-the-mouth chicken and chickpeas with bite in a rich and spicy tomato sauce, to be nothing short of irresistible. It's a very satisfying and warming meal indeed, and just what I yearn for on a cold winter's night seated in front of the fireplace with some fresh, crusty bread and a glass of red wine.

This one's always gone down a treat at home, appealing to both the traditional and more contemporary tastes found in a family of three generations. Incorporating chickpeas into the recipe adds much more sustenance to our diet, replacing some of our meat intake with one of nature's best sources of protein.

2 tablespoons olive oil
2 teaspoons cumin seeds
$3/4$ teaspoon salt, or to taste
1 small onion, thinly sliced
4 garlic cloves, finely chopped
1 teaspoon turmeric
1 teaspoon ground ginger
2 teaspoons ground coriander
400g can tomatoes, blended until
  smooth
4 chicken thighs on the bone or
  4 chicken thigh fillets, skinned
400g can chickpeas, rinsed and
  drained
2 tablespoons grated (peeled) fresh
  root ginger
2–6 green chillies, chopped
1 teaspoon garam masala
chopped fresh coriander, to season

Pour the olive oil into a deep saucepan, add 1 teaspoon of the cumin seeds and cook over a low-medium heat until the seeds start to pop – this should take no longer than 2–3 minutes. Add the salt and onion and fry until the onion is light brown in colour, remembering to stir frequently – this should take no more than about 5 minutes.

Stir in the garlic and fry for about 1–2 minutes or until it is a light brown colour. Sprinkle in the turmeric, mix well and cook for about 20 seconds. Add the ground ginger and 1 teaspoon of the ground coriander and mix well. Add the tomatoes and cook for about 10 minutes or until the excess juices in the saucepan have dried off, remembering to keep stirring occasionally.

Add the chicken thighs to the pan, mix well and cook until they are sealed all over, stirring constantly – this should take no more than about 5 minutes.

Add the chickpeas and enough boiling water to just cover the chicken thighs. Leave to simmer over a gentle heat, uncovered, for 30–45 minutes or until the chicken is cooked and tender, stirring occasionally.

About 10 minutes prior to the end of cooking, mix through the fresh ginger, chillies and the remaining cumin seeds and ground coriander.

Season with the garam masala and chopped coriander. Serve with your choice of sides.

**One serving =
225%+ RDA
antioxidants**

Antibacterial
chilli, coriander,
cumin, garlic,
ginger, turmeric

Antifungal
chilli, coriander,
cumin, garlic,
ginger, turmeric

Antiviral
garlic, turmeric

Anti-inflammatory
chilli, coriander,
cumin, garlic,
ginger, turmeric

Analgesic
chilli

Indian Superfood

Spicy Prawns in a Dry Seaweed Masala

If, like me, you're a fan of prawns and crispy seaweed, you'll fall for this recipe – hook, line and sinker. Spicy sea salad replaces the use of traditional spinach and, boy oh boy, what a Herculean difference it makes; they go together like Ben and Jerry's!

Sea salad incrusts the prawns not only with a dramatic flavour, but also with the most immense range of minerals available to us in the ocean, or on Earth. In fact, in the Orient, it is known as the 'secret elixir' to a long life.

And, if all this isn't enough to get you running into the kitchen already, how about a recipe that's more about assembling and heating, rather than complex preparation and cooking? Chop-chop, I'd say – but then again, there is no chopping required either!

Serves 2

1 tablespoon olive oil
1 teaspoon cumin seeds
$1/_2$ teaspoon turmeric
$1/_3$ teaspoon chilli powder
3 tablespoons sea salad (available at health-food shops)
240g cooked peeled king prawns
salt, to taste (optional)

lemon wedges, to garnish

Heat a non-stick wok over a high heat until it is very hot. Pour the olive oil into the wok and heat until it is almost smoking – this should take no more than 1 minute.

Add the cumin seeds and cook until they start popping – this should take no longer than 1 minute. Sprinkle in the turmeric and chilli powder and mix well. Add the sea salad, mixing it thoroughly into the spices.

Throw the prawns in, mix well and stir-fry until heated through. Season to taste with salt, if desired.

Garnish with lemon wedges and serve with pilau.

One serving =
100%+ RDA
antioxidants

Antibacterial
chilli, cumin,
turmeric

Antifungal
chilli, cumin,
turmeric

Antiviral
turmeric

Anti-inflammatory
chilli, cumin,
turmeric

Analgesic
chilli

Chickpeas with Sea Salad and Star Anise

Serves 4

Up until about now, it would have been unheard of to have chickpeas, sea salad and tomato knocking around together on the same plate. It was as if they were separated by caste and sent to the four corners of the earth – doomed to live separately for an eternity. It just wasn't the done thing to put this trio into the same room, let alone for them to share a plate. But now that they have banded and bonded, I hope they play together and stay together; because they sure do make a great team.

The luscious and twangy tomato sauce is diffused with the sweet floral perfume of the star anise which also doubles up to help relieve aching joints. Floating around in the sauce are fleshy chickpeas – one of nature's best sources of plant proteins. Hanging onto the chickpeas, you will find the 'salty'-tasting sea salad, which offers the most immense range of minerals found in any food.

2 tablespoons olive oil
1 tablespoon mustard seeds
1 teaspoon fennel seeds
1/2 teaspoon nigella seeds
8 garlic cloves, finely chopped
1 tablespoon grated (peeled) fresh root ginger
2–4 green chillies, finely chopped, to taste
1/2 teaspoon turmeric
1/2 teaspoon chilli powder
200g tomato purée
6 star anise
1 teaspoon ground ginger
1 teaspoon salt, or to taste
1 teaspoon sugar

2 tablespoons sea salad (available from health-food shops)
2 x 400g cans chickpeas, rinsed and drained

chopped fresh coriander, to garnish

Pour the olive oil into a deep saucepan, add the mustard, fennel and nigella seeds and cook over a high heat until the mustard seeds start to pop – this will take no more than 1–2 minutes. Remove the pan from the heat and allow the oil to cool for a moment or two.

Add the garlic and cook over a medium heat until the garlic begins to sizzle. Add the fresh ginger and chillies and fry until the ginger is golden brown in colour, stirring all the time – this will take 2–3 minutes (if the garlic and ginger stick to the pan, add a few drops of cold water). Stir in the turmeric and chilli powder and cook for a further 20 seconds.

Add the tomato purée and heat through, then add the star anise, ground ginger, salt, sugar, sea salad and 750ml boiling water and bring to a simmer. Stir in the chickpeas and simmer over a medium heat, uncovered, for 10 minutes.

Garnish with the chopped coriander. Serve with your choice of sides.

One serving = 210%+ RDA antioxidants

Antibacterial
chilli, coriander, fennel, garlic, ginger, mustard, nigella, star anise, turmeric

Antifungal
chilli, coriander, garlic, ginger, mustard, nigella, turmeric

Antiviral
garlic, turmeric

Anti-inflammatory
chilli, coriander, garlic, ginger, mustard, nigella, turmeric

Analgesic
chilli, fennel, nigella

" The essential oil of nigella has tested under stringent laboratory conditions as a potent analgesic and anti-inflammatory drug."

Isfahan University of Medical Sciences, Iran[16]

Beef and Tomato Rogan Josh

Serves 4

Like an old trusted friend, this recipe churns out consistently good results each and every time. It's a stereotypical rich-tasting rogan josh, with no bells or whistles – no need for any fuss or rush. All it needs from you is about 20 minutes' preparation time and then you can leave it to slow-cook on the stove, whilst you pop on your slippers and relax. It's just what you need when you get home on a cold winter's night and want to forget the world outside of the front door.

Traditionally, the use of so much tomato in Indian cooking is unthinkable. It's as if the entire Indian people 'could' have an allergy to them and, therefore, minimise their use. It certainly took me a fair few years to develop my tomatoey taste buds. I used to wriggle like a worm when fed the tangy sauces – but I guess I'm not the only one.

Although my Mum loves to eat truckloads of raw tomatoes, she still twitches at the thought of so many in her curry – quite peculiar when you come to think of it. But, now that most of us have acquired a taste for tomatoes and since they work so incredibly well with meat, there really is nothing holding us back from including some of the ethos of the Mediterranean diet into the nation's favourite cuisine. Serve it to close friends and family; they will love you for it.

2 tablespoons olive oil
10 green cardamom pods, lightly crushed
1 teaspoon cumin seeds
$\frac{1}{2}$ teaspoon nigella seeds
$\frac{3}{4}$ teaspoon salt, or to taste
1 small onion, thinly sliced
6 garlic cloves, finely chopped
1 teaspoon turmeric
2 teaspoons garam masala

3 x 400g cans tomatoes, blended until smooth
3 tablespoons grated (peeled) fresh root ginger
2–6 green chillies, chopped
500g lean beef, diced
chopped fresh coriander, to season

Pour the olive oil into a deep saucepan, add the cardamom pods and cumin and nigella seeds and cook over a low-medium heat until the seeds start to pop – this should take no longer than 2–3 minutes. Add the salt and onion and fry until the onion is light brown in colour, remembering to stir frequently – this should take no more than 5 minutes.

Stir in the garlic and fry for about 1–2 minutes or until a light brown colour. Sprinkle in the turmeric, mix well and cook for about 20 seconds.

Add half of the garam masala and mix well. Pour in a third of the tomatoes, together with the ginger and chillies, and cook for about 10 minutes or until the excess juices in the saucepan have dried off, remembering to keep stirring occasionally.

Add the beef to the pan, mix well and cook until it is sealed all over, stirring constantly – this should take no more than 5 minutes.

Add the remaining tomatoes and bring to a gentle simmer. Leave to simmer over a gentle heat, uncovered, for 30 minutes, then cover and simmer for a further 30 minutes or until the meat is tender. Remember to stir occasionally.

Season with the remaining garam masala and the chopped coriander. Serve with your choice of sides.

One serving = 210%+ RDA antioxidants

Antibacterial
cardamom, chilli, coriander, cumin, garlic, ginger, nigella, turmeric

Antifungal
cardamom, chilli, coriander, cumin, garlic, ginger, nigella, turmeric

Antiviral
garlic, turmeric

Anti-inflammatory
cardamom, chilli, coriander, cumin, garlic, ginger, nigella, turmeric

Analgesic
chilli, nigella

Oven-Roasted Baby Aubergines and Tomatoes in Yogurt Sauce

Serves 3–4

In many parts of Asia, aubergine is considered to be the 'king of vegetables'. And, for me, no three words could sum it up more exactingly. Aubergine lends itself wholeheartedly to the flavours of whatever it is that you happen to be cooking it in. Its flesh softens, almost appearing to 'open up' and absorb flavours like a sponge, taking on a character that was once totally alien to it. There is no vegetable that's quite as committed as the beloved aubergine.

Notably, whilst being effective at controlling bad cholesterol, aubergines also contain the highest amount of nicotine found in any edible plant, perhaps another reason for its popularity? Mum loves aubergines so much that she even sings to them 'bataun, bataun meh tenoo khakay batoon', which is a fatalistic jingle that roughly translates to English as 'aubergine, aubergine, I can only tell you how sweet your flesh tastes after first biting in to you'.

In this particular recipe, the baby aubergines are not sliced at all and are instead pricked with a fork, leaving much of their flesh cloaked by their mysterious purple-black coat, so that you can taste their own bitter-sweetness accentuated lovingly by oven-baking. It's an incredibly appealing low-carbohydrate vegetarian recipe for those amongst us who are seeking a meal that simply refuses to compromise by way of good looks, great taste and a simple preparation. Try it with naans or chapattis and extra yogurt on the side.

16 whole baby aubergines, stalks trimmed
2 large vine-ripened tomatoes

2 tablespoons olive oil
2 teaspoons cumin seeds
3/4 teaspoon salt, or to taste
1 small onion, sliced
4 garlic cloves, chopped
2–4 green chillies, finely chopped (optional)
1 teaspoon turmeric
1 tablespoon tomato purée
4 tablespoons low-fat Greek yogurt

Preheat the oven to 200°C/fan 180°C/Gas Mark 6. Prick each whole baby aubergine a few times with a fork. Place the whole aubergines and tomatoes on a baking tray and bake in the centre of the oven for approximately 15–25 minutes or until the aubergines are soft to touch.

Meanwhile, pour the olive oil into a deep saucepan, add the cumin seeds and cook over a low-medium heat until the seeds start to pop – this should take no longer than 2–3 minutes. Add the salt and onion and fry until the onion is light brown in colour, remembering to stir frequently – this should take no more than 5 minutes.

Stir in the garlic and chillies and fry for about 1–2 minutes or until the garlic is a light brown colour. Sprinkle in the turmeric and cook for about 20 seconds. Add the tomato purée, mix well and heat through. Pour in the yogurt, mixing thoroughly, and heat through.

Once the aubergines and tomatoes are finished baking, remove from the oven, cut the tomatoes into quarters and mix them into the yogurt curry mixture with the whole baby aubergines. Cook for 5 minutes, stirring occasionally.

Serve with your choice of sides.

One serving =
195%+ RDA
antioxidants

Antibacterial
chilli, cumin, garlic, turmeric

Antifungal
chilli, cumin, garlic, turmeric

Antiviral
garlic, turmeric

Anti-inflammatory
chilli, cumin, garlic, turmeric

Analgesic
chilli

Chicken 'Stew' with Yellow Split Peas and Courgette

Serves 4–6

When I come home to my Mum's, this is exactly the sort of dish I hope she has cooked for me. It's typical of her rustic Punjabi home-cooking style and, for me, one of a handful of recipes which nourish my mind, body and soul; leaving me feeling satiated, relaxed and sheltered.

In the Punjab, we don't truly have a concept of 'comfort food'. In fact, most other Indians consider Punjabi food on the whole to be a complete comfort cuisine. And, it's an accurate assumption, for no other regional Indian kitchen has so many recipes that are as hearty as ours. From stuffed parathas to rich slow-cooked dahls and creamy meat curries, Punjabis tend to prefer eating 'comfortably', all the time.

In this recipe, I adore how the chicken melts hopelessly into the stew, blending in with the mushy yellow peas and courgette – both of which also help lower the incidence of cardiovascular diseases and reduce cholesterol. Try it dished up with crispy chapattis or crusty fresh bread, and some of Mum's Mint Chutney (page 148). And, enjoy!

500g skinless, boneless chicken breasts, cut in half
210g dried yellow split peas
1 tomato, finely chopped
3/4 teaspoon salt, or to taste
1/2 teaspoon turmeric
2 tablespoons grated (peeled) fresh root ginger
1 teaspoon ground ginger
5 black cardamom pods, lightly crushed (optional)
2 teaspoons cumin seeds
1 courgette, cut into small bite-size cubes

2 tablespoons olive oil
1 teaspoon freshly ground black pepper
1 teaspoon nigella seeds
1 small onion, thinly sliced
6 garlic cloves, finely chopped
2–6 green chillies, chopped

chopped fresh coriander, to garnish

Place the chicken, yellow split peas, tomato, salt, turmeric, fresh ginger, ground ginger, cardamom pods, if using, and 1 teaspoon of the cumin seeds in a deep saucepan. Pour in 1.6 litres boiling water and mix well. Heat gently until the water returns to a simmer, then cook, uncovered, for 1 hour, remembering to stir occasionally to avoid sticking. If the sauce thickens too much, you may need to add a little more boiling water. Stir in the courgette after 40 minutes of cooking.

In the meantime, pour the olive oil into a frying pan, add the black pepper, nigella seeds and remaining cumin seeds and cook over a low-medium heat until the seeds start to pop – this should take no longer than 2–3 minutes.

Add the onion and fry until it is light brown in colour, remembering to stir frequently – this should take no more than 5 minutes. Add the garlic and chillies, mix well and fry for about 2–4 minutes or until the garlic is a golden brown colour. Remove from the heat and set aside.

Once the yellow peas are ready, mix the spice mixture into them and simmer for just a few minutes.

Garnish with the chopped coriander. Serve with your choice of sides.

One serving = 155%+ RDA antioxidants

Antibacterial
cardamom, chilli, coriander, cumin, garlic, ginger, nigella, pepper, turmeric

Antifungal
cardamom, chilli, coriander, cumin, garlic, ginger, nigella, turmeric

Antiviral
garlic, turmeric

Anti-inflammatory
cardamom, chilli, coriander, cumin, garlic, ginger, nigella, turmeric

Analgesic
chilli, nigella

Pumpkin with Coconut and Lamb

Serves 4–6

This recipe is inspired by my encounters with Her Excellency Reena Pandey, Ambassador of India, who loved nothing more than showing her Turkish friends how adding a simple tarka of superspices and some coconut to the unassuming pumpkin could turn it into something nearly as fabulous as herself. In-between cooking for friends, shopping with the German Ambassador's wife, flying around with her sari jutting out in Lakshmi Mittal's helicopter, and reading newspapers upside down, Her Excellency managed to represent the affairs of India and its people with utmost diligence.

Although I am not an Indian citizen (yet), she even found time to extend her support to my cause; once even loaning to me her huge brass Ganesh murti for use at the food promotion at the Mövenpick Hotel. Her Excellency is an ideal role model and has shaped my perception of what to expect of an Ambassador – and my, what a mighty standard she has set. So, this one is for you, Your Excellency. Just as you do to your pumpkin, I have added a simple tarka and coconut milk to completely transform and refresh my lamb and pumpkin.

There isn't a long list of ingredients in this recipe because the four main flavours of pumpkin, lamb, coconut and ginger are exactly what I want you to experience. And, of course, pumpkin isn't fabulous without a reason. It's loaded with beta-carotene which provides the body with vitamin A and protects our cells from the destructive effects of free radicals.

2 tablespoons olive oil
1 teaspoon each mustard seeds and fenugreek seeds
$1/2$ teaspoon nigella seeds
$3/4$ teaspoon salt, or to taste
1 small onion, thinly sliced
6 garlic cloves, finely chopped
1 teaspoon turmeric
400g can tomatoes, blended until smooth
500g lean lamb (preferably leg), diced
400g (prepared weight) pumpkin, peeled, deseeded and diced
400ml light coconut milk
3 tablespoons grated (peeled) fresh root ginger
2–6 green chillies, chopped

chopped fresh coriander, to garnish

Pour the olive oil into a deep saucepan, add the mustard, fenugreek and nigella seeds and cook over a low-medium heat until the seeds start to pop – this should take no longer than 2–3 minutes. Add the salt and onion and fry until the onion is light brown in colour, remembering to stir frequently – this should take no more than 5 minutes.

Stir in the garlic and fry for about 1–2 minutes or until a light brown colour. Sprinkle in the turmeric, mix well and cook for about 20 seconds. Pour in the tomatoes and cook for about 10 minutes or until the excess juices in the saucepan have dried off, remembering to keep stirring occasionally.

Add the lamb to the pan, mix well and cook until it is sealed all over, stirring constantly – this should take no more than 5 minutes.

Add the pumpkin, coconut milk and enough boiling water to cover the lamb, then bring to a simmer. Leave to simmer, uncovered, for 30 minutes, then cover and simmer for a further 20 minutes, stirring occasionally.

Stir in the ginger and chillies, then cover and simmer for a further 10 minutes or until the meat is tender. Remember to stir occasionally.

Garnish with the chopped coriander. Serve with your choice of sides.

One serving = 200%+ RDA antioxidants	Antifungal chilli, coriander, fenugreek, garlic, ginger, mustard, nigella, turmeric
Antibacterial chilli, coriander, fenugreek, garlic, ginger, mustard, nigella, turmeric	**Antiviral** garlic, turmeric
	Anti-inflammatory chilli, coriander, fenugreek, garlic, ginger, mustard, nigella, turmeric
	Analgesic chilli, fenugreek, nigella

Indian Superfood

Seafood Stew with Chickpeas and Saffron

Serves 4

Made entirely with low fat omega-3 rich seafood and plant proteins, this is probably one of the healthiest stews you will come across.

Ocean-fresh seafood, saffron and tomatoes weave their magic by imbuing creaminess into this warming and satisfying stew. Chickpeas add their own texture, and a richness more associated with heavier meat stews, which contrasts pleasingly with that of the seafood.

It's ideal for midweek suppers when you want something fast and easy to prepare but still crave an ample meal. Exceedingly good served with either fresh bread or traditional Indian sides.

2 tablespoons olive oil
1 cinnamon stick
1 teaspoon each cumin seeds and
 fennel seeds
3/4 teaspoon salt, or to taste
1 small onion, sliced
4 garlic cloves, crushed
1 tablespoon grated (peeled) fresh root
 ginger
2–4 green chillies, finely chopped
1 teaspoon turmeric
400g can chopped tomatoes
a large pinch of saffron
300g white fish fillets, cut into large
 bite-size pieces
200g mixed fresh (prepared) seafood
 (such as mussels, king prawns and
 squid rings)
400g can chickpeas, rinsed and
 drained
chopped fresh coriander, to garnish

Pour the olive oil into a deep saucepan, add the cinnamon stick and cumin and fennel seeds and cook over a low-medium heat until the seeds start to pop – this should take no longer than 2–3 minutes. Add the salt and onion and fry until the onion is light brown in colour, remembering to stir frequently – this should take no more than 5 minutes.

Stir in the garlic, ginger and chillies and fry for about 1–2 minutes or until the garlic is a light brown colour. Sprinkle in the turmeric and cook for about 20 seconds. Add the tomatoes and saffron and cook for about 10 minutes or until the excess juices in the saucepan have dried off. Remember to keep stirring occasionally.

Add 400ml boiling water to the pan, return to a simmer, then leave to simmer, uncovered, for 10 minutes, stirring from time to time.

Stir in the fish, seafood and chickpeas and return to a simmer. Cook over a gentle heat, uncovered, for 5 minutes or until the seafood is cooked through.

Garnish with the chopped coriander and serve with your choice of sides.

One serving =
220%+ RDA
antioxidants

Antibacterial
chilli, cinnamon, coriander, cumin, fennel, garlic, ginger, saffron, turmeric

Antifungal
chilli, cinnamon, coriander, cumin, fennel, garlic, ginger, saffron, turmeric

Antiviral
cinnamon, garlic, turmeric

Anti-inflammatory
chilli, cinnamon, coriander, cumin, fennel, garlic, ginger, saffron, turmeric

Analgesic
chilli, fennel

Chicken with Cabbage

Serves 4–6

I'm not exactly sure what it is about the combination of chicken and cabbage that works so well together. Perhaps it's the natural sweetness of cabbage that enriches all the other flavours. Whatever happens inside the saucepan between the two is all good, because this curry tastes great. It's mouthwateringly rich and spicy and entirely Indian in its aroma and taste.

Cooking cabbage with chicken curry means we also add phytonutrients known as glucosinolates, which eliminate free radicals by stimulating the body's own antioxidant response. Try this one on someone who claims not to like cabbage.

2 tablespoons olive oil
¹/₂ teaspoon nigella seeds
1 teaspoon fennel seeds
³/₄ teaspoon salt, or to taste
1 small onion, thinly sliced
6 garlic cloves, finely chopped
1 teaspoon turmeric
1 tablespoon curry powder
1 teaspoon ground ginger
2 teaspoons garam masala
¹/₂ x 400g can tomatoes, blended until smooth
2–6 green chillies, chopped
3 tablespoons grated (peeled) fresh root ginger
500g skinless, boneless chicken breasts, cut in half
¹/₄ white or green cabbage (approximately 300g), finely shredded
1 tablespoon tomato purée
chopped fresh coriander, to season

Pour the olive oil into a deep saucepan, add the nigella and fennel seeds and cook over a low-medium heat until the seeds start to pop – this should take no longer than 2–3 minutes. Add the salt and onion and fry until the onion is light brown in colour, remembering to stir frequently – this should take no more than 5 minutes.

Stir in the garlic and fry for about 1–2 minutes or until a light brown colour. Sprinkle in the turmeric, mix well and cook for about 20 seconds. Add the curry powder, ground ginger and 1 teaspoon of the garam masala and mix well. Add the tomatoes, chillies and fresh ginger and cook for about 5 minutes or until the excess juices in the saucepan have dried off, remembering to keep stirring occasionally.

Add the chicken to the pan, mix well and cook until sealed all over, stirring constantly – this should take about 5 minutes.

Mix the cabbage into the chicken. Add the tomato purée and enough boiling water to cover the chicken, then bring to a simmer. Leave to simmer, uncovered, for 30 minutes, stirring occasionally.

Once it's finished cooking, using a pair of tongs, remove the chicken pieces from the saucepan to a plate. Using a hand-held blender, blitz the sauce until it's smooth.

Return the chicken to the saucepan. Season with the remaining garam masala and the chopped coriander and heat through. Serve with your choice of sides.

One serving = 195%+ RDA antioxidants

Antibacterial
chilli, coriander, fennel, garlic, ginger, nigella, turmeric

Antifungal
chilli, coriander, fennel, garlic, ginger, nigella, turmeric

Antiviral
garlic, turmeric

Anti-inflammatory
chilli, coriander, fennel, garlic, ginger, nigella, turmeric

Analgesic
chilli, fennel, nigella

Beef with Puy Lentils

Serves 4–5

Savoury pieces of tender beef, contrast with a tangy aromatic curry and sweet Puy lentils, which burst in the mouth, releasing their vibrant and earthy juices like small volcanoes. This recipe has a very wholesome and good-for-you feel about it; in all probability, because lentils lend vitamins and minerals to places where we wouldn't normally expect to find them. So, there's no excuse not to eat healthily all of the time, whilst still enjoying your food.

Cardamom stands out as one of the dominant flavours in this recipe, its sweet aromas accentuated more by those of the Puy lentils. What's also most agreeable about this recipe is that you essentially throw nearly all of the ingredients into a saucepan and get on with your life, only coming back to fry a few superspices and to season. Serve with crispy chapattis, bread or even 'creamy' mashed potato.

500g lean beef, diced
100g Puy lentils
4 tablespoons tomato purée
³/₄ teaspoon salt, or to taste
1 teaspoon turmeric
3 tablespoons grated (peeled) fresh root ginger
1 teaspoon ground ginger
10 green cardamom pods, lightly crushed
2 teaspoons garam masala
2 tablespoons olive oil
1 small onion, thinly sliced
6 garlic cloves, finely chopped
2–6 green chillies, chopped

chopped fresh coriander, to garnish

Place the beef, lentils, tomato purée, salt, turmeric, fresh ginger, ground ginger, cardamom pods and 1 teaspoon of the garam masala in a deep saucepan. Pour in 1.5 litres boiling water and mix well. Heat gently until the water returns to a simmer, then cook, uncovered, for 1 hour or until the meat is tender, remembering to stir occasionally to avoid sticking. If the lentils thicken too much, you may need to add a little more boiling water.

In the meantime, pour the olive oil into a frying pan, add the onion and fry over a low-medium heat until it turns light brown in colour, remembering to stir frequently – this should take no more than 5 minutes. Add the garlic and chillies, mix well and fry for about 2–4 minutes or until the garlic is a golden brown colour. Mix through the remaining garam masala.

Once the meat is tender, stir the spice mixture into the meat mixture and simmer for just a few minutes.

Garnish with the chopped coriander. Serve with your choice of sides.

One serving = 180%+ RDA antioxidants

Antibacterial
cardamom, chilli, coriander, garlic, ginger, turmeric

Antifungal
cardamom, chilli, coriander, garlic, ginger, turmeric

Antiviral
garlic, turmeric

Anti-inflammatory
cardamom, chilli, coriander, garlic, ginger, turmeric

Analgesic
chilli

" Recently we assessed the effects of turmeric extract on irritable bowel syndrome symptomology in otherwise healthy adults. 500 volunteers were screened for IBS. 207 suitable volunteers were randomised. One or two tablets of turmeric extract were taken daily for 8 weeks and the volunteers monitored. During the assessment, IBS prevalence decreased significantly in both groups between screening and baseline (41% and 57%), with a further significant drop of 53% and 60% between baseline and after treatment, in the one- and two-tablet groups respectively. A post-study analysis revealed abdominal pain/discomfort score reduced significantly by 22% and 25% in the one and two-tablet group respectively, the difference tending toward significance. Approximately two thirds of all subjects reported an improvement in symptoms after treatment, and there was a favourable shift in self-reported bowel pattern. There were no significant differences between groups. CONCLUSIONS: Turmeric may help reduce IBS symptomology."

The University of Reading[22]

Baked Vegetables with Marinated Tofu and Chickpeas

Serves 4–6

With savoury marinated tofu, chickpeas, roasted vegetables and a whole bulb of garlic, this recipe is definitely vegetarian food fit enough for He-Man. In fact, it's so meaty that it reminds me of my first visit to the Tao Buffet Restaurant in Old Compton Street, London. Wrapped up in the hustle and bustle of everyday life, Sarah and I sat down to dinner. After a few platefuls of various dishes, we began to realise that all the 'meat' had a similar light taste about it and, perhaps, it wasn't meat at all. That was when we realised we had stumbled into a vegan restaurant. What we had been eating all along was vegetarian meat, made by extracting gluten from wheat protein and compressing and flavouring it into seitan, which tastes so much like meat that many vegetarians prefer to avoid it altogether.

With the spread of Buddhism in ancient China, came vegetarianism, and monks in China are believed to have first come up with the technique of producing seitan. Unlike their neighbours in India, the Chinese had been meat eaters for millennia, and felt the need to satisfy cravings with a vegetarian alternative. Two thousand years on and Chinese Buddhists can now imitate meat within a hair's breadth.

Although this recipe doesn't use seitan, it does use marinated tofu which also does a good job of imitating meat, and in the same way will satisfy a carnivorous appetite. To boot, the US FDA (US Food and Drug Administration) granted official approval for health claims that soy products, such as tofu, reduce cholesterol.

With the distinct flavours of Indian superspices, Oriental marinated tofu, chickpeas and baked vegetables running around like maniacs on the rampage, your taste buds are in for a real treat.

1 aubergine (about 300g), pricked with a fork
500g vine-ripened tomatoes
1 whole bulb of garlic
2 tablespoons olive oil
2 teaspoons cumin seeds
1 teaspoon nigella seeds
3/4 teaspoon salt, or to taste
1 small onion, sliced
2 tablespoons grated (peeled) fresh root ginger
4 garlic cloves, chopped
1 teaspoon turmeric
1 teaspoon garam masala
2–4 green chillies, chopped
150g marinated tofu pieces
400g can chickpeas, rinsed and drained
plenty of chopped fresh coriander, to season

Preheat the oven to 200°C/fan 180°C/Gas Mark 6. Place the whole aubergine and tomatoes on a baking tray and bake in the centre of the oven for 45 minutes or until they are soft; add the whole bulb of garlic halfway through cooking.

Remove the vegetables from the oven and allow them to cool a little. Peel the roasted cloves of garlic and place in a bowl. Remove the stalk from the aubergine. Roughly chop the aubergine and tomatoes and place in the bowl with the roasted garlic cloves. Set aside.

Pour the olive oil into a deep saucepan, add the cumin and nigella seeds and cook over a low-medium heat until the seeds start to pop – this should take no longer than 2–3 minutes. Add the salt and onion and fry until the onion is a light brown colour – this should take no longer than 5 minutes. Remember to stir frequently.

Add the ginger and chopped garlic and cook until the garlic is a light brown colour – this should take about 2–3 minutes. Sprinkle in the turmeric and garam masala, mix well and cook for 20 seconds.

Now add the roasted garlic, aubergine, tomatoes, chillies, tofu and chickpeas, mixing well. Bring to a simmer, then cook over a gentle heat, uncovered, for 10 minutes, stirring frequently.

Season with the chopped coriander. Serve with your choice of sides.

One serving =
205%+ RDA
antioxidants

Antibacterial
chilli, coriander, cumin, garlic, ginger, nigella, turmeric

Antifungal
chilli, coriander, cumin, garlic, ginger, nigella, turmeric

Antiviral
garlic, turmeric

Anti-inflammatory
chilli, coriander, cumin, garlic, ginger, nigella, turmeric

Analgesic
chilli, nigella

Chicken with Sun-Dried Tomatoes and Roasted Garlic

Serves 4–6

With a breath of fresh air, this recipe proves to us that it's possible for healthy Indian food to taste rich, without having to be 'dry' at all. Just like how Indian pickles are used to add a dynamic flavour to our meals, sun-dried tomatoes and roasted garlic impart an intensely rich and tangy flavour to this recipe, without adding any fat. Naturally, sun-dried tomatoes also contain no water, and therefore are a concentrated source of lycopene. So, add more or less, as per your taste; as long as you like tomatoes, you cannot go wrong!

I remember cooking this once for my Anglo-Indian friend, Deborah, who was visiting her then-boyfriend Ian in Baldock. She was expecting dinner guests and had me ferried over to do the cooking. After a lot of frantic chopping and cooking, Deborah paid me in kind with a few glasses of champagne and then sent me packing home, for she had to greet her dinner guests with the obligatory Namastes, and serve to them 'her' Indian feast for which they had been longing.

This is one of my favourite meals; I love it served over a mound of pilau to soak up the moreish juices. I don't use sun-dried tomatoes in oil; if you do, there'll be no need to soak them.

1 whole garlic bulb
50–100g sun-dried tomatoes, or to taste
2 tablespoons olive oil
1 teaspoon black peppercorns
2 teaspoons cumin seeds
1 teaspoon each fennel seeds and mustard seeds
1/2 teaspoon nigella seeds
1/2 teaspoon salt, or to taste

1 small onion, thinly sliced
6 garlic cloves, finely chopped
1 teaspoon turmeric
1 teaspoon ground ginger
2 teaspoons garam masala
400g can tomatoes, blended until smooth
2 tablespoons sun-dried tomato paste
700g chicken joints, skinned
3 tablespoons grated (peeled) fresh root ginger
2–6 green chillies, chopped
chopped fresh coriander, to season

Preheat the oven to 200°C/fan 180°C/Gas Mark 6. Bake the bulb of garlic in the centre of the oven for 15–20 minutes or until soft. Remove and leave to cool. Once cool, remove the cloves from the bulb and peel them. Set the peeled garlic cloves aside.

Place the sun-dried tomatoes in a small dish and cover with boiling water. Set aside.

Pour the olive oil into a deep saucepan, add the peppercorns and cumin, fennel, mustard and nigella seeds and cook over a low-medium heat until the seeds start to pop – this should take no longer than 2–3 minutes. Add the salt and onion and fry until the onion is light brown in colour, remembering to stir frequently – this should take no more than 5 minutes.

Stir in the chopped garlic and fry for about 1–2 minutes or until a light brown colour. Sprinkle in the turmeric and ground ginger, mix well and cook for about 20 seconds.

Stir in 1 teaspoon of the garam masala and mix well. Add the tomatoes, tomato paste and roasted garlic cloves and cook

for about 10 minutes or until the excess juices in the saucepan have dried off. Remember to keep stirring occasionally. In the meantime, remove the sun-dried tomatoes from the water, draining off the excess water, then coarsely chop the tomatoes.

Add the chicken joints and sun-dried tomatoes to the saucepan, mix well and cook until the chicken is sealed all over, stirring constantly – this should take about 5 minutes.

Pour in enough boiling water to just cover the chicken. Return the water to a simmer, then leave to simmer over a gentle heat, uncovered, for 20 minutes, stirring occasionally.

Mix through the fresh ginger and chillies and continue simmering for 10–25 minutes or until the chicken is tender and cooked to your liking.

Season with the remaining garam masala and the chopped coriander. Serve with your choice of sides.

One serving = 260%+ RDA antioxidants

Antibacterial
chilli, coriander, cumin, fennel, garlic, ginger, mustard, nigella, pepper, turmeric

Antifungal
chilli, coriander, cumin, fennel, garlic, ginger, mustard, nigella, turmeric

Antiviral
garlic, turmeric

Anti-inflammatory
chilli, coriander, cumin, fennel, garlic, ginger, mustard, nigella, turmeric

Analgesic
chilli, fennel, nigella

Cauliflower Florets and King Prawns in a Rich Spicy Cashew Sauce

Serves 4–6

If you need more proof that healthy Indian food tastes fabulicious, here we have an awesome-foursome of nourishing cauliflower, prawns, tomatoes and cashews. An unorthodox kinship that just works really well.

Cauliflower adds wholesome body; prawns, satisfying mastication; and the cashew and tomato paste, an opulence which binds it all together. It's rather like a jungle curry – fresh and spicy, and also very light.

I was first served a similar dish, and introduced to this mélange, by my friend, Dr. Mandakini, who hails from the coastal regions just outside of Hyderabad, in India. As a South Indian, she is inclined to lighter tastes than those we commonly associate with in the North.

Back in Birmingham, she would serve it up to us in her ravishing green sari with 'mountains' of rice, and then, shortly after, play the guitar, singing her beloved Christian hymns – sometimes as a special treat, in Russian, too. The eclectic Dr. Mandakini, her nutritious cooking and sing-alongs, always made for a memorable night indeed.

2 tablespoons olive oil
1 teaspoon each cloves and black peppercorns
1 teaspoon each cumin seeds and mustard seeds
$3/4$ teaspoon salt, or to taste
1 small onion, thinly sliced
6 garlic cloves, finely chopped
1 teaspoon turmeric
1 teaspoon garam masala
400g can tomatoes, blended until smooth
2–6 green chillies, chopped
2 tablespoons grated (peeled) fresh root ginger
25g unsalted cashews
400g cauliflower florets
240g cooked peeled king prawns
chopped fresh coriander and desiccated coconut, to season

Pour the olive oil into a deep saucepan, add the cloves, peppercorns and cumin and mustard seeds and cook over a low-medium heat until the seeds start to pop – this should take no longer than 2–3 minutes. Add the salt and onion and fry until the onion is light brown in colour, remembering to stir frequently – this should take no more than 5 minutes.

Stir in the garlic and fry for about 1–2 minutes or until a light brown colour. Sprinkle in the turmeric, mix well and cook for about 20 seconds. Add the garam masala and mix well. Add the tomatoes, chillies and ginger and cook for about 10 minutes or until the excess juices in the saucepan have dried off. Remember to keep stirring occasionally.

In the meantime, process the cashews in a food processor until they resemble fine breadcrumbs.

Add the cauliflower to the spicy sauce in the pan, together with the cashews, mix well and heat through.

Pour in enough boiling water to just cover the cauliflower. Return the water to the boil, then leave to simmer over a gentle heat, uncovered, for 12–15 minutes or until cooked to your liking, stirring occasionally.

Add the prawns, season with the chopped coriander and a handful of coconut and heat through.

Serve with your choice of sides.

One serving = 235%+ RDA antioxidants

Antibacterial
chilli, cloves, cumin, garlic, ginger, mustard, pepper, turmeric

Antifungal
chilli, cloves, coriander, cumin, garlic, ginger, mustard, turmeric

Antiviral
cloves, garlic, turmeric

Anti-inflammatory
chilli, cloves, cumin, garlic, ginger, mustard, nigella, turmeric

Analgesic
chilli, cloves

Indian Superfood

Best-Ever Chicken Tikka Masala

Serves 4–6

Chicken tikka masala is the nation's favourite dish and one of my 'guilty' food pleasures too. I have succumbed many a time to its rich and creamy sorcery as it somehow finds its way past my lips without a great deal of effort. It was a particularly fond friend of mine in Turkey, where I worked in the restaurant trade. Countless nights would end with Melissa and I soaking up the cream-gilded sauce with naans as soft as feather pillows. All very nice at the time, but not so for one's chassis; I am still paying now, having being taken from my svelte McLaren-like physique into one more distinguishable with a Hummer.

So, keeping all that in mind, this chicken tikka masala is a 'best ever' because it is rich and 'creamy' but with a great deal less fat. In fact, the oil in the coconut milk actually helps us to burn more fat and, therefore, it won't hang onto your body as an unwanted guest, unlike its very distant cousin the dairy cream.

Plentiful use of ginger helps with blood circulation and counteracts the sluggish feel associated after finishing off the nation's favourite dish. Even so, if you are in an occasionally indulgent mood, you can substitute some of the coconut milk with cream – but keeping the Hummer in mind.

2 tablespoons olive oil
1 teaspoon cloves
15 green cardamom pods, lightly crushed
1 small onion, thinly sliced
6 garlic cloves, finely chopped
2 teaspoons ground ginger
3 tablespoons tandoori masala powder
5 tablespoons tomato purée
3 tablespoons sugar
2 tablespoons grated (peeled) fresh
   root ginger

2–4 green chillies, finely chopped
500g skinless, boneless chicken
   breasts, cut into bite-size pieces
800ml light coconut milk
salt, to taste

chopped fresh coriander, to garnish
   (optional)

Pour the olive oil into a deep saucepan, add the cloves and cardamom pods and cook over a low-medium heat until the oil is hot and the cloves and cardamom pods start to release their aroma – this should take no longer than 2–3 minutes. Add the onion and fry until it is light brown in colour, remembering to stir frequently – this should take no more than 5 minutes.

Stir in the garlic and fry for about 1–2 minutes or until a light brown colour. Sprinkle in the ground ginger and tandoori masala powder, mix well and cook for about 20 seconds. Add the tomato purée, sugar, fresh ginger and chillies, mix well and cook until the tomato purée is heated through – this should take no longer than 1–2 minutes.

Add the chicken to the pan, mix well and cook until sealed all over, stirring all the time – this should take no more than 5 minutes.

Pour in the coconut milk and mix well. Bring to a gentle simmer, then cook, uncovered, for 25 minutes, remembering to stir occasionally to avoid any sticking.

Season to taste with salt. Garnish with the chopped coriander and serve with your choice of sides.

One serving =
235%+ RDA
antioxidants

Antibacterial
cardamom, chilli, cloves, coriander, garlic, ginger

Antifungal
cardamom, chilli, cloves, coriander, garlic, ginger

Antiviral
cloves, garlic

Anti-inflammatory
cardamom, chilli, cloves, coriander, garlic, ginger

Analgesic
chilli, cloves

Chicken with Turnip and Cinnamon

Serves 4–6

You cannot get much more traditional in taste than this particular dish. It's a recipe which, in a sniff, transports me back to my childhood jaunts at my grandmother's house in the rural Punjab. On foggy winter nights, we would be bathed in water, pumped warm from the water basin. A day's worth of dust washed away by an exotic lather of neem and turmeric soap.

For dinner, Grandma would feed us each a bowlful of Chicken with Turnip and Cinnamon and flaky chapattis; wholesome nourishment to keep the winter chill far from our young bones. At bedtime and in our manji's with clay lanterns flickering, we would listen intently to our grandparents telling ancient tales of when demons, gods and goddesses roamed the Earth.

This recipe, once thought to be lost with a dying generation of bedtime stories, can now be savoured again. Like a child falling into a heavy sleep, the earthy turnip melts blissfully into the bounty of superspices, making for an intensely rich and 'creamy' sauce that is the perfect backdrop for the large and juicy pieces of chicken. Although turnip is a starchy vegetable, it contains only a third of the amount of calories of a potato. To boot, it has the cancer-fighting power of its cruciferous cousins. Plentiful superspices warm the body from top to toe. I can't think of better food to come home to on a cold and frosty night.

2 tablespoons olive oil
1 teaspoon each coriander seeds, mustard seeds and cumin seeds
¹/₂ teaspoon each nigella seeds, fennel seeds and fenugreek seeds

³/₄ teaspoon salt, or to taste
1 small onion, thinly sliced
6 garlic cloves, finely chopped
1 teaspoon turmeric
2 teaspoons garam masala
¹/₂ 400g can tomatoes, blended until smooth
3 tablespoons grated (peeled) fresh root ginger
500g skinless, boneless chicken breasts, cut in half
200g (prepared weight) turnip or swede, chopped into small chunks
1 cinnamon stick
2–6 green chillies, chopped
chopped fresh coriander, to season

Pour the olive oil into a deep saucepan, add the coriander, mustard, cumin, nigella, fennel and fenugreek seeds and cook over a low-medium heat until the seeds start to pop – this should take no longer than 2–3 minutes. Add the salt and onion and fry until the onion is light brown in colour, remembering to stir frequently – this should take no more than 5 minutes.

Stir in the garlic and fry for about 1–2 minutes or until a light brown colour. Sprinkle in the turmeric and 1 teaspoon of the garam masala, mix well and cook for about 20 seconds. Add the tomatoes and 2 tablespoons of the fresh ginger and cook for about 5 minutes or until the excess juices in the saucepan have dried off. Remember to keep stirring occasionally.

Add the chicken to the pan, mix well and cook until the chicken is sealed all over, stirring constantly – this should take about 5 minutes.

Add the turnip and cinnamon stick and mix through. Pour in enough boiling water to just cover the chicken. Return the water to a simmer, then leave to simmer, uncovered, for 20 minutes, stirring occasionally.

Stir in the remaining fresh ginger, then cook for a further 10 minutes.

Once the chicken mixture has finished cooking, using a pair of tongs, remove the chicken pieces and cinnamon stick from the saucepan to a warm plate. Discard the cinnamon stick. Using a hand-held blender, blitz the sauce until it is smooth.

Return the chicken to the saucepan. Season with the chillies, the remaining garam masala and the chopped coriander and heat through. Serve with your choice of sides.

One serving = 285%+ RDA antioxidants	Antiviral cinnamon, garlic, turmeric
Antibacterial chilli, cinnamon, coriander, cumin, fennel, fenugreek, garlic, ginger, mustard, nigella, turmeric	**Anti-inflammatory** chilli, cinnamon, coriander, cumin, fennel, fenugreek, garlic, ginger, mustard, nigella, turmeric
Antifungal chilli, cinnamon, coriander, cumin, fennel, fenugreek, garlic, ginger, mustard, nigella, turmeric	Analgesic chilli, fennel, fenugreek, nigella

Pilchard Keema with Green Peas

Serves 4

Wow, this is another one of those recipes that has me clapping my hands in raptures and licking my lips in sweet anticipation! It's the coming of seafood in the guise of keema which gets me so enthralled. I love both seafood and keema and this is their splendid culinary communion.

When my siblings and I were younger, this used to be one of our firm favourites that Mum brought us up on. She would serve it to us with onion rings, lemon wedges and hot crispy chapattis; I can still recollect flaky pieces of chapatti, hiding inside it the warm and spicy pilchard keema, and how the peas would pop in my mouth interspersing their sweet juices into the hot curry flavours.

I must admit that nowadays I tend to opt for it with rice. Albeit, I say it reluctantly because rice is foreign to the Punjabi kitchen and, therefore, those who single it out for favouritism are likewise singled out for an interrogation – it wouldn't be the first time I would be accused of having a Bengali lineage. Mixing the two together is, for me, an instant seafood biryani. The soft bed of pilau, combined with the spicy pilchards and peas jumping up and down on top of it, is bliss.

And, if you aren't jumping for joy just yet, maybe you will when you realise that pilchards and superspices are an inexpensive source of vital omega-3 fatty acids and anti-inflammatory compounds; this could be just what the doctor would prescribe you.

2 x 425g cans pilchards in tomato sauce
2 tablespoons olive oil
1 teaspoon cumin seeds
1/2 teaspoon nigella seeds
2 black cardamom pods, lightly crushed (optional)
1/2 teaspoon salt, or to taste
1 small onion, thinly sliced
6 garlic cloves, finely chopped
1 teaspoon turmeric
2 tablespoons grated (peeled) fresh root ginger
1 teaspoon ground ginger
2 teaspoons garam masala
2 large handfuls of green peas (fresh or frozen)
2–6 green chillies, chopped
chopped fresh coriander, to season

lemon wedges and onion slices, to serve

Remove and discard the bones from the pilchards. Set the flesh aside, reserving the tomato sauce separately.

Pour the olive oil into a deep saucepan, add the cumin and nigella seeds and the cardamom pods, if using, and cook over a low-medium heat until the seeds start to pop – this should take no longer than 2–3 minutes. Add the salt and onion and fry until the onion is light brown in colour, remembering to stir frequently – this should take no more than 5 minutes.

Stir in the garlic and fry for about 1–2 minutes or until a light brown colour. Sprinkle in the turmeric, mix well and cook for about 20 seconds. Add the tomato sauce from the pilchards, the fresh ginger, ground ginger and 1 teaspoon of the garam masala.

Mix well and cook for about 2–3 minutes or until the oil starts to split from the tomato sauce, remembering to keep stirring occasionally.

Mix the pilchards into the sauce in the pan, then continue to cook, uncovered, for 15 minutes, remembering to stir frequently.

A few minutes prior to the end of cooking, mix through the green peas, chillies, chopped coriander and remaining garam masala and heat through.

Serve with lemon wedges, onion slices and your choice of sides.

One serving = 165%+ RDA antioxidants

Antibacterial
cardamom, chilli, coriander, cumin, garlic, ginger, nigella, turmeric

Antifungal
cardamom, chilli, coriander, cumin, garlic, ginger, nigella, turmeric

Antiviral
garlic, turmeric

Anti-inflammatory
cardamom, chilli, coriander, cumin, garlic, ginger, nigella, turmeric

Analgesic
chilli, nigella

Indian Superfood

Salmon and Potato Biryani with Cherry Tomatoes, Lime and Coriander

Serves 4

Out of the abundant types of biryanis, the most widely recognised one which can be found in restaurants all over the world is the saffron-coloured biryani, which originates from the kitchens of Nizams of Hyderabad, who at their peak, in the mid 18th century, were amongst the wealthiest rulers on earth. For hours on end, royal chefs would combine together a baffling array of spices, rice and meats, layering them into earthen dishes before closing them shut with a lid, sealed airtight by wet dough, and baking.

What makes my recipe unique is that it pays homage to authenticity, whilst at the same time being accessible to even a novice chef.

As the word beryan suggests, the spices, meat and rice are fried before being baked together. Conversely, the superfood twist is given to the biryani by replacing the meat with omega-3 rich salmon. The mélange of traditional Indian superspices with salmon and fresh lime leaves and coriander, is nothing short of breathtaking.

2 tablespoons olive oil
2 teaspoons cumin seeds
1 teaspoon black peppercorns
10 green cardamom pods, lightly crushed
1 small onion, thinly sliced
4 garlic cloves, finely chopped
1 tablespoon grated (peeled) fresh root ginger
2 green chillies, coarsely chopped (optional)
2 tablespoons mild curry powder
350g salmon fillets, skinned and cut into large bite-size pieces
400g basmati rice
12 kaffir lime leaves, fresh or frozen (available at Oriental grocers)
1 rounded teaspoon salt, or to taste

1 potato, diced into cubes no larger than 1.5cm
1 punnet of cherry tomatoes (about 200g), sliced in half
chopped fresh coriander, to season (optional)

lime wedges, onion salad, extra green chillies and raita, to serve

Pour the olive oil into a deep saucepan, add the cumin seeds, peppercorns and cardamom pods and cook over a low-medium heat until the seeds start to pop – this should take no more than 2–3 minutes. Add the onion and cook until it is a light brown colour, stirring frequently – this should take no more than 5 minutes.

Add the garlic, ginger and chillies and continue cooking for about 2–3 minutes or until the garlic is brown in colour. Add the curry powder, mix well and cook for about 20 seconds.

Add the salmon pieces and cook until they are sealed all over (not cooked through), making sure to stir gently to avoid breaking the salmon into small pieces – this should take about 2–3 minutes. Remove the pan from the heat, then remove the salmon pieces from the pan to a warm plate, brushing off any excess spice mixture that may have stuck to them back into the saucepan. Set the salmon aside.

Return the saucepan with the spice mixture to the heat and add the rice. Continue cooking and stirring frequently until the rice turns from slightly translucent to very white in colour – this process should take only about 2–3 minutes. Remove the pan from the heat.

Transfer the rice mixture into a microwave-safe dish (at least 22 x 7cm), add the lime leaves and salt and pour in 790ml boiling water. Mix with a fork. Microwave, uncovered, for 6 minutes on HIGH at 700W, or for 5$^{1}/_{2}$ minutes on HIGH at 800W, or for 5 minutes on HIGH at 900W.

Mix well with a fork. Microwave, uncovered, for further 5 minutes on HIGH at 700W, or for a further 4$^{1}/_{2}$ minutes on HIGH at 800W, or for a further 4 minutes on HIGH at 900W.

Mix well with a fork. Add the salmon pieces and potato cubes, making sure to cover them with the rice. Cover the dish and microwave for a further 7 minutes on HIGH at 700W, or for a further 6 minutes on HIGH at 800W, or for a further 5 minutes on HIGH at 900W.

Take the biryani out of the microwave. Stir in the cherry tomatoes and cover. Leave to stand for 10 minutes. Season with the chopped coriander, if using, and mix well.

Serve immediately with lime wedges, onion salad, extra green chillies and raita.

One serving = 175%+ RDA antioxidants

Antibacterial
cardamom, chilli, coriander, cumin, garlic, ginger, pepper

Antifungal
cardamom, chilli, coriander, cumin, garlic, ginger

Antiviral
garlic

Anti-inflammatory
cardamom, chilli, coriander, cumin, garlic, ginger

Analgesic
chilli

Chicken with Orange and Apricots

Serves 4

Imam Bayildi is one of Turkey's most famous aubergine and olive oil recipes. Legend has it that, upon tasting, the Imam fainted from pleasure. Despite the fact that my recipe contains no aubergine, it's the Imam's chaste repercussion from sampling food that best sums up this chicken with orange and apricots. Chicken melting off the bone and coated in a caramelised sauce of orange and apricots, bustling with the splendid warmth of the cinnamon, cloves and aphrodisiac cardamom, is enough to take one's breath away.

So, if you want someone to propose to you, this is what I recommend you cook for them. And, if on the perchance, your lover does faint, you can always carry him/her over your shoulder to home, and wait eagerly for the proposal to come through.

On a more austere note, the apricots and orange juice bolster our intake of vitamin C, which we need for healthy teeth and gums – all very important for civilised courting rituals.

2 tablespoons olive oil
1 cinnamon stick
10 green cardamom pods, lightly
  crushed
1 teaspoon cloves
1 teaspoon cumin seeds
3/4 teaspoon salt, or to taste
1 small onion, thinly sliced
6 garlic cloves, finely chopped
1 teaspoon turmeric
2 tomatoes, finely chopped
2–6 green chillies, chopped
1 teaspoon ground ginger
700g chicken joints, skinned
2 handfuls of dried apricots, roughly
  chopped
700ml orange juice

Pour the olive oil into a deep saucepan, add the cinnamon stick, cardamom pods, cloves and cumin seeds and cook over a low-medium heat until the seeds start to pop – this should take no longer than 2–3 minutes. Add the salt and onion and fry until the onion is light brown in colour, remembering to stir frequently – this should take no more than 5 minutes.

Stir in the garlic and fry for about 1–2 minutes or until it is a light brown colour. Sprinkle in the turmeric, mix well and cook for about 20 seconds. Add the tomatoes, chillies and ground ginger and cook for about 5 minutes or until the tomatoes are cooked through and any excess juices in the saucepan have dried off, remembering to keep stirring occasionally.

Add the chicken to the pan, together with the apricots, mix well and cook until the chicken is sealed all over, stirring constantly – this should take no more than about 5 minutes.

Pour in the orange juice and bring to a simmer. Leave to simmer over a gentle heat, uncovered, for 30–45 minutes or until the chicken is cooked and tender, stirring frequently to avoid sticking.

Serve with your choice of sides.

One serving = 300%+ RDA antioxidants

Antibacterial
cardamom, chilli, cinnamon, cloves, cumin, garlic, ginger, turmeric

Antifungal
cardamom, chilli, cinnamon, cloves, cumin, garlic, ginger, turmeric

Antiviral
cinnamon, cloves, garlic, turmeric

Anti-inflammatory
cardamom, chilli, cinnamon, cloves, cumin, garlic, ginger, turmeric

Analgesic
chilli, cloves

Kale and Potatoes in a Rich Tomato Masala

Serves 4

For individuality in taste quite like no other vegetable, kale comes out tops. It has a strong, earthy flavour and a firm and crunchy texture, which it retains even after cooking. A part of the cruciferous family, kale is linked with cancer prevention. Paired with melting potatoes in a tangy, spicy tomato sauce, each mouthful is as vibrant and colourful as a Bollywood film production. If you haven't yet embraced kale with a song and dance, now is the perfect time.

2 tablespoons olive oil
$1/2$ teaspoon each cumin seeds and nigella seeds
1 teaspoon mustard seeds
$3/4$ teaspoon salt, or to taste
1 small onion, thinly sliced
4 garlic cloves, finely chopped
1 teaspoon turmeric
2 tomatoes, finely chopped
2 tablespoons grated (peeled) fresh root ginger
2–4 green chillies, chopped
400g can tomatoes, blended until smooth
200g kale (tough stems removed), shredded
2 large potatoes, diced into cubes no larger than 1.5cm

Pour the olive oil into a deep saucepan, add the cumin, nigella and mustard seeds and cook over a low-medium heat until the seeds start to pop – this should take no longer than 2–3 minutes. Add the salt and onion and fry until the onion is light brown in colour, remembering to stir frequently – this should take no more than 5 minutes.

Stir in the garlic and fry for about 1–2 minutes or until a light brown colour. Sprinkle in the turmeric, mix well and cook for about 20 seconds. Add the chopped tomatoes, ginger and chillies and cook for about 5 minutes or until the tomatoes are cooked through and any excess juices in the saucepan have dried off. Remember to keep stirring occasionally.

Pour in the blended tomatoes, mix well and bring to a simmer. Add the kale and potatoes and return to a simmer. Cover and cook gently for about 20–25 minutes or until the potatoes are tender, stirring occasionally.

Serve with your choice of sides.

One serving =
200%+ RDA
antioxidants

Antibacterial
chilli, cumin, garlic, ginger, mustard, nigella, turmeric

Antifungal
chilli, cumin, garlic, ginger, mustard, nigella, turmeric

Antiviral
garlic, turmeric

Anti-inflammatory
chilli, cumin, garlic, ginger, mustard, nigella, turmeric

Analgesic
chilli, nigella

" The antifungal activity of nigella seed extract and thymoquinone, a phytochemical compound derived from it, was tested against eight species of dermatophytes (fungi that commonly cause skin disease in humans and animals). Nigella and thymoquinone inhibited fungal growth, denoting the potentiality of nigella as a source of antidermatophyte drugs and supporting its use in folk medicine for the treatment of fungal skin infections."

King Faisal University, Dammam, Saudi Arabia[17]

Lamb with Carrots and Star Anise

Serves 4–5

My appetite was first whetted for this recipe in Edgbaston, one early morning after a late night. I accidentally stumbled upon a Tupperware container hidden at the back of the refrigerator, which I opened to reveal a mishmash of diced meat and carrots, a combination that I had never come across. Although a little suspicious, I was driven by sheer curiosity and hunger. So, I popped some into the microwave to heat. Timidly, and unaware of my flatmate's cooking skills, I took a small bite, which was then followed by a mouthful and before I knew it I had nearly finished it all. The sweet carrots and savoury meat in a dry masala worked together befittingly. Neither of the two overpowered the other. Mouthfuls of chunky pieces of meat yo-yoed flawlessly with the candied spicy carrots.

Later that day, I asked Sarah where she had come across the recipe, to which she replied that her mother in Pakistan had been making it forever and a day. I felt somewhat sheepish for not 'keeping up with the Khans'; so here is my version, using the mandatory sacrificial lamb to make up for my inadequacy.

My inclusion of star anise adds an intense flavour that works alluringly well with the sweet carrots and adds a more sophisticated feel to this rustic dish. The rich colour found in carrots is due to the vast amount of beta-carotene that is contained within them. Once carrots are eaten, the body converts the beta-carotene into nature's richest source of vitamin A. And, if you are planning a late night, there are plenty of analgesic superspices in this recipe to make it an ideal supper.

2 tablespoons olive oil
12 star anise
1 teaspoon each cumin seeds and fennel seeds
1/2 teaspoon nigella seeds
1 teaspoon salt, or to taste
1 small onion, thinly sliced
1 teaspoon turmeric
2 teaspoons garam masala
400g can tomatoes, blended until smooth
1 tablespoon paprika
500g lean lamb (preferably leg), diced
4 large carrots, diced
3 tablespoons grated (peeled) fresh root ginger
6 garlic cloves, finely chopped
2–6 green chillies, chopped
chopped fresh coriander, to season

Pour 1 tablespoon olive oil into a deep saucepan, add the star anise, cumin, fennel and nigella seeds and cook over a low-medium heat until the seeds start to pop – this should take no longer than 2–3 minutes. Add the salt and onion and fry until the onion is light brown in colour, remembering to stir frequently – this should take no more than 5 minutes.

Sprinkle in the turmeric, mix well and cook for about 20 seconds. Add 1 teaspoon of the garam masala and mix well. Add the tomatoes and paprika and cook for about 10 minutes or until the excess juices in the saucepan have dried off, remembering to keep stirring occasionally.

Add the lamb to the pan, mix well and cook until sealed all over, stirring constantly – this should take no more than about 5 minutes. Add the carrots and heat through.

Pour in 500ml boiling water. Simmer gently, uncovered, for 1 hour, remembering to stir from time to time. If the sauce dries out, add a little more boiling water.

Stir in the ginger and continue to simmer, uncovered, for a further 10 minutes or until the meat is tender.

Pour the remaining olive oil into a small frying pan, add the garlic and fry over a medium heat for about 2–3 minutes or until a golden brown colour.

Mix the fried garlic, remaining garam masala, the chillies and chopped coriander into the lamb mixture and continue to simmer for just a few moments.

Serve with your choice of sides.

One serving = 280%+ RDA antioxidants

Antibacterial
chilli, coriander, cumin, fennel, garlic, ginger, nigella, paprika, star anise, turmeric

Antifungal
chilli, coriander, cumin, fennel, garlic, ginger, nigella, paprika, turmeric

Antiviral
garlic, turmeric

Anti-inflammatory
chilli, coriander, cumin, fennel, garlic, ginger, nigella, paprika, turmeric

Analgesic
chilli, fennel, nigella, paprika

Chocolate and Chicken Curry

Serves 2

I first came across chocolate curry in my days at RAJ TV, where I was gainfully employed as an Asian Keith Floyd, visiting restaurants and chatting with their chefs whilst tasting food on camera – well somebody had to do it!

Iqbal was the very charismatic proprietor of Sweet Chillies in Yardley Wood, who first mentioned chocolate curry to me, disclosing that it was popular with the ladies. I don't actually recall seeing it on his menu at the time; so, maybe I'd had too much wine, or perhaps he was just pulling my leg. But still, it made perfectly good sense to bring together a passion for Indian food with chocolate.

So, here is my version for the ladies, and gentlemen. If you are fond of chicken tikka masala, you should be smitten by this one too. It's a rich and silky curry with the uniquely bittersweet taste of chocolate. It can be made richer still with the inclusion of a few pieces of dark chocolate.

And, since this is 'allegedly' a Brummie recipe, it requires Bournville cocoa; so, none of that fancy Belgian chocolat – s'il vous plaît. Cocoa also releases antioxidants and feel good endorphins into our body and that's why it's widely known as an aphrodisiac. In fact, cocoa has been a chi-chi superfood ever since the savvy Aztec Indians first laid their hands on it, mixing it with spices to make a drink. Cardamom further intensifies these aphrodisiac properties. Perhaps this one's best for Valentine's Day?

3 teaspoons cocoa powder
400ml light coconut milk
2 tablespoons olive oil
1/2 teaspoon cloves
7 green cardamom pods, lightly crushed
1/2 teaspoon salt, or to taste
1 small onion, finely chopped
3 garlic cloves, finely chopped
2 teaspoons ground ginger
1/2–1 teaspoon chilli powder
2 skinless, boneless chicken breasts, cut into bite-size pieces
4 teaspoons sugar, or to taste
chopped fresh coriander, to season

Place the cocoa in a large bowl. Slowly pour in the coconut milk, stirring all the time until you have a smooth mixture. Set aside.

Pour the olive oil into a deep saucepan, add the cloves and cardamom pods and cook over a medium heat until the oil is hot and the cloves and cardamom pods start to release their aroma – this should take no longer than 2–3 minutes. Add the salt and onion and fry until the onion is light brown in colour, remembering to stir frequently – this should take no more than 5 minutes.

Stir in the garlic and fry for about 1–2 minutes or until a light brown colour. Sprinkle in the ginger and chilli powder, mix well and cook for about 20 seconds. Add the chicken to the pan and cook until sealed all over, stirring all the time – this should take no more than 5 minutes.

Pour in the cocoa mixture, together with the sugar and bring to a gentle simmer. Cook, uncovered, for 10 minutes, remembering to stir to avoid any sticking.

Remove the chicken from the pan to a warm plate and set aside. Remove and

discard the cardamom pods and cloves. Transfer the sauce to a food processor. Season with chopped coriander and blitz until smooth.

Return the sauce and chicken pieces to the saucepan and heat through. Serve with your choice of sides.

One serving = 225%+ RDA antioxidants

Antibacterial
cardamom, chilli, coriander, cloves, garlic, ginger

Antifungal
cardamom, chilli, cloves, coriander, garlic, ginger

Antiviral
cloves, garlic

Anti-inflammatory
cardamom, chilli, cloves, coriander, garlic, ginger

Analgesic
chilli, cloves

Green Tea Chicken

Serves 4

If you're looking for a novel way to increase your intake of antioxidising green tea goodies that also simultaneously boost the body's metabolic rate, or you just like eating a curry that stands out from the crowd, this one is for you.

Surprisingly, green tea makes a huge impact on the taste or, more to the point, the aftertaste of the curry. Somewhat like an alchemist, it removes much of the lingering secondary response to the superspices. Each mouthful is as yummy as ever. Only, after you have swallowed, there is little evidence of ever having eaten curry. It's as if the Listerine fairy comes in and cleans and dusts down after each and every mouthful – most bamboozling indeed.

2 green teabags
2 tablespoons olive oil
1 cinnamon stick
1 teaspoon cumin seeds
1/2 teaspoon each fennel seeds and
   nigella seeds
3/4 teaspoon salt, or to taste
1 small onion, thinly sliced
6 garlic cloves, finely chopped
1 teaspoon turmeric
3 teaspoons garam masala
1 teaspoon ground ginger
1/2 400g can tomatoes, blended until
   smooth
2–6 green chillies, chopped
3 tablespoons grated (peeled) fresh
   root ginger
700g chicken joints, skinned or 500g
   skinless, boneless chicken breasts,
   cut in half
chopped fresh coriander, to season

Place the green teabags in a small saucepan and pour over 500ml boiling water. Set aside.

Pour the olive oil into a separate deep saucepan, add the cinnamon stick and cumin, fennel and nigella seeds and cook over a low-medium heat until the seeds start to pop – this should take no longer than 2–3 minutes. Add the salt and onion and fry until the onion is light brown in colour, remembering to stir frequently – this should take no more than 5 minutes.

Stir in the garlic and fry for about 1–2 minutes or until a light brown colour. Sprinkle in the turmeric, mix well and cook for about 20 seconds. Add 1 teaspoon of the garam masala and the ground ginger and mix well. Add the tomatoes, chillies and fresh ginger and cook for about 5 minutes or until the excess juices in the saucepan have dried off. Remember to keep stirring occasionally.

Add the chicken to the pan, mix well and cook until sealed all over, stirring constantly – this should take no more than 5 minutes.

In the meantime, bring the small pan containing the green tea to the boil, then remove the teabags.

Add the hot tea to the chicken mixture and bring to a simmer. Leave to simmer over a gentle heat, uncovered, for 30–45 minutes or until the chicken is cooked and tender, stirring occasionally. 10 minutes prior to the end of cooking, mix through 1 teaspoon of the remaining garam masala.

Season with the remaining garam masala and the chopped coriander. Serve with your choice of sides.

One serving =
320%+ RDA
antioxidants

Antibacterial
chilli, cinnamon, coriander, cumin, fennel, garlic, ginger, nigella, turmeric

Antifungal
chilli, cinnamon, coriander, cumin, fennel, garlic, ginger, nigella, turmeric

Antiviral
cinnamon, garlic, turmeric

Anti-inflammatory
chilli, cinnamon, coriander, cumin, fennel, garlic, ginger, nigella, turmeric

Analgesic
chilli, fennel, nigella

Indian Superfood

Stir-Fried King Prawns and Baby Spinach

Serves 2-3

Crisp and salty-tasting prawns are entwined by earthy baby spinach leaves and spicy batons of ginger. You can taste each and every ingredient individually in this stir-fry. It sure won me over in no time at all, and of course it takes hardly any time to prepare, either.

Try this recipe on one of those nights when you don't feel like cooking at all. Just one serving will provide up to 150% of your daily vitamin A requirement.

1 tablespoon olive oil
$1/2$ teaspoon nigella seeds
a piece of fresh root ginger (no larger than the size of a small matchbox), peeled and cut into small batons
4 garlic cloves, sliced
$1/2$ teaspoon turmeric
240g cooked peeled king prawns
2–6 green chillies, finely chopped
200g baby spinach leaves
salt, to taste

Heat a non-stick wok over a high heat until it is very hot. Pour the olive oil into the wok and heat until the oil is almost smoking – this should take no more than 1 minute.

Add the nigella seeds and cook until they sizzle – this should take no longer than 1 minute. Add the ginger and garlic and stir-fry until light brown in colour – this should take no longer than 2 minutes. Sprinkle in the turmeric and mix well.

Throw the prawns and chillies into the wok and stir-fry until heated through. Add the spinach to the wok and stir-fry for 1–2 minutes or until the spinach leaves are wilted. Season to taste with salt.

Serve with your choice of sides.

One serving =
185%+ RDA
antioxidants

Antibacterial
chilli, garlic, ginger, nigella, turmeric

Antifungal
chilli, garlic, nigella, turmeric

Antiviral
garlic, turmeric

Anti-inflammatory
chilli, garlic, ginger, nigella, turmeric

Analgesic
chilli, nigella

Pomegranate, Blueberry and Acai Superfruit Chicken

Serves 4

It doesn't take a rocket scientist, or even Gurpareet, to figure this recipe contains a previously-inconceivable gang of superfoods. The posse is led by the Amazonian acai berry, which contains an extraordinary concentration of cancer-fighting antioxidants known as anthocyanins – up to thirty times more than red wine! However, blueberry and pomegranate aren't too far behind acai either.

Together, the berries also have a remarkable impact on the taste buds. Their combined sweetness teases out the 'heat' from within the chillies, making for a fruity curry that is fiery yet sweet and sour. Using a fruit smoothie also induces a spectacularly rich and silky texture to the curry. If you don't want HOT – go easy on the chillies.

2 tablespoons olive oil
1 teaspoon cloves
$\frac{1}{2}$ teaspoon each fenugreek seeds and nigella seeds
2 garlic cloves, finely chopped
3 tablespoons grated (peeled) fresh root ginger
1 teaspoon turmeric
2–6 green chillies, chopped
$\frac{3}{4}$ teaspoon salt, or to taste
2 tablespoons tomato purée
300ml pomegranate, blueberry and acai smoothie (see Cook's Tip)
500g skinless, boneless chicken breasts, cut into bite-size pieces

a handful of pomegranate seeds and chopped fresh coriander, to garnish

Pour the olive oil into a deep saucepan, add the cloves and fenugreek and nigella seeds and cook over a high heat until the seeds start to sizzle – this should take no more than 1–2 minutes. Remove the pan from the heat and allow the oil to cool for a moment or two.

Add the garlic and ginger to the pan and cook over a low-medium heat until they are a golden brown colour, stirring frequently – this should take no more than 2–3 minutes (if the garlic and ginger stick to the pan, add a few drops of cold water). Add the turmeric, mix well and cook for about 20 seconds.

Now add the chillies, salt, tomato purée and fruit smoothie, mix well and bring to a rapid simmer.

Add the chicken to the pan, mix well and bring to a gentle simmer, then cook, uncovered, for 10 minutes or until the chicken is cooked and tender, remembering to stir occasionally.

Garnish with the pomegranate seeds and chopped coriander. Serve with your choice of sides.

Cook's Tip
I used an Innocent Pomegranate, Blueberry & Acai superfruit smoothie. If you cannot find it, a smoothie containing any one of the mentioned fruits will suffice, so long as it's thick and sweet.

One serving = 330%+ RDA antioxidants

Antibacterial
chilli, cloves, coriander, fenugreek, garlic, ginger, nigella, turmeric

Antifungal
chilli, cloves, coriander, fenugreek, garlic, ginger, nigella, turmeric

Antiviral
cloves, garlic, turmeric

Anti-inflammatory
chilli, cloves, coriander, fenugreek, garlic, ginger, nigella, turmeric

Analgesic
chilli, cloves, fenugreek, nigella

Beef with Beetroot, Potato and Star Anise

Serves 4

In this recipe, the condensing beetroot juice 'mutates' the masala sauce to a ghoulish blood red colour. Star anise gives it even more of a spooky look. I think this recipe is ideal for a Halloween party. Perhaps, you can tell the kids it's a curry made from spiders' meat and vampire blood. Just don't tell them how nutritious it is. You don't want to put the little terrors off their dinner! Nitrate contained in beetroot leads to a reduction in oxygen uptake, making running around less tiring for them.

2 tablespoons olive oil
10 star anise
1 teaspoon each mustard seeds and
 cumin seeds
1/2 teaspoon nigella seeds
3/4 teaspoon salt, or to taste
1 small onion, thinly sliced
6 garlic cloves, finely chopped
1 teaspoon turmeric
2 teaspoons garam masala
1 teaspoon ground ginger
1/2 400g can tomatoes, blended until
 smooth
2–6 green chillies, chopped
3 tablespoons grated (peeled) fresh
 root ginger
500g lean beef, diced
700ml beetroot juice
1 potato, cut into large bite-size pieces
1 tablespoon lemon juice
chopped fresh coriander, to season

lemon wedges, to garnish

Pour the olive oil into a deep saucepan, add the star anise and mustard, cumin and nigella seeds and cook over a low-medium heat until the seeds start to pop – this should take no more than 2–3 minutes. Add the salt and onion and fry until the onion is light brown in colour, remembering to stir frequently – this should take no more than 5 minutes.

Add the garlic and cook until it is a golden brown colour, stirring frequently – this should take no more than 2–3 minutes. Add the turmeric and 1 teaspoon of the garam masala, mix well and cook for about 20 seconds. Mix through the ground ginger, then add the tomatoes, chillies and fresh ginger. Cook for about 5 minutes or until the excess juices in the saucepan have dried off, remembering to keep stirring occasionally.

Add the beef to the pan, mix well and cook until sealed all over, stirring constantly – this should take no more than 5 minutes.

Pour in the beetroot juice and bring to a simmer. Leave to simmer, uncovered, for 30 minutes, stirring occasionally.

Add the potato and lemon juice to the pan and mix well. Continue simmering for another 30 minutes or until the meat is tender, stirring occasionally. If the sauce dries out too much, add a little extra beetroot juice or water.

Season with the remaining garam masala and the chopped coriander. Garnish with the lemon wedges. Serve with your choice of sides.

One serving =
240%+ RDA antioxidants

Antibacterial
chilli, coriander, cumin, garlic, ginger, mustard, nigella, star anise, turmeric

Antifungal
chilli, coriander, cumin, garlic, ginger, mustard, nigella, turmeric

Antiviral
garlic, turmeric

Anti-inflammatory
chilli, coriander, cumin, garlic, ginger, mustard, nigella, turmeric

Analgesic
chilli, nigella

Salmon and Red Lentil Kedgeree

Serves 4–6

Allegedly, during the days of the British Raj, the Scottish kedgeree travelled to India where it metamorphosed into the local Indian populous as a vegetarian lentil version. Ever since, the two kedgerees have remained apart by keeping their distinct identities. The Scottish one is made with salmon and the Indian version without it. In true Indian style, my recipe marries the two kedgerees together, putting any differences well and truly behind.

You see, 'we' Indians believe that a marriage can solve all disputes. It's a dish which echoes the deep sea salmon flavours of Scotland with those of exotic India, harmoniously. A match made in heaven. Whether you're Scottish or Indian, or anything in-between, I am sure that you will agree this kedgeree tastes better than the rest.

And, with salmon, basmati rice, cumin and butter, imparting their spiffy flavours, it's easy to see, or taste rather, why this one's a winner. It's a complete one-pot meal, bringing together two extraordinary superfoods – salmon and lentils.

Now, did I mention that Indians don't widely accept that kedgeree was introduced to the subcontinent? They claim to have been eating lentils and rice cooked together for millennia. So, even after a song and a dance, some brouhaha's will never be agreed upon.

160g red lentils
150g basmati rice
1½ teaspoons salt, or to taste
3 tomatoes, finely chopped
2–6 green chillies, chopped
¾ teaspoon turmeric

3 tablespoons grated (peeled) fresh root ginger
4 teaspoons cumin seeds
2 tablespoons olive oil
1 teaspoon mustard seeds
½ teaspoon nigella seeds
1 small onion, thinly sliced
6 garlic cloves, finely chopped
400g salmon fillet, skinned and cut into large bite-size pieces
a handful of green peas (fresh or frozen)
chopped fresh coriander and a knob of butter, to season

Place the lentils, rice, salt, tomatoes, chillies, turmeric, ginger and 2 teaspoons of the cumin seeds in a deep saucepan. Pour in 1.8 litres boiling water. Place over a high heat and return to the boil, then reduce the heat to low and simmer, uncovered, for 30 minutes. Remember to stir frequently to avoid sticking. If the mixture thickens too much, you may need to add a little more boiling water.

At the end of cooking, the kedgeree should have a thick consistency similar to that of porridge; and the lentils should be cooked to a pulp, but the grains of rice will still be distinguishable.

In the meantime, pour the olive oil into a frying pan, add the mustard and nigella seeds and the remaining cumin seeds and cook over a low-medium heat until the seeds start to pop – this should take no longer than 2–3 minutes. Add the onion and fry until it is light brown in colour, remembering to stir frequently – this should take no more than 5 minutes.

Stir in the garlic and fry for about 2–3 minutes or until it is a light brown colour. Add the salmon pieces and cook until they are sealed all over (not cooked through), making sure to stir gently to avoid breaking the salmon into small pieces – this should take about 2–3 minutes.

Once the lentil mixture is ready, add the salmon and spice mixture to the kedgeree, together with the peas, stir to mix, then simmer for 5 minutes or until the salmon is cooked through.

Season with the chopped coriander and serve with a knob of butter.

One serving = 265%+ RDA antioxidants

Antibacterial
chilli, coriander, cumin, garlic, ginger, mustard, nigella, turmeric

Antifungal
chilli, coriander, cumin, garlic, ginger, mustard, nigella, turmeric

Antiviral
garlic, turmeric

Anti-inflammatory
chilli, coriander, cumin, garlic, ginger, mustard, nigella, turmeric

Analgesic
chilli, nigella

Sides

For many of us, sides invoke a blurry-eyed déjà vu of late nights down at the local Indian curry house, tearing apart, haphazardly, fluffy naans and crispy tandoori rotis, and soaking up the delicious sauces sitting at the bottom of our plate, much of it landing on our best shirt. Fortunately, now that we are a little bit older and wiser, I think it is safe enough to learn how to make our very own sides.

In this chapter, we have the classic naan with the incredible superfood twist – for example, the mouthwatering and exotic Seaweed and Roasted Pumpkin Seed Naan. Let's not forget to mention the cooling superfood raitas, including one made with the soothing properties of banana. As you might expect, there are recipes for many pilau and vegetable dishes, also.

One of the most innovative recipes is the Spaceman's Quinoa Pilau, aptly named because NASA is considering quinoa as a possible food crop for space voyages. It's food that is out of this world.

New Potatoes and Baby Spinach

Serves 4

Here we have a lightning-fast take on another one of the nation's favourite dishes, aloo palak. With the basic ingredients already being pretty much healthy, I haven't done a huge amount of changing to it. Of course, as you've probably become to expect of me by now, I've greatly cut down on fat content and cooking time – without sacrificing the taste. It's a broody combination of sweet-tasting new baby potatoes and baby spinach, spruced up with garlic and batons of ginger in a light and spicy jus.

Potatoes are a powerhouse of carbohydrates, which our body needs, certainly, for fuel. But, much to the surprise of many amongst us, they are also a source of vitamins B6 and C, and contain manganese, potassium, fibre and phytonutrients that act as antioxidants against free radicals. So I'll have you know the sweet-tasting new baby potatoes aren't just sacrificing themselves for you in vain. And, this recipe is ready at the speed of light; so, buckle down and hold onto your handbag, or manbag!

1 tablespoon olive oil
1 teaspoon each cumin seeds and nigella seeds
¹/₂ teaspoon mustard seeds
a piece of fresh root ginger (no larger than the size of a small matchbox), peeled and cut into small batons
4 garlic cloves, sliced
1 teaspoon turmeric
6 baby new potatoes, cooked, drained and cut into quarters
1–6 green chillies, finely chopped
400g baby spinach leaves
salt, to taste

Heat a non-stick wok over a high heat until it is very hot. Pour the olive oil into the wok and heat until the oil is almost smoking – this should take no more than 1 minute. Add the cumin, nigella and mustard seeds and cook until they start to pop – this should take no longer than 1–2 minutes. Stir in the ginger and garlic and stir-fry until they are light brown in colour – this should take no longer than 2 minutes. Sprinkle in the turmeric and mix well.

Throw the potatoes and chillies into the wok and stir-fry until heated through. Gradually add the spinach to the wok, mixing it through, then stir-fry for 2–3 minutes or until the spinach leaves have wilted.

Season to taste with salt. Serve.

One serving =
185%+ RDA antioxidants

Antibacterial
chilli, cumin, garlic, ginger, mustard, nigella, turmeric

Antifungal
chilli, cumin, garlic, ginger, mustard, nigella, turmeric

Antiviral
garlic, turmeric

Anti-inflammatory
chilli, cumin, garlic, ginger, mustard, nigella, turmeric

Analgesic
chilli, nigella

Sweet Potatoes with Peppers

Serves 4–6

I first had this dish when prepared for me by my pabhi, who had just come to my parents' country home in Blunham after marrying my brother. There was much anticipation for her as to how her first recipe would turn out at her new in-laws' home. Indian fathers cherish nothing more than being fed by their daughters-in-law. As children, they were nurtured by their mother, and as they grew into adults and married, they would be fed by their wife, and when she was too old to carry on, the baton was passed onto their daughters-in-law. And, so the cycle went on, as it had for millennia. This was the Indian way.

But, modern times have brought along the winds of change. And, nothing is quite the way it used to be. Now, most Indians feed themselves; perhaps, the exception being the likes of my Dad, who seem to struggle with time or, time with them. The main thing is that I still remember my pabhi's first dish of aloo Shimla mirch in a good way. Ever since then, she hasn't cooked a whole lot more; maybe because she isn't very adept in the kitchen. And, that's probably why she chose such a simple first dish to cook for her in-laws.

My version takes out the ghee traditionally used to make this recipe; instead, relying on 'creamy' sweet potatoes to impart the same quality, as well as over 100% of your minimum daily vitamin A requirement – that's a whole lot more than what ghee has ever had to offer. Velvety sweet potatoes and sharp-tasting green peppers are an assuredly novel match. More excitement than you would expect from a sides recipe.

Indian Superfood

2 tablespoons olive oil
1 teaspoon fennel seeds
$1/2$ teaspoon each nigella seeds, fenugreek seeds and cumin seeds
$3/4$ teaspoon salt, or to taste
1 small onion, thinly sliced
4 garlic cloves, finely chopped
1 teaspoon turmeric
400g can tomatoes, blended until smooth
2 tablespoons grated (peeled) fresh root ginger
2–4 green chillies, chopped
4 small sweet potatoes, peeled and cut into small bite-size pieces
3 green peppers, deseeded and diced

chopped fresh coriander, to garnish

Pour the olive oil into a deep saucepan, add the fennel, nigella, fenugreek and cumin seeds and cook over a low-medium heat until the seeds start to pop – this should take no longer than 2–3 minutes. Add the salt and onion and fry until the onion is light brown in colour, remembering to stir frequently – this should take no more than 5 minutes.

Stir in the garlic and fry for about 1–2 minutes or until a light brown colour. Sprinkle in the turmeric, mix well and cook for about 20 seconds. Add the tomatoes, ginger and chillies and cook for about 10 minutes or until the excess juices in the saucepan have dried off, remembering to keep stirring occasionally.

Add the sweet potatoes and peppers, mix well and bring to a simmer. Cover and cook gently for about 20–30 minutes or until the sweet potatoes are soft, stirring occasionally.

Garnish with the chopped coriander and serve.

One serving = 165%+ RDA antioxidants

Antibacterial
chilli, coriander, cumin, fennel, fenugreek, garlic, ginger, nigella, turmeric

Antifungal
chilli, coriander, cumin, fennel, fenugreek, garlic, ginger, nigella, turmeric

Antiviral
garlic, turmeric

Anti-inflammatory
chilli, coriander, cumin, fennel, fenugreek, garlic, ginger, nigella, turmeric

Analgesic
chilli, fennel, fenugreek, nigella

Lotus Roots in Yogurt and Tomato Masala

Serves 3–4

For me, this recipe conjures up an image of a Hindu goddess floating on a lotus flower in a serene lake. It's an effigy of unadulterated exoticism which transports me back to a visit to Pushkar, one of India's oldest settlements and a beautiful white walled city in the desert state of Rajasthan, built around a lake oasis. In fact, in Hindi, Pushkar means born due to a flower. According to Hindu legends, the gods set free a swan with a lotus in its beak, and Pushkar is where the lotus fell. Ancient Indian texts also report the use of lotus root for illnesses, including diarrhoea and fever.

And, with an incomparable flavour, all of its own, the root of the resplendent lotus flower will not disappoint. It's a nutty-tasting vegetable with a firm texture and plenty of bite – perhaps something like an overlap between water chestnut and bamboo shoot, but yet with its own uniqueness. It's most definitely one of my favourite vegetables and I suggest everyone should try it at least once; be it even just for dinnertime discussion, it is well worth hunting it down, with merely a walk to the local Indian or Oriental grocery store. Move over diva; hello, goddess!

2 tablespoons olive oil
$1/2$ teaspoon black peppercorns
1 teaspoon cumin seeds
$1/2$ teaspoon mustard seeds
$1/2$ teaspoon salt, or to taste
1 small onion, sliced
4 garlic cloves, chopped
2–4 green chillies, finely chopped (optional)
$1/2$ teaspoon turmeric
$1/2$ 400g can tomatoes, blended until smooth
1 tablespoon tomato purée
4 tablespoons low-fat Greek yogurt
400g can lotus roots, rinsed, drained and thinly sliced

chopped fresh coriander, to garnish

Pour the olive oil into a deep saucepan, add the peppercorns and cumin and mustard seeds and cook over a low-medium heat until the seeds start to pop – this should take no longer than 2–3 minutes. Add the salt and onion and fry until the onion is light brown in colour, remembering to stir frequently – this should take no more than 5 minutes.

Stir in the garlic and chillies, if using, and fry for about 1–2 minutes or until the garlic is a light brown colour. Sprinkle in the turmeric, mix well and cook for about 20 seconds. Add the tomatoes and cook for 5 minutes or until the excess juices in the saucepan have dried off, remembering to stir frequently.

Mix through the tomato purée and heat, then pour in the yogurt, mixing thoroughly, and allow it to heat through.

Add the lotus roots and mix well, then cover and simmer gently for 10 minutes, stirring frequently.

Garnish with the chopped coriander and serve.

One serving = 90%+ RDA antioxidants	
Antibacterial chilli, coriander, cumin, garlic, mustard, pepper, turmeric	**Antiviral** garlic, turmeric
	Anti-inflammatory chilli, coriander, cumin, garlic, mustard, turmeric
Antifungal chilli, coriander, cumin, garlic, mustard, turmeric	**Analgesic** chilli

Samphire Stir-Fried with Mustard and Nigella

Serves 3–4

I have to concede that samphire is quite possibly the most debonair of the Indian Superfood side dishes. It starts off as a rather craggy-and-unassuming-looking vegetable. After washing and drying, it's given the simplest possible tarka in a wok. And, for such little effort, we are rewarded handsomely with beautiful stems of samphire entwined together like how I imagine the mythical Medusa's serpents to be. Samphire cooked in this manner falls nothing short of a stunning dining experience.

The crunchy and charcoaled-tasting stems are naturally salty, and biting through their pleasant spicy exterior; and into their interior we are greeted with savouriness, analogous to having a warm and gentle blast of sea-spray splashed inside of one's mouth. Try them served with Scallops with Red Caviar and Spicy Chilli Oil or even by themselves with pilau; and if you have some left over, mix them through natural yogurt for a crunchy and refreshing raita.

Samphire is also a digestive aid and a source of vitamin C. At the time of writing, samphire is available from good fishmongers only during the summer months. So, as the saying goes, 'Make hay while the sun shines'.

1 tablespoon olive oil
$1/2$ teaspoon mustard seeds
$1/3$ teaspoon nigella seeds
$1/3$ teaspoon each turmeric and chilli powder
200g samphire

lemon wedges, to serve

Crisp Roasted Baby Potatoes with Spiced Sea Green Crust

Serves 4–6

Heat a non-stick wok over a high heat until it is very hot. Pour the olive oil into the wok and heat until the oil is almost smoking – this should take no more than 1 minute.

Add the mustard and nigella seeds and cook until they start to pop – this should take no longer than 1 minute. Sprinkle in the turmeric and chilli powder and mix well.

Throw the samphire into the wok and stir-fry until heated through.

Serve with the lemon wedges.

One serving = 45%+ RDA antioxidants	
Antibacterial chilli, mustard, nigella, turmeric	**Antiviral** turmeric
	Anti-inflammatory chilli, mustard, nigella, turmeric
Antifungal chilli, mustard, nigella, turmeric	**Analgesic** chilli, nigella

[34] "Turmeric has been shown to exhibit antioxidant, anti-inflammatory, antiviral, antibacterial, antifungal and anticancer activities and thus has a potential against various malignant diseases, diabetes, allergies, arthritis, Alzheimer's disease, and other chronic illnesses. Considering the recent scientific bandwagon that multi-targeted therapy is better than mono-targeted therapy for most diseases, turmeric can be considered an ideal 'Spice for Life'."

The University of Texas, US[21]

My word – just the mere mention of the Indian Superfood alternative to Bombay aloo and I am drooling in my seat; and that's saying something, because I'm not a hardcore fan of potatoes. The crunchy exterior of the potatoes is coated with salty and spicy flavours, which contrast with their 'creamy' core. It's a spanking way to seduce any 'would-be-victims' into joining the potato fan club. It's also swift and easy to prepare. Once you've sliced the potatoes, you're almost at the finish line.

Astonishingly, potatoes contain phytonutrients which act as antioxidants against free radicals that cause damage to the body. Cumin seeds and sea salad possess curative properties for the common cold and flu, which makes this recipe especially great on a cold winter's day. Serve with any of the Indian Superfood recipes or, if you prefer, with grilled meat and salad.

800g baby new potatoes, cut in half
2 tablespoons olive oil, plus extra for roasting the potatoes
1 heaped teaspoon cumin seeds
1 teaspoon turmeric
$\frac{3}{4}$ teaspoon salt, or to taste
4 tablespoons sea salad (available from health-food shops)

Preheat the oven to 200°C/fan 180°C/Gas Mark 6. Rub the potatoes in the extra olive oil, place them in a single layer on a baking tray and bake in the centre of the oven for about 15–20 minutes or until golden brown and cooked through. (If preferred, the potatoes can be boiled rather than baked.)

Meanwhile, pour the remaining 2 tablespoons olive oil into a deep frying pan, add the cumin seeds and cook over a medium heat until the cumin seeds begin to pop and release their flavour – this should take no more than 2–3 minutes.

Add the turmeric and salt and stir. Mix in the sea salad and stir, then remove the pan from the heat.

When the potatoes are cooked, add them to the spiced sea salad mixture, stir to mix, then serve.

One serving = 145%+ RDA antioxidants
Antibacterial cumin, turmeric
Antifungal cumin, turmeric
Antiviral turmeric
Anti-inflammatory cumin, turmeric

Lotus Roots in Yogurt and Tomato Masala, page 130   *Samphire Stir-Fried with Mustard and Nigella, page 130*

Indian Superfood

Crisp Roasted Baby Potatoes with Spiced Sea Green Crust, page 131

Foolproof Pilau

Serves 4

Like boiling water, making perfect pilau should be amongst the very simplest of things that one can do in the kitchen. However, unless we are taught how, even the easiest task can turn out to be a treacherous affair. If you follow my recipe with meticulous attention, I assure you that it will surpass all other pilau recipes in its ease of preparation and perfect-each-time results.

At the touch of a button, the mystery of how to cook light and fluffy pilau, as well as putting your microwave to good use, will be unravelled in front of your very own eyes; and from this day forward the sound of 'ping' will be the only way to cook rice.

Do give the cardamom, cumin and garlic pilaus a try. It's truly remarkable how the individual superspices stand out and transform each pilau into a distinctive one, whilst at the same time adding antioxidants.

200g basmati rice
a knob of butter (optional)
$1/_3$ teaspoon salt, or to taste
400ml boiling water

Place all of the ingredients into a large microwave-safe bowl and mix with a fork.

Microwave, uncovered, for 4 minutes on HIGH at 700W, or for $3^1/_2$ minutes on HIGH at 800W or for 3 minutes on HIGH at 900W.

Mix with a fork. Microwave, uncovered, for a further 4 minutes on HIGH at 700W, or for a further $3^1/_2$ minutes on HIGH at 800W, or for a further 3 minutes on HIGH at 900W.

Mix with a fork. Cover the bowl and microwave for a further 4 minutes on HIGH at 700W, or for a further $3^1/_2$ minutes on HIGH at 800W, or for a further 3 minutes on HIGH at 900W.

Take the pilau out of the microwave and leave it to stand, covered, for 10 minutes.

Fluff the rice with a fork and serve.

For cardamom pilau
Add 10 green cardamom pods, lightly crushed, with the rest of the ingredients (at the beginning, before cooking).

For cumin pilau
Add 1 teaspoon cumin seeds with the rest of the ingredients (at the beginning, before cooking).

For garlic pilau
Add 1 tablespoon dried garlic flakes with the rest of the ingredients (at the beginning, before cooking).

Mustard Seed Pilau with Steamed Oyster Mushrooms

Serves 4–6

Oyster mushrooms, mustard seeds, ginger and coriander push this pilau to new heights. It's much like stir-fried rice, but so much fresher and lighter-tasting, and with very little added fat. Oyster mushrooms also add a satisfying meatiness to the pilau whilst penetrating it with a powerful property that stimulates our immune system. Very moreish indeed.

1 tablespoon olive oil
1 teaspoon mustard seeds
1 garlic clove, chopped
1 tablespoon grated (peeled) fresh root ginger
1–2 green chillies, finely chopped (optional)
125g oyster mushrooms
200g basmati rice
$1/_2$ teaspoon salt, or to taste
chopped fresh coriander, to season (optional)

Pour the olive oil into a deep saucepan, add the mustard seeds and cook over a low-medium heat until the seeds begin to pop – this will take no longer than 2–3 minutes. Add the garlic, ginger and chillies, mix well and cook until the garlic is aromatic – this will take no more than 1–2 minutes.

Add the mushrooms and mix well, coating them with the spices. Cook for 1–2 minutes or until the mushrooms start to wilt. Remove the mushrooms from the saucepan to a warm plate, brushing off any excess spice mixture that may have stuck to them back into the saucepan. Set the mushrooms aside.

Place the spice mixture, rice, salt and 400ml boiling water into a large microwave-safe bowl and mix with a fork.

Spaceman's Quinoa Pilau

Serves 3-4

Microwave, uncovered, for 4 minutes on HIGH at 700W, or for 3$\frac{1}{2}$ minutes on HIGH at 800W or for 3 minutes on HIGH at 900W. Mix with a fork. Microwave, uncovered, for a further 4 minutes on HIGH at 700W, or for a further 3$\frac{1}{2}$ minutes on HIGH at 800W, or for a further 3 minutes on HIGH at 900W.

Mix with a fork. Cover the bowl and microwave for a further 4 minutes on HIGH at 700W, or for a further 3$\frac{1}{2}$ minutes on HIGH at 800W, or for a further 3 minutes on HIGH at 900W.

Take the pilau out of the microwave, place the mushrooms on top of the rice and leave it to stand, covered, for 10 minutes.

Fluff the rice with a fork, season with chopped coriander and serve.

One serving = 35%+ RDA antioxidants

Antibacterial
chilli, coriander, garlic, ginger, mustard

Antifungal
chilli, coriander, ginger, garlic, mustard

Antiviral
garlic

Anti-inflammatory
chilli, coriander, garlic, ginger, mustard

Analgesic
chilli

When I first came across quinoa, I couldn't imagine what it would taste like. Even today, although I have now used it in my cooking many times, it's hard for me to describe the flavour. Occasionally, I think perhaps it's rather like a cross between basmati rice and couscous. At other times I beg to differ because it has its own uniqueness. To sum it up, weighing quinoa up to anything else would be like comparing noodles with spaghetti – case dismissed. This recipe sparkles with gems of cumin seeds, which add a nutty aroma that's out of this world.

Quinoa itself isn't just a grain with a pretty face; nothing could be so much further from the truth. It's a complete protein, meaning that it contains all nine essential amino acids normally found in meat and is, therefore, reputed to be the world's healthiest grain – so-very good in fact that even NASA plans to take it into space on long-duration manned space flights. Personally, I prefer it served on Earth and in the comfort of my home, with saucy chicken, meat or lentil curries.

1 tablespoon olive oil
1 heaped teaspoon cumin seeds
$\frac{3}{4}$ teaspoon salt, or to taste
1 small onion, thinly sliced
1 carrot, grated
200g quinoa
a handful of green peas (fresh or frozen)

Pour the olive oil into a deep saucepan, add the cumin seeds and cook over a medium heat until the seeds begin to pop – this should take no more than 2–3 minutes.

Add the salt and onion and cook over a low-medium heat until the onion is soft, stirring frequently – this should take no more than 5 minutes. As soon as the onion is soft, add the carrot and cook for 2–3 minutes. Add the quinoa and cook for a further 2–3 minutes, stirring all the time.

Add 1 litre boiling water to the pan, bring back to the boil, then boil the quinoa hard, uncovered, for 10 minutes, stirring occasionally with a fork.

Reduce the quinoa to a simmer, then cover and cook until the water is absorbed, stirring occasionally with a fork – this should take no longer than 15 minutes.

Remove the pan from the heat, add the peas and stir with a fork. Cover the pan and leave to stand for 5 minutes before serving.

One serving = 85%+ RDA antioxidants

Antibacterial
cumin

Antifungal
cumin

Anti-inflammatory
cumin

Goji Berry and Green Pea Pilau

Serves 4–6

This is pretty much the basic pilau recipe my Mum fed me on from a young age. It was how I thought all rice was made until I was much older. In fact, Punjabis possess a queer snobbery for their pilau recipe. Rather peculiar, considering we have never been the traditional connoisseurs of rice. I remember my grandmother was once served plain boiled rice. She threw it back at her servants, saying that boiled rice was for the labourers and not for her. Even my Mum would 'snarl' at rice cooked in any other way than the traditional Punjabi method, saying the pure white grains of boiled rice would remind her of teeth and, therefore, put her off her dinner.

For a people who rarely eat rice, the Punjabi obsession with their pilau is nothing short of baffling. But, once you experience its multifaceted flavours, you will be able to appreciate, just a little, where the burning passion takes root from. Like most of their foods, it's very satisfying indeed; enough so that you can even enjoy it by itself with just a knob of butter or a dollop of natural yogurt.

I remember it was the first rice dish I taught myself to cook when leaving home. It took me years to get it right, so, I thought I'd share it with you. You can also throw in a few black cardamom pods for added depth of flavour – I remember Mum doing so on special occasions. The superfood twist is brought into full swing with the inclusion of ruby-coloured goji berries which add loads of vitamin C, as well as a wonderful and slightly fruity, almost tea-like flavour.

1 tablespoon olive oil
1 cinnamon stick
1 heaped teaspoon cumin seeds
1 small onion, thinly sliced
1 carrot, grated
200g basmati rice
$^1/_2$ teaspoon salt, or to taste
a small handful of dried goji berries
a handful of green peas (fresh or frozen)

Pour the olive oil into a deep saucepan, add the cinnamon stick and cumin seeds and cook over a low-medium heat until the seeds begin to pop – this should take no more than 2–3 minutes. Add the onion and cook until it is soft, stirring frequently – this should take no more than 5 minutes. As soon as the onion is soft, add the carrot and cook for 2–3 minutes, stirring frequently.

Place the onion mixture, rice, salt and 400ml boiling water into a large microwave-safe bowl and mix with a fork.

Microwave, uncovered, for 4 minutes on HIGH at 700W, or for 3$^1/_2$ minutes on HIGH at 800W or for 3 minutes on HIGH at 900W.

Mix with a fork. Microwave, uncovered, for a further 4 minutes on HIGH at 700W, or for a further 3$^1/_2$ minutes on HIGH at 800W, or for a further 3 minutes on HIGH at 900W.

Mix with a fork. Cover the bowl and microwave for a further 4 minutes on HIGH at 700W, or for a further 3$^1/_2$ minutes on HIGH at 800W, or for a further 3 minutes on HIGH at 900W.

Take the pilau out of the microwave, add the goji berries and peas on top of the rice and leave it to stand, covered, for 10 minutes.

Fluff the rice with a fork and serve.

One serving = 140%+ RDA antioxidants

Antibacterial
cinnamon, cumin

Antifungal
cinnamon, cumin

Antiviral
cinnamon

Anti-inflammatory
cinnamon, cumin

Indian Superfood

Naan

Makes 4 naans

As with most other breads, we have bonded somewhat idiosyncratically with naans. We realise they are an indispensable part of the Indian cuisine and essential for soaking up delicious sauces sitting at the bottom of our plate, yet presume they are tedious in preparation and therefore voiding the possibility of ever making them at home. Why do we shy away from baking? Not being a baker myself, I have first-hand experience and can say without presumption that naan-baking is one of the easier kitchen 'tasks' that we can ever undertake; it's all about time management, really.

Knead the dough in the morning – it's therapeutic and can be considered a warm up for starting the day. Let it rest until lunch or dinner – it needs a good breather after taking a bashing from you. Roll out and bake just as your mains are ready to be served. And, if you do have a diva-like aversion to baking, the naans and yourself don't have to go anywhere near an oven – simply cook them on a dry frying pan, like you would chapattis.

If you like your naans to be thin and crispy, roll them out thinner, and for thick doughy naans, like the ones we often find in restaurants, roll them out smaller and fatter. Fancy them plain, then omit the superspices. And if, like me, you have a penchant for garlic naans, simply spread them with a little garlic butter.

You see, this recipe is as easy and flexible as you want it to be. However, there's always a catch, and just a few things that aren't adjustable. For, if you presume to fall for the Seaweed and Roasted Pumpkin Seed Naan, the Cranberry and Almond Naan or even the Sweet Sesame Seed and Sultana Naan, you will have to make them at home as you won't find them anywhere else; at least not yet!

2 tablespoons olive oil, plus a little extra
75g natural yogurt
1 tablespoon honey
50ml semi-skimmed milk
310g plain flour, plus extra for dusting
1/2 teaspoon salt
1/2 sachet (3.5g) fast-action dried yeast
1/2 teaspoon each nigella seeds and fennel seeds
rock salt, for sprinkling

In a small bowl, whisk together 2 tablespoons olive oil, the yogurt, honey and milk. Heat the mixture until it is warm (hand-hot), using either a microwave oven or a saucepan on top of the stove. Set aside.

Place the 310g flour, 1/2 teaspoon salt and the yeast into a large mixing bowl and combine. Make a well in the middle of the flour mixture.

Pour the warm yogurt mixture slowly into the well while stirring with a wooden spoon and mixing into the flour. When the fluids are combined with the flour to make a dough (the dough may be slightly sticky at this stage), knead for 10 minutes in the bowl (or on a lightly floured work surface) to make a firm, yet elastic dough ball – the dough ball needs to be of a pliable texture, therefore, you may need to add a few drops of cold water to get the right consistency.

Roll this dough ball in a little extra olive oil, then cover the bowl with a clean kitchen towel. Place the bowl in a warm place and allow the dough to rest for 2 hours or until it has doubled in size.

Once the dough is ready, preheat the oven to its maximum temperature setting or preheat the grill to its maximum setting, leaving a baking tray to heat at the top of the oven or under the grill. Split the dough into 4 equal portions. Roll each portion in the palm of your hands until you have a smaller dough ball. Push this dough ball flat on a clean work surface until it resembles a thick disc in shape.

Using a rolling pin, roll this disc out into a teardrop shape approximately 22cm long x 17cm wide (if you like your naans thin and crispy, roll them out to a larger size of about 28 x 19cm). Repeat the process until you have 4 naans in total. (If the dough sticks to the work surface or rolling pin, use extra flour for dusting.)

Brush the naans on one side with a little water and on each naan press down equal amounts of the nigella and fennel seeds and a pinch of rock salt. Prick the naans with a fork.

Place one naan at a time at the top of the oven or under the grill on the hot baking tray and cook for 2–3 minutes or until the naan has puffed up and cooked through with some golden brown patches. Repeat until all the naans are cooked.

Drizzle the naans with extra olive oil and serve immediately.

| One serving =
20%+ RDA
antioxidants | Anti-inflammatory
nigella |
|---|---|
| Antibacterial
fennel, nigella | Analgesic
fennel, nigella |
| Antifungal
nigella | |

Naan, page 137

Tandoori-Style Soy Milk Roti, page 141

Indian Superfood

Wholegrain Spelt Flour Chapattis, page 144

Seaweed and Roasted Pumpkin Seed Naan

Cranberry and Almond Naan

Sweet Sesame Seed and Sultana Naan

Makes 4 naans

Impress try-hard guests with a jet-set naan that's abounding with an invigorating symphony of savoury deep sea and sweet roasted pumpkin seed flavours.

1 quantity Naan dough (see page 137)
a large handful of sea salad (available from health-food shops)
a large handful of pumpkin seeds

Follow the basic naan recipe and roll out the dough into teardrop shapes.

Brush the naans on one side with a little water and press down on each naan equal amounts of the sea salad and pumpkin seeds with the nigella and fennel seeds and a pinch of rock salt. Prick the naans with a fork.

Place one naan at a time at the top of the oven or under the grill on the hot baking tray and cook for 2–3 minutes or until the naan has puffed up and cooked through with some golden brown patches. Repeat until all the naans are cooked.

Drizzle the naans with extra olive oil and serve immediately.

One serving = 15%+ RDA antioxidants	Anti-inflammatory nigella
	Analgesic
Antibacterial fennel, nigella	fennel, nigella
Antifungal nigella	

Makes 4 naans

A Peshawari-inspired naan, with a cosmo-kick to it. It's got a yummy flavour and is 'berry' good for you.

1 quantity Naan dough (see page 137)
a large handful each of dried cranberries and flaked almonds

Follow the basic naan recipe and roll out the dough into teardrop shapes.

Brush the naans on one side with a little water and press down on each naan equal amounts of the dried cranberries and flaked almonds with the nigella and fennel seeds and a pinch of rock salt. Prick the naans with a fork.

Place one naan at a time at the top of the oven or under the grill on the hot baking tray and cook for 2–3 minutes or until the naan has puffed up and cooked through with some golden brown patches. Repeat until all the naans are cooked.

Drizzle the naans with extra olive oil and serve immediately.

One serving = 50%+ RDA antioxidants	Anti-inflammatory nigella
	Analgesic
Antibacterial fennel, nigella	fennel, nigella
Antifungal nigella	

Makes 4 naans

Scattered with cholesterol-lowering sesame seeds, this naan is not only delicious but also incredibly energising. Finger-licking good, and not a chicken in sight!

1 quantity Naan dough (see page 137)
a large handful each of pumpkin seeds, sesame seeds and sultanas

extra honey and natural yogurt, to serve

Follow the basic naan recipe and roll out the dough into teardrop shapes.

Brush the naans on one side with a little water and press down on each naan equal amounts of the pumpkin seeds, sesame seeds and sultanas. Omit the nigella seeds, fennel seeds and rock salt. Prick the naans with a fork.

Place one naan at a time at the top of the oven or under the grill on the hot baking tray and cook for 2–3 minutes or until the naan has puffed up and cooked through with some golden brown patches. Repeat until all the naans are cooked.

Drizzle the naans with extra honey. Serve immediately with yogurt.

One serving = 30%+ RDA antioxidants

Tandoori-Style Soy Milk Roti

Makes 6 rotis

Tandoori rotis are a hybrid of naan and chapatti. Like naans, they are made with plain flour, and, just as chapattis are, they are rolled into thin discs, which are then slapped onto the fiercely hot interior wall of a tandoor oven for cooking the way we do naans. My Mum often recollects to me her memories of visiting her village's communal tandoor as a child, where she would collect rotis for occasions when meat was being served to special guests at home. In 1960s' rural Punjab, entertaining guests at home was the proviso – taking them out to dinner would be to dishonour them.

Given there is no longer a communal bakery, when Mum is in India she still gets her fix by visiting her sister's roadside dhaba for a few rotis with dahl – it's one of her few exceptions to her 'no eating out' rule.

In this recipe, I haven't done a great deal of changing to the main ingredient, plain flour, as we do need the elasticity that it offers us. Instead, for the superfood twist, I've used soy milk which adds omega-3 fatty acids in a place we'd never expect to find them. For a change, try brushing with a little garlic butter.

300g plain flour, plus extra for dusting
$1/2$ teaspoon salt
$1/2$ sachet (3.5g) fast-action dried yeast
150ml soy milk
2 tablespoons olive oil, plus a little extra

Place the flour, salt and yeast into a large mixing bowl and mix. Make a well in the middle of the flour mixture.

Pour the milk and 2 tablespoons olive oil slowly into the well, while stirring with a wooden spoon and mixing into the flour. When the fluids are combined with the flour to make a dough (the dough may be slightly sticky at this stage), knead for 10 minutes in the bowl (or on a lightly floured work surface) to make a firm, yet elastic dough ball – the dough ball needs to be of a pliable texture, therefore, you may need to add a few drops more of soy milk to get the right consistency.

Roll this dough ball in a little extra olive oil, then cover the bowl with a clean kitchen towel. Place the bowl in a warm place and allow the dough to rest for 2 hours or until it has doubled in size.

Split the dough into 6 equal portions and roll each portion between the palms of your hands until you have a dough ball. Push the dough ball flat on a clean work surface until it resembles a thick disc in shape. Using a rolling pin, roll it out into a round roti shape (approximately 20cm in diameter).

Repeat the process until you have 6 rotis in total. (If you find the dough sticking to the work surface or the rolling pin, use extra flour for dusting.)

Heat a large, heavy-based frying pan over a high heat. Once the pan is very hot, reduce to a medium heat. Place a roti in the pan and cook on each side until cooked through with some brown patches – this should take no more than 2–3 minutes for each side. Repeat until all the rotis are cooked.

Drizzle the rotis with extra olive oil and serve immediately.

Wholemeal Pumpkin and Caraway Seed Bread

Makes 1 loaf (Serves 6)

In India, we don't have a tradition of baking loaves of bread. Sure, we have marvellous flatbreads such as naans, chapattis and rotis that have travelled as far as England, becoming a part of the indigenous food culture. Yet still, we don't have anything that even closely resembles a loaf of bread which we could, say, make a cheese sandwich from, or dip slices of into a bowl of soup or curry.

Sometimes I wonder how charismatic it would be if children in India skipped down dusty and narrow streets to communal bakers to pick up loaves of piping hot bread for dinner, like they do in Morocco. But, I am fantasising and borrowing from another culture, something that simply is not mine. Children of India are much more likely to run into a sacred cow or a paan walla's stand barricading the winding streets, on their way back home from a sweet shop and, perhaps, returning with bagfuls of freshly fried samosas and jalebis.

So, this recipe is my compromise between what we have here in England, or even in Morocco, with what's truly Indian. This dense, damper-style of bread is made from basic naan dough. Instead of being rolled out into individual naans, the dough is baked whole, demonstrating the versatility of the Indian kitchen beautifully.

Although from the outside it may have a somewhat foreign appearance, rest assured this bread is 100% Indian to the core. You don't even need any special equipment to make it – not even a loaf tin. No excuses for not giving this recipe a once over. Try experimenting with different spices, or even leaving them out altogether.

Enjoy this bread for breakfast, lunch or dinner, and remember that people who consume wholemeal flour bread are less likely to be overweight or suffer from heart disease, than those who don't.

2 tablespoons olive oil
75g natural yogurt
1 tablespoon honey
75ml semi-skimmed milk
170g strong wholemeal flour
130g strong white flour, plus extra for dusting
1/2 teaspoon salt
1/2 sachet (3.5g) fast-action dried yeast
1 teaspoon each caraway seeds and cumin seeds
a small handful of pumpkin seeds

In a small bowl, whisk together the olive oil, yogurt, honey and milk. Heat the mixture until it is warm (hand-hot), using either a microwave oven or a saucepan on top of the stove. Set aside.

Place the flours, salt, yeast and caraway, cumin and pumpkin seeds into a large mixing bowl and combine. Make a well in the middle of the flour mixture.

Pour the warm yogurt mixture slowly into the well while stirring with a wooden spoon and mixing into the flour. When the fluids are combined with the flour to make a dough (the dough may be slightly sticky at this stage), knead for 10 minutes in the bowl (or on a lightly floured work surface) to make a firm, yet elastic dough ball – the dough ball needs to be of a pliable texture, therefore, you may need to add a few drops more of cold water to get the right consistency.

Make two diagonal cuts into the top of the dough ball and dust with some of the extra flour, then cover the bowl with a clean kitchen towel. Place the bowl in a warm place and allow the dough to rest for 2 hours.

Once the dough is ready, preheat the oven to 200°C/fan 180°C/Gas Mark 6. Place the dough ball on a floured baking tray. Bake in the centre of the oven for 10 minutes, then reduce the oven temperature to 180°C/fan 160°C/Gas Mark 4 and bake for a further 30 minutes or until the loaf is dark brown in colour.

Remove from the oven and transfer to a wire rack to cool. Serve in slices.

One serving =
20%+ RDA
antioxidants

Antibacterial
cumin

Antifungal
cumin

Anti-inflammatory
cumin

Analgesic
caraway

Indian Superfood

Wholegrain Spelt Flour Chapattis

Tamarind Reduction

Makes 6 chapattis

How can I ever forget chapattis? These 'flying saucers' of bread are what Mum fed me on to make me "grow big and strong". The love affair started when I grew my first teeth and she soaked a chapatti in a little curry and fed me, gently melting into carbohydrate bliss; I have never looked back.

Still, I can't just blame Mum for my addiction. To be totally frank, I am a Punjabi Jatt descending from wheat farmers. From the fertile plains of the Punjab, farmers feed their families, and also the entire nation, with wheat flour. Eventually, wives and mothers all over India knead this flour with water to make dough from which they roll out crispy, hot chapattis to be had with nearly every meal. If you're not part of the Indian chapatti hierarchy and taught how to make them from a very young age, or your name isn't Houdini, you'll appreciate the addition of plain flour and olive oil in this recipe. It just makes the dough so much more obedient when kneading.

However, if you wish to make a wheat-free version of this recipe, omit the plain flour, substituting it for spelt flour, and using more water accordingly. If you have wheat intolerance, tread carefully. Although spelt is wheat-free, it's still very similar to wheat and therefore its proteins won't suit all.

250g wholegrain spelt flour
150g plain flour, plus extra for dusting
2 tablespoons olive oil, plus a little extra
rock salt, for sprinkling

Place the flours into a large mixing bowl and combine. Make a well in the middle of the flour. Pour 2 tablespoons olive oil and 180ml cold water slowly into the well, while stirring with a wooden spoon and mixing into the flour. When the fluids are combined with the flour to make a dough (the dough may be slightly sticky at this stage), knead for 10 minutes in the bowl (or on a lightly floured work surface) to make a firm, yet elastic dough ball – the dough ball needs to be of a pliable texture, therefore, you may need to add a few drops more of cold water to get the right consistency.

Cover the dough ball with a clean kitchen towel and leave it to rest for 10 minutes.

Split the dough into 6 equal portions and roll each portion in the palm of your hands until you have a smaller dough ball. Push the dough ball flat on a clean work surface until it resembles a thick disc in shape. Using a rolling pin, roll it out into a round chapatti shape (approximately 22cm in diameter).

Repeat the process until you have 6 chapattis in total. (If you find the dough sticking to the work surface or the rolling pin, use extra flour for dusting.)

Heat a large, heavy-based frying pan over a high heat. Once the pan is very hot, reduce to a medium heat. Place a chapatti in the frying pan and cook on each side until cooked through with some brown patches – this should take no more than 2–3 minutes for each side. Repeat until all the chapattis are cooked.

Drizzle the chapattis with extra olive oil, sprinkle with rock salt and serve immediately.

Makes approximately 250ml

In India, sauces made from tamarind are an indispensable accompaniment to almost all vegetarian nibbles; from samosas to gol gappas served roadside, or in the Ram Bagh Palace in Jaipur, they will always come accompanied with tamarind chutney. It's an Indian institution, and to break it, is nothing short of blasphemous.

My recipe further intensifies the already tangy tamarind flavours, resulting in a refreshing and sweet-and-sour sauce that has an ability to make the hair on the back of your neck stand in attention. Once prepared, it can be refrigerated and used at later instances.

In South India, tamarind is also prepared as a soup to treat the common cold; the steaming hot soup has a flushing effect and, when taken, causes the nose and eyes to water, thus, clearing nasal blockage. Studies have also demonstrated that tamarind substantially increases the bioavailability of aspirin and ibuprofen. So, if you're burdened with a cold, dual-acting tamarind reduction, added to a steaming hot bowl of chicken broth, may be worth a go.

100g piece of dried tamarind block, cut into bite-size pieces
3 tablespoons sweet chilli sauce
2 tablespoons sugar
1/2 teaspoon salt
1/2 teaspoon chilli powder
a large handful each of fresh coriander leaves and fresh mint leaves, chopped

Pour 1 litre boiling water into a deep saucepan and add the tamarind. Return the water to the boil, then reduce to a simmer. Using a potato masher, mash the tamarind pieces into the simmering water (being careful not to

Indian Superfood

splash yourself). Mix in the sweet chilli sauce, sugar, salt and chilli powder and continue to simmer over a low heat, uncovered, for 30 minutes (stirring very occasionally, if you wish).

Remove the pan from the heat and pour the contents into a blender. Sprinkle in the coriander and mint leaves. Blitz until smooth. Pour the contents of the blender through a large sieve placed over a bowl, keeping the juice and throwing out the tamarind flesh that is collected in the sieve – it may take some time for the tamarind juice to drain as it's quite pulpy, but you can press or stir the mixture through the sieve to help it on its way, if you like. Cover and chill in the refrigerator for 2 hours before using.

Store in an airtight container in the refrigerator for up to 7 days.

One serving (1 tablespoon) = 3%+ RDA antioxidants

Antibacterial
chilli, coriander, mint, tamarind

Antifungal
chilli, coriander, mint

Anti-inflammatory
chilli, coriander

Analgesic
chilli

Indian Superfood

Spicy Chilli Oil

Makes approximately 500ml flavoured oil

I was first introduced to the 'hair-raising' delights of chilli oil in a small 'hidden' trattoria in Leichardt, the Italian quarter of Sydney. It was one of those clichéd eateries with chequered plastic tablecloths run by 'Mamma'. The food was great, and in fact much better than most ristorantes I came to know later. As to be expected, the atmosphere was also wholly Italian, and positively noisy. I never could tell whether 'Mamma' was arguing with her customers or simply trying to run the business in the best possible manner after guzzling down a bottle of chilli oil.

My Spicy Chilli Oil recipe also includes a symphony of Indian superspices that play out on the taste buds like a flavoured musical. The best thing about it is that it adds heat to food without overpowering, unlike many traditional Indian pickles. So, if like me, you're just after heat, you will adore it. If you are a bit of a toughie, you can even make an impromptu chilli pickle by pouring it over freshly chopped chillies.

Perhaps it would be surprising to know that this 'heart-stopper' of a recipe is also loaded with chilli and olive oil antioxidants that guard against heart disease.

500ml olive oil
10 green cardamom pods, lightly crushed
5 cloves
1 cinnamon stick
1 teaspoon each cumin seeds and mustard seeds
1–2 tablespoons dried red chilli flakes, as per your taste
1 tablespoon dried garlic flakes

Pour 350ml olive oil into an airtight sterilised jar and set aside.

Pour the remaining olive oil into a small saucepan, add the cardamom pods, cloves, cinnamon stick and cumin and mustard seeds and cook over a high heat until the seeds start to pop – this will take no more than 2–3 minutes. Remove the pan from the heat and immediately stir in the chilli and garlic flakes.

Pour the hot spiced oil into the jar with the olive oil and allow it to cool. After some time, shake the jar gently to combine. Seal the jar and leave it to stand overnight at room temperature before using.

Store in a cool, dark place and use as required.

**One serving
(1 tablespoon) =
20%+ RDA
antioxidants**

Antibacterial
cardamom, chilli, cinnamon, cloves, cumin, garlic, mustard

Antifungal
cardamom, chilli, cinnamon, cloves, cumin, garlic, mustard

Antiviral
cinnamon, cloves, garlic

Anti-inflammatory
cardamom, chilli, cinnamon, cloves, cumin, garlic, mustard

Analgesic
chilli, cloves

Mum's Mint Chutney

Walnut Chutney

Makes about 450ml

Serves 4–6

Mum's Mint Chutney is the chutney-world equal of the English summertime drink, Pimms. No other chutney is quite as refreshing in taste as this one. Every mouthful reminds me of the summer just gone and of the one I am longing for.

The pure and refreshing mint appeases the digestive tract and soothes the tummy, whilst cooling the body. It's an indispensable mealtime accompaniment. Mum also recommends it for sandwiches. You can keep it refrigerated for up to one week.

100g bunch of fresh mint, washed and dried
2 large Granny Smith eating apples
2 small onions, cut into quarters
1–6 green chillies
salt, to taste

Remove all the leaves from the mint stalks and place them in a food processor. Discard the stalks.

Peel, core and quarter the apples, then add them to the food processor, together with the onions, chillies and salt. Process all the ingredients together until you have a pesto-like consistency (you may need to add a few drops of cold water to achieve the right consistency).

Serve immediately or store in an airtight container in the refrigerator for up to 1 week.

One serving (1 tablespoon) = 25%+ RDA antioxidants	Antifungal chilli, mint
	Anti-inflammatory chilli
Antibacterial chilli, mint	Analgesic chilli

High up in the valleys of Kashmir, almond, cherry, pomegranate and walnut trees blossom in the springtime like the Garden of Eden. There is no other place on the Indian subcontinent quite like it, where one can indulge so freely in the finest of nature's bounty of fruits and nuts.

Year in, year out, just as the seasons always come and go, Auntie Zehra will collect basketfuls of walnuts, preparing them into her legendary chutney. It's so celebrated, in fact, that people vying for the last of it have been known to cause trouble in paradise.

Tasting somewhat like an exotic pesto, it can accompany all kinds of foods and is even great when spread in sandwiches. Walnuts also contain the powerful antioxidant melatonin, which induces sleep and dreaming. This chutney could well be your ticket to paradise. It is best served immediately.

200ml natural yogurt
10g bunch of fresh coriander, chopped
10g bunch of fresh mint leaves, chopped
2–6 green chillies, finely chopped (optional)
a large pinch of chilli powder
salt, to taste
100g walnuts

Place the yogurt, coriander, mint, chillies, if using, chilli powder and salt in a food processor and blitz until smooth.

Add the walnuts and blend in short spurts, turning the food processor on and off until the walnut pieces are blended – the chutney will have a grainy texture.

Serve immediately.

One serving = 130%+ RDA antioxidants

Antibacterial
chilli, coriander, mint

Antifungal
chilli, coriander, mint

Anti-inflammatory
chilli, coriander

Analgesic
chilli

Punch and Gusto Fresh Coriander Salsa

Makes approximately 700ml

Coriander is very much recognised for its diuretic and relaxant properties. Therefore, a good helping of this flavour-laden salsa not only livens up the taste buds, but also brings an authentic Indian flavour to mealtimes and, ultimately, it helps you to feel more serene. You can keep it refrigerated for up to one week.

2 large tomatoes
1 large Granny Smith eating apple
1 small onion, cut into quarters
80g chopped fresh coriander
1 garlic clove, peeled
1–6 green chillies
1 teaspoon lemon juice
salt, to taste

Start by making a few small and not-very-deep surface cuts in the tomatoes and place them in a deep bowl. Pour in enough boiling water to cover the tomatoes and allow them to sit in the water for 2–3 minutes.

In the meantime, peel, core and quarter the apple and place in a food processor.

Drain the tomatoes, then peel off and discard the skins. Place the tomatoes in the food processor, together with the onion, chopped coriander, garlic, chillies and lemon juice and blitz until you have a pesto-like consistency (you may need to add a few drops of cold water to achieve the right consistency). Season to taste with salt.

Serve immediately or store in an airtight container in the refrigerator for up to 1 week.

One serving (1 tablespoon) = 8%+ RDA antioxidants

Antibacterial
chilli, coriander, garlic

Antifungal
chilli, coriander, garlic

Antiviral
garlic

Anti-inflammatory
chilli, coriander, garlic

Analgesic
chilli

Baby Spinach Raita

Serves 2–3

This wonderfully earthy and peasant-like raita is made up entirely of superfoods. Yogurt balances pH levels in the stomach, aiding digestion, spinach contains antioxidants that give us overall protection, and phytochemicals derived from garlic interrupt a multitude of diseases.

For vaguely little effort, it's a very gratifying recipe indeed. In fact, I sometimes find myself eating it on its own, as a meal, with just some crispy naan or bread.

1 garlic clove, finely chopped
a pinch of chilli powder
1 tablespoon olive oil, plus extra for drizzling
75g baby spinach leaves, washed and dried
225ml natural yogurt
salt, to taste

Place the garlic, chilli powder and 1 tablespoon olive oil in a frying pan and cook over a medium heat for 1–2 minutes or until the garlic is almost golden brown in colour.

Add the spinach, cover and cook over a medium-low heat for 5 minutes, stirring occasionally. Remove the lid and continue cooking until all the moisture has evaporated, stirring occasionally. Remove the pan from the heat and allow the spinach mixture to cool.

Once cool, mix the spinach mixture into the yogurt in a bowl. Season to taste with salt and serve, drizzled with some extra olive oil.

Serve immediately or store in an airtight container in the refrigerator for up to 2–3 days.

One serving = 30%+ RDA antioxidants

Antibacterial
chilli, garlic

Antifungal
chilli, garlic

Antiviral
garlic

Anti-inflammatory
chilli, garlic

Analgesic
chilli

Banana Raita

Serves 4

Based on its eccentricity and my constant need to provoke stirring conversation, this is probably one of my favourite raitas. To get tongues wagging, it has the perfect balance of savoury, sweet, spicy, sour and hot. It is the flavour of South India, whipped up into a raita in seconds. You might have guessed, but just in case you didn't, I'll let you know that even Banana Raita counts towards one of your 5-a-day. This raita is best served immediately.

1 teaspoon mustard seeds
1 teaspoon olive oil
1 ripe banana
1-2 green chillies, finely chopped
450ml natural yogurt
salt, to taste

chopped fresh coriander, to garnish

Place the mustard seeds and olive oil in a small frying pan and cook over a high heat for 1-2 minutes or until the seeds start to pop. Remove the pan from the heat and allow the oil to cool.

Peel and slice the banana. In a bowl, combine the sliced banana, oil and mustard seed mixture, chillies and yogurt, mixing well. Season to taste with salt.

Garnish with chopped coriander and serve immediately.

One serving = 25%+ RDA antioxidants	Antifungal chilli, coriander, mustard
Antibacterial chilli, coriander, mustard	Anti-inflammatory chilli, coriander, mustard

Indian Superfood

Coriander Raita

Mint Raita

Serves 3-4

Serves 3–4

Fresh coriander raita does for your taste buds what a shower does for you. It invigorates. Simultaneously, coriander also neutralises free radicals. So, without ado, we had better set our kamikaze friends loose. This energising raita is also great served as a dip.

A sweet and refreshing raita that's ideal for balancing full-bodied Indian flavours. Mint and yogurt soothe the digestive tract and the stomach. This raita is also perfect served as a dip.

450ml natural yogurt
20g bunch of fresh coriander, finely
    chopped
1/2 small onion, finely chopped
a large pinch of chilli powder
salt and freshly ground black pepper,
    to taste

450ml natural yogurt
20 fresh mint leaves, finely chopped
1 teaspoon dried mint
1/2 small red onion, finely chopped
1/2 teaspoon sugar
a large pinch of chilli powder
salt and freshly ground black pepper,
    to taste

Combine all of the ingredients in a bowl, mixing well. Cover and refrigerate for at least 1 hour before serving – this marinating time allows the coriander flavours to fully develop into the yogurt.

Combine all of the ingredients in a bowl, mixing well. If you have time, cover and refrigerate for at least 1 hour before serving – this marinating time allows the minty flavours to fully mature into the yogurt.

Serve or store in an airtight container in the refrigerator for up to 2–3 days.

Serve or store in an airtight container in the refrigerator for up to 2–3 days.

One serving =
17%+ RDA
antioxidants

Antifungal
chilli, coriander

Antibacterial
chilli, coriander,
pepper

Anti-inflammatory
coriander

Analgesic
chilli

One serving =
17.5%+ RDA
antioxidants

Antifungal
chilli, mint

Analgesic
chilli

Antibacterial
chilli, mint, pepper

" *Black pepper finds an extensive application in antibacterial preparations belonging to the Ayurvedic system of medicine. The petroleum ether extract of the berries was isolated. Under laboratory conditions, all of the isolated compounds were active against Bacillus subtilis, Bacillus sphaericus, Staphylococcus aureus, Klebsiella aerogenes and Chromobacterium violaceum strains.* "

Indian Institute of Chemical Technology, Hyderabad, India[18]

Walnut Chutney, page 148

Banana Raita, page 150

Indian Superfood

Passion Fruit and Ginger Raita, page 154

Passion Fruit and Ginger Raita

Serves 3–4

Sweet and spicy with crunchy bites of fruity and sour passion fruit rubble, this raita has a distinguished character. As you'd expect, it's the passion fruit that gives it va-va-voom. Passion fruit contains potassium – in fact, weight for weight, it contains as much potassium as you'd find in a banana hiding inside a bodybuilder's lunchbox – which means it helps your muscles and nerves function with oomph.

1 teaspoon cumin seeds
1 teaspoon olive oil
450ml natural yogurt
1 passion fruit, halved and pulp and seeds scooped out
2 green chillies, finely chopped (optional)
1 teaspoon finely grated (peeled) fresh root ginger
1 teaspoon sugar
salt, to taste
chopped fresh coriander, to season

Place the cumin seeds and olive oil in a small frying pan and cook over a high heat for 1–2 minutes or until the seeds start popping. Remove the pan from the heat and allow the oil to cool.

In a bowl, combine the oil and cumin seed mixture with all the remaining ingredients, mixing well.

Serve immediately or store in an airtight container in the refrigerator for up to 2–3 days.

One serving = 45%+ RDA antioxidants

Antibacterial
chilli, coriander, cumin, ginger

Antifungal
chilli, coriander, cumin, ginger

Anti-inflammatory
chilli, coriander, cumin, ginger

Analgesic
chilli

Garlic Raita

Serves 3–4

Pungent Garlic Raita can also be used as a dip and, perhaps surprisingly, as a ferocious medicinal potion. Garlic has long been accepted as a powerful antimicrobial, destroying bacteria and infection-causing viruses. If you have a sore throat, try eating Garlic Raita last thing before sleeping at night – after brushing your teeth.

In some parts of the Arab world, parents feed their young adolescents dishes flavoured with large amounts of raw garlic to keep them away from the opposite sex – a novel form of birth control.

Use more or less garlic as per your taste or needs. For something really different, try making it with roasted garlic.

450ml natural yogurt
4 garlic cloves, finely chopped
2 spring onions, thinly sliced
salt and freshly ground black pepper, to taste

Combine all of the ingredients in a bowl, mixing well. If you have time, cover and refrigerate for at least 1 hour before serving – this marinating time allows the garlicky flavours to fully develop into the yogurt.

Serve or store in an airtight container in the refrigerator for up to 2–3 days.

One serving = 15%+ RDA antioxidants

Antibacterial
garlic, pepper

Antifungal
garlic

Antiviral
garlic

Anti-inflammatory
garlic

Sea Salad and Roasted Cumin Raita

Serves 2–3

This is one of many Indian Superfood recipes where the blend of ingredients was never originally destined to meet. With sea salad from China and yogurt from India, and the two cuisines haplessly afraid of one another, the 'cold-war' was as glacial as the Himalayan mountain range dividing the two countries. It was as if, somehow, the Chinese believed yogurt would drown the sea salad, and the Indians thought sea salad would curdle the yogurt. The misconception of each other's cuisines was based on delusions.

All in all, sea salad and yogurt are an ace source of iodine, needed by the thyroid to regulate a healthy metabolism. This raita has a fresh and clean finish that will have heads nodding with approval, in both India and China. It's best served immediately.

One serving = 60%+ RDA antioxidants

Antibacterial
chilli, cumin

Antifungal
chilli, cumin

Anti-inflammatory
chilli, cumin

Analgesic
chilli

**1 teaspoon cumin seeds
a handful of sea salad (available from
   health-food shops)
a pinch of chilli powder
225ml natural yogurt
salt, to taste**

Place the cumin seeds in a small, dry frying pan and roast over a medium heat for 1–2 minutes or until the seeds begin to pop. Mix in the sea salad and continue roasting for 1 minute, shaking the pan once or twice.

Transfer the mixture to a bowl. Add the chilli powder, yogurt and salt and stir to mix. Serve immediately.

Light Bites

This chapter is for those 'foragers' amongst us who just aren't satisfied with eating three set meals a day. It is intended for that time when the tummy rumbles for a tad more nourishment. You will find a handful of carefully-selected and moreish bites that can be enjoyed as either canapés, entrées or as a light meal and, if you really must, as an accompaniment to a night-in with the television.

If you do happen to be keeping up with the Beckhams, there is the very chic Oyster Pakoras with Punch and Gusto Fresh Coriander Salsa. For those of us pushed for time, we have a velvety-rich Chickpea Mousse, which can be ready to eat in minutes. I think it's about time we all started to undertake some serious snacking.

Bollywood Popcorn

Serves 2

Except for a few poor sods with dentures or a broken tooth (that includes me), there aren't many of us out there who don't love eating popcorn; in all likeliness, probably because it generally coincides with a fun outing to the cinema too. It's definitely one of my favourite pastimes.

My recipe is somewhat inspired by my wonderful and wacky Christian evangelist friend Dr. Mandakini, from Hyderabad, who once made me popcorn with chilli, and by Mum who has been making popcorn in the microwave using recycled brown paper bags from Mr. Maqsood's green grocery store, for years.

Popcorn is also inexpensive to make from scratch and contains more antioxidants and fibre than most other snack foods. So, grab yourself a movie and make some. It will save you a pocket load of dosh, as well as fat and calories on the convenience food you get at the supermarket.

70g popcorn kernels
$\frac{1}{2}$ teaspoon curry powder
a large pinch of chilli powder (optional)
a knob of butter
salt, to taste

Place the popcorn kernels, curry powder, chilli powder, if using, butter and salt in a microwaveable multi-purpose cooking bag. Tie the bag loosely at the top, leaving plenty of room for the kernels to pop.

Microwave for 6 minutes on HIGH at 700W, or for $5\frac{1}{2}$ minutes on HIGH at 800W, or for 5 minutes on HIGH at 900W or until the kernels go from popping hard to hardly popping at all.

Leave to stand for 1 minute. Shake the bag and serve.

**One serving =
30%+ RDA
antioxidants**

Antibacterial
chilli

Antifungal
chilli

Anti-inflammatory
chilli

Analgesic
chilli

Salmon Pakoras with Coriander Raita

Serves 4–6

Fish pakoras are typical of Punjabi roadside dhaba fare and are the Indian answer to the Turkish mezze – savoury morsels of food to be appreciated with a cold drink. They are also cherished by many Indian 'vegetarians', who see them as a way of bridging their love of meat with their ethical lifestyles.

At wedding parties, I often share my portion of fish pakoras with the older Indian ladies who are somewhat reluctant to eat meat in public, afraid of being labelled by ancient Hindu social custom as heathen carnivores from kala pani. Or, perhaps they just don't want to share something that tastes so damn fine, confining me to the more carnal pleasures of meat kebabs.

So, make plenty to share with your friends. If my experiences are anything to go by, they will go down a treat. If you do happen to have one drink too many and behave like a junglie, it's also good to know that ajwain is used as a hangover remedy. Salmon adds another superfood pirouette to these Amritsari-style pakoras with a good dose of omega-3 fatty acids. Serve with Coriander Raita and, if you do make a meal of it, with salad and pilau.

500g salmon fillets, skinned and cut into large bite-size pieces
2 tablespoons tandoori masala powder
1 onion, cut into quarters
4 garlic cloves, peeled
1 tablespoon grated (peeled) fresh root ginger
2–6 green chillies
7 tablespoons gram flour
$3/4$ teaspoon salt, or to taste
1 teaspoon garam masala
1 teaspoon ajwain
1 teaspoon coriander seeds

olive oil or vegetable oil, for shallow frying
Coriander Raita (see page 151), a few lemon wedges and salad, to serve

In a large mixing bowl, rub the salmon pieces in the tandoori masala powder and set aside – all of the masala should stick to the salmon and there should be no excess spices at the bottom of the mixing bowl.

To prepare the pakora batter, place the onion, garlic, ginger, chillies, gram flour, salt, garam masala, ajwain, coriander seeds and 4 tablespoons cold water in a food processor and blend until you have a batter that resembles a runny porridge – to get the right consistency you may need to add more cold water or gram flour.

Pour the batter into the large mixing bowl containing the salmon and mix, making sure each piece of salmon is thoroughly coated.

Pour enough oil into a deep saucepan so that the oil is at least 3cm deep, then heat over a high heat until the oil is almost smoking. Reduce the heat to medium-high.

Take the salmon pieces out of the batter individually, shaking off any excess batter mixture (discard any leftover batter). Fry in small batches in the hot oil for 3–4 minutes or until the salmon pieces are floating near the top of the oil. Remove with a spatula and drain on kitchen paper.

Serve the salmon pakoras immediately with the coriander raita, lemon wedges and salad.

These are best served as nibbles with drinks.

One serving = 125%+ RDA antioxidants

Antibacterial
ajwain, chilli, coriander, garlic, ginger

Antifungal
ajwain, chilli, coriander, garlic, ginger

Antiviral
garlic

Anti-inflammatory
ajwain, chilli, coriander, garlic, ginger

Analgesic
chilli

Indian Superfood

Scallops with Red Caviar and Spicy Chilli Oil

Serves 2–4

There's not a lot you need to do with scallops. They have their own naturally rich and buttery taste which is enhanced, even more so, by the contrasting turmeric and aromatic basil flavours. Red caviar accentuates the ocean-fresh bouquet further.

Scallops are rich in zinc which is exceptionally imperative for healthy skin and is essential for maintaining a buoyant immune system and improving resistance to infections.

This recipe makes an impressive dinner or cocktail party hors d'oeuvre. For a more substantial meal, serve with buttered Wholemeal Pumpkin and Caraway Seed Bread and salad.

1 tablespoon Spicy Chilli Oil (see page 147), plus extra for drizzling
1 tablespoon olive oil, plus extra for frying
$\frac{1}{2}$ teaspoon turmeric
12 fresh scallops (if possible, on their shells)
12 large fresh basil leaves
6 teaspoons red caviar

lime wedges, to serve
buttered bread and salad, to serve (optional)

In a bowl, mix together 1 tablespoon each of the spicy chilli oil and olive oil with the turmeric. Add the scallops, stir to mix and leave to marinate for a few moments.

Place a frying pan over a low-medium heat, pour in a little extra olive oil and heat until hot. Cook the basil leaves in the oil for about 10 seconds on each side or until they are a brighter shade of green. Remove from the pan to a plate and set aside.

Heat the same frying pan over a high heat until hot, then reduce to a medium-high heat. Place the scallops in the hot pan and cook for about 1–2 minutes on each side or until they are firm to touch.

Place the scallops on their shells, or onto a plate, and drizzle with some extra spicy chilli oil. Garnish each scallop with a basil leaf and $\frac{1}{2}$ teaspoon of the red caviar, and serve. (If you are not using red caviar, you will need to season the scallops with a pinch of rock salt, prior to serving.)

Serve with the lime wedges and buttered bread and salad, if desired.

One serving = 80%+ RDA antioxidants

Antibacterial
basil, chilli, turmeric

Antifungal
chilli, turmeric

Antiviral
basil, turmeric

Anti-inflammatory
basil, chilli, turmeric

Analgesic
chilli

Chickpea Mousse

Serves 3–4

We should never judge a book by its cover, and this recipe is a prime example of those pearls of wisdom – it's an authentic Indian adaptation of the Arabic hummus. Just like biryani, which originates from Persia, India also has its own recipe for hummus. Naturally, our adaptation uses ingredients that are indigenous to the subcontinent, so there is no tahini or parsley; instead, they are replaced with sesame oil and fresh coriander. And, consequently, our velvety Chickpea Mousse has a distinctly uplifting flavour that is at the same time bursting full of the titillating aromas of fresh coriander and chilli.

It's chock-a-block full of protein, calcium and minerals, including zinc, which helps regulate the body's metabolic rate and wound-healing. Serve as either a dip or spread, or as a balanced main meal with plenty of vegetable sticks and fresh naan or bread.

2 x 400g cans chickpeas, rinsed and drained
2 garlic cloves, peeled
1 green chilli
juice of 1 large lemon
50ml low-fat Greek yogurt
2 tablespoons olive oil
1 tablespoon sesame oil
$3/4$ teaspoon salt, or to taste
1 teaspoon freshly ground black pepper
a large handful of fresh coriander leaves

Place all the ingredients in a food processor and blend until a smooth, airy and light, mousse-like texture is attained.

Serve with naan or any other fresh bread and vegetable sticks.

Store in an airtight container in the refrigerator for up to 3 days.

One serving = 45%+ RDA antioxidants

Antibacterial
chilli, coriander, garlic, pepper

Antifungal
chilli, coriander, garlic

Antiviral
garlic

Anti-inflammatory
chilli, coriander, garlic

Analgesic
chilli

Lamb Kofta Kebabs with Cashews

Serves 4–6

These koftas are the smaller and rounder cousins of the seekh kebab, and are the ones most preferred by Indians as hors d'oeuvres. Quite possibly they are favoured by virtue of being petit and, therefore, helping Indians to keep their meat-eating under a firm discipline, as prescribed by Ayurveda. They are also easier to prepare when compared to their longer cousins.

All throughout my childhood, and up until recently, I cannot remember a wedding reception without these being served alongside flowing Patiala Peg shots of whisky or white rum. In fact, if these kebabs were not presented at a wedding reception, I would be thoroughly disappointed. My wedding was kebab-free and now I am liberated of my wife, too.

To counterbalance the 'unhealthy' image of meat kebabs, I include in this recipe a generous helping of cashew nuts which contain phytosterols that prevent the accumulation of fats in artery walls, reduce cholesterol and dilate blood vessels, therefore, reducing blood pressure and the possibility of heart complaints and stroke. All very good news if you want to stay fit for your special day.

Serve these meaty treats with Mint Raita and a salad, if you like. And, if you want to make a meal of them, they can be stuffed into pittas or served with pilau.

50g unsalted cashews
1 small onion, cut into quarters
4 garlic cloves, peeled
4 tablespoons tandoori masala powder
3 teaspoons cumin seeds
2 teaspoons ground ginger (optional)
2–12 green chillies, chopped (optional)
40g bunch of fresh coriander, coarsely
    chopped
1 large egg
salt, to taste
500g minced lamb
olive oil, for greasing

salad and Mint Raita (see page 151), to
    serve

Preheat the oven to 200°C/fan 180°C/ Gas Mark 6. Place the cashews in a food processor and blend until they resemble breadcrumbs. Add the onion, garlic, tandoori masala powder, cumin seeds, ginger, chillies, chopped coriander, egg and salt and blitz until you have a thick paste.

Add the minced lamb and blitz so that the meat passes completely through the blade three times and is thoroughly combined.

Divide the meat mixture into 20 equal portions. Shape each portion into a small round ball, then flatten into a disc. Place the koftas on an oiled baking tray. Bake at the top of the oven for 15 minutes, turning over once halfway through.

Serve with salad and Mint Raita.

One serving = 65%+ RDA antioxidants

Antibacterial
chilli, coriander, cumin, garlic, ginger

Antifungal
chilli, coriander, cumin, garlic, ginger

Antiviral
garlic

Anti-inflammatory
chilli, coriander, cumin, garlic, ginger

Analgesic
chilli

Oyster Pakoras with Punch and Gusto Fresh Coriander Salsa

Serves 2–4

Profoundly inspired by an air of simplicity from the Japanese kitchen, these pakoras skilfully match the right amount of spice to complement the tantalising and fresh ocean flavours of the oysters, without overwhelming them.

For me, they are little morsels of utopia. And, if you're new to oysters, this is definitely the way to go before trying them raw. Their little pakora batter jumpsuits just make them so much more appealing than when they are naked, for beauty is in the eye of the beholder.

Naturally, and as you might expect, oysters aren't celebrated as a superfood without justification – they are, in fact, nature's highest source of zinc, which is essential for the body's immune function and wound-healing capacity.

1 onion, cut into quarters
4 garlic cloves, peeled
1 green chilli
7 tablespoons gram flour
$3/4$ teaspoon salt
1 teaspoon garam masala
12 oysters 'shucked' and on the half shell
olive oil or vegetable oil, for shallow frying

6 teaspoons Punch and Gusto Fresh Coriander Salsa (see page 149), a few lemon wedges and chopped fresh dill, to serve

First, you will need to prepare the pakora batter. To do this, place the onion, garlic, chilli, gram flour, salt, garam masala and 3 tablespoons cold water into a food processor and blend until you have a batter that resembles a 'runny' porridge mixture – to get the right consistency you may need to add a little more cold water or gram flour.

Pour the batter into a bowl. Mix the oysters into the batter, making sure they are thoroughly coated.

Pour enough oil into a deep saucepan so that the oil is at least 3cm deep, then heat over a high heat until the oil is almost smoking.

Take the oysters out of the batter individually, shaking off any excess batter mix (discard any leftover batter). Fry in the hot oil for 15–20 seconds or until the oysters are golden brown all over – you may need to turn them over in the oil. Remove with a spatula and drain on kitchen paper.

Serve the oyster pakoras immediately on their shells, each with a $1/2$ teaspoon dollop of the coriander salsa, a squeeze of lemon and a pinch of chopped dill.

These are best served on their own.

One serving = 35%+ RDA antioxidants

Antibacterial
chilli, coriander, dill, garlic

Antifungal
chilli, coriander, dill, garlic

Antiviral
garlic

Anti-inflammatory
chilli, coriander, dill, garlic

Analgesic
chilli

" Under test conditions, dill extract exhibited antibacterial activity against a panel of rapidly growing mycobacteria known to cause tuberculosis and leprosy."

University of London[14]

Indian Superfood

Roasted Masala Almonds

Serves 12+

For as long as I can remember, Mum has always roasted almonds with her own spice mixture, turning the nourishing kernels into something spectacular. She used to try to keep them hidden from Dad, who, if given the chance, would devour them in an instant. Mum failed dismally.

A few high protein almonds are a great way to fill up in-between meals. Or serve to guests with pre-dinner cocktails.

300g whole natural (unblanched) almonds
1 teaspoon garam masala
$1/2$ teaspoon each paprika, dried red chilli flakes and freshly ground black pepper
1 heaped teaspoon rock salt
2 tablespoons Spicy Chilli Oil (see page 147)

Preheat the oven to 210°C/fan 190°C/ Gas Mark $6^{1}/_{2}$. Place the almonds onto a baking tray. Bake in the centre of the oven for 7 minutes or until the almonds have developed a fragrant aroma.

In the meantime, in a large bowl, mix together the garam masala, paprika, chilli flakes, black pepper, rock salt and Spicy Chilli Oil.

When the almonds have finished baking, add them to the spice mixture and mix until thoroughly combined. Set aside to cool before serving.

Store in an airtight container for up to 7 days.

One serving = 40%+ RDA antioxidants

Antibacterial
cardamom, chilli, cinnamon, cloves, cumin, garlic, mustard, paprika, pepper

Antifungal
cardamom, chilli, cinnamon, cloves, cumin, garlic, mustard, paprika

Antiviral
cinnamon, cloves, garlic

Anti-inflammatory
cardamom, chilli, cinnamon, cloves, cumin, garlic, mustard, paprika

Analgesic
chilli, cloves, paprika

Sweet Potato and Pea Fritters

Serves 4+

I'm not a huge fan of potatoes, and consequently I'd never been a devotee of the aloo tikki either. That was until I used sweet potato in the recipe. It was as if an Indian fairy had transformed, with a wave of her wands, the aloo tikki into something stupendously good. The natural sugariness of the sweet potato draws out the flavours of the superspices more so than regular potato.

These fritters have an irresistibly crispy and almost caramelised exterior which contrasts wonderfully with the rich, 'creamy' and spicy core. I once served them at a dinner party in London, overlooking St. Paul's Cathedral, to dinner guests who had requested minimal use of spicing; and much to my surprise these highly-seasoned nibbles were gobbled down within seconds!

If you need justification to indulge in starchy foods, I will have you know that sweet potato will help keep your tummy feeling fuller for longer by stabilising blood sugar levels and, also, caraway has long been recognised as an appetite suppressant.

Serve as pre-dinner canapés with drinks or as a light meal with raita and salad. If you like, the Punch and Gusto Fresh Coriander Salsa can be substituted for sweet chilli sauce.

500g sweet potatoes, peeled and cut into large bite-size pieces
1 tablespoon olive oil, plus extra for frying
2 teaspoons cumin seeds
1 teaspoon caraway seeds
1 tablespoon ground coriander
1 teaspoon each turmeric and chilli powder

200g fresh or frozen petit pois, defrosted if necessary
3/4 teaspoon salt
3 tablespoons gram flour
40g dried breadcrumbs
2 tablespoons grated (peeled) fresh root ginger
3 spring onions, finely chopped
20g bunch of fresh coriander, chopped
1 egg yolk

Punch and Gusto Fresh Coriander Salsa (see page 149), to serve

Cook the sweet potatoes in a deep pan of boiling water for approximately 15 minutes or until tender. Drain, then rinse the sweet potatoes under cold running water until cool and drain again. Place in a mixing bowl and set aside. (To minimise the loss of nutrients, the sweet potatoes may be steamed or cooked in the microwave, instead of boiling.)

Pour 1 tablespoon olive oil into a deep saucepan, add the cumin and caraway seeds and cook over a medium heat until the seeds begin to pop – this will take no longer than 2–3 minutes. Remove the pan from the heat and immediately add the ground coriander, turmeric and chilli powder. Mix well.

Add the cooked sweet potatoes and petit pois to the spice mixture and mash well. Mix through the salt, gram flour, breadcrumbs, ginger, spring onions, chopped coriander and egg yolk until thoroughly combined.

Divide the mixture into 16 equal portions. Shape each portion into a small round patty.

Heat some extra olive oil in a frying pan over a medium heat. Cook the patties in the hot oil until they are golden brown, turning once – this should take about 2–3 minutes for each side.

Remove with a spatula and drain well on kitchen paper. Serve with the coriander salsa.

One serving = 205%+ RDA antioxidants

Antibacterial
chilli, coriander, cumin, ginger, turmeric

Antifungal
chilli, coriander, cumin, ginger, turmeric

Antiviral
turmeric

Anti-inflammatory
chilli, coriander, cumin, ginger, turmeric

Analgesic
caraway, chilli

Cocktails and Refreshments

A friend of mine commented that this chapter of the book is a rather novel way of getting your 5-a-day, and she is absolutely right. Although I would say it is more of a fun way to bolster vitamins and nutrients in your diet. With *Indian Superfood*, at last, we are given an option to take in extra nutrients, whilst washing away the worries of the day by means of a cooling beverage. An added benefit, to something that is already so very good.

You will find alcoholic and non-alcoholic beverages aplenty. From the Pomegranate Summer Cooler to the Mango and Blueberry Smoothie Lassi or Spiced Green Tea, there is no thirst that will remain unquenched. It really is this simple. On a more serious note, alcohol is most definitely an occasional indulgence and should be used sparingly.

Mango and Blueberry Lassi Smoothie

Serves 2

Mangoes hail from the tropics and blueberries from more temperate climes. In the not-too-distant past, sheer distance reduced their chances of a liquefaction, to the minimum – that's until now. Thanks to globalisation, all this has changed and their commingling is now possible.

Nothing quite compares to the extreme refreshment and antioxidising goodies of raw mango and blueberries blended with natural yogurt and ice. These two fruits were made for one another. Try it at breakfast time, for an energising launch to the day.

175g prepared mango flesh, diced
100g blueberries
200ml natural yogurt
a large handful of ice, plus extra to serve
sugar, to taste

Put all the ingredients into a blender and blend together until smooth.

Place the extra ice in tall glasses and pour in the lassi smoothie. Serve immediately.

**One serving =
110%+ RDA
antioxidants**

Mango and Ginger Lassi Smoothie

Serves 2

Ever wondered what to drink with an Indian meal? Well, this could well be the inamorato.

Mango contains the enzymes mangiferin and lactase, which aid digestion and intestinal health. Raw ginger and natural yogurt further amplify the digestive effect and, when liquefied with the ice, also refresh the palate – an ideal accompaniment to a spicy meal.

175g prepared mango flesh, diced
1 teaspoon finely grated (peeled) fresh root ginger
300ml natural yogurt
a large handful of ice, plus extra to serve
sugar, to taste

Put all the ingredients into a blender and blend together until smooth.

Place the extra ice in tall glasses and pour in the lassi smoothie. Serve immediately.

**One serving =
30%+ RDA
antioxidants**

Antibacterial
ginger

Antifungal
ginger

Anti-inflammatory
ginger

Strawberry and Mint Lassi

Serves 2–3

My fresh Strawberry and Mint Lassi captures the very essence of the English summertime. Nothing could purport to be as English as this Anglo-Indian lassi. In-between the crushed ice, darting around like tennis balls at a microscopic Wimbledon Tournament, are anthocyanins bursting with sheer enthusiasm just to get into our body and protect us from the signs of ageing – all very good if we have happened to be out in the sun. Mint, yogurt and ice work collectively as a trilogy of coolants.

Keep this flawless thirst-quencher for long, hot afternoons.

250g strawberries, hulled
a few fresh mint leaves, plus extra to decorate
200ml natural yogurt
a large handful of ice, plus extra to serve
sugar, to taste

Put all the ingredients into a blender and blend together until smooth.

Place the extra ice in tall glasses and pour in the lassi smoothie.

Decorate each serving with an extra mint leaf and serve immediately.

**One serving =
120%+ RDA
antioxidants**

Antibacterial
mint

Antifungal
mint

Indian Superfood

Pomegranate Summer Cooler

Mango Cocktail

Serves 1

Serves 1

Fragrant pomegranate, chai spices and mint jostle together to gently refresh and seduce the taste buds. Each sip can be likened to being taken out on a warm night, in a shikara, for a dip in the middle of a serene lake. If there was one drink from paradise, this would be it.

This smooth cocktail is a real crowd-pleaser. It's ideal for sipping poolside or in the company of friends, with some light bites. In some parts of the world, mango is also taken as a supplement for sexual potency – so, go easy on your guests.

ice
a few fresh mint leaves
25ml Chai Vodka (see page 176)
15ml Cointreau
chilled fresh pomegranate juice drink, to taste
1 cinnamon stick

25ml vodka
150ml mango pulp/purée
15ml Cointreau
15ml lime juice
8 fresh mint leaves
ice

Place a tall glass in the refrigerator to chill.

Half-fill a tall glass with ice and sprinkle over a few leaves of mint. Pour in the chai vodka and Cointreau. Top up with pomegranate juice drink.

Pour the vodka, mango pulp, Cointreau and lime juice into a cocktail shaker and add 7 of the mint leaves with some ice. Shake for 30 seconds.

Decorate with the cinnamon stick and serve.

Place plenty of extra ice in the chilled glass and pour in the cocktail, without straining. Garnish with the remaining mint leaf and serve immediately.

Antibacterial
cardamom, cinnamon, cloves, mint

Antibacterial
mint

Antifungal
cardamom, cinnamon, cloves, mint

Antifungal
mint

Antiviral
cinnamon, cloves

Anti-inflammatory
cardamom, cinnamon, cloves

Analgesic
cloves

Strawberry and Mint Lassi, page 172

Mango Cocktail, page 173

Indian Superfood

Pomegranate Summer Cooler, page 173

Spiced Green Tea (Kahwa), page 177

Cocktails and Refreshments

Chai Spice-Infused Bloody Mary

Chai Vodka

Serves 1

Chai spices lift the traditional Bloody Mary to dizzying heights, giving it a potent pick-me-up quality, not normally associated with it.

a large handful of ice
25ml 'Chai Vodka' (see right)
125ml tomato juice or V8 juice
Worcestershire sauce, to taste
Tabasco sauce, to taste
salt and white pepper (or freshly ground black pepper), to taste

peeled mooli, cut into a long thin baton, to garnish

Place the ice in a tall glass and top with the chai vodka. Pour in the tomato juice and a good glug of both the Worcestershire and Tabasco sauces.

Sprinkle over salt and pepper to taste. Garnish with the baton of mooli and serve.

Antibacterial
cardamom, cinnamon, cloves

Antifungal
cardamom, cinnamon, cloves

Antiviral
cinnamon, cloves

Anti-inflammatory
cardamom, cinnamon, cloves

Analgesic
cloves

Makes 700ml

Superspices add an exotic hustle and bustle to vodka. One sip and you're transported to a busy Indian bazaar with its heady waft of agarbatti and chai. Use in place of regular vodka to spice up your drinks.

700ml good quality vodka
2 cinnamon sticks
20 green cardamom pods, lightly crushed
10 cloves

Pour the vodka into a clean 1 litre glass bottle or jar. Add in all the spices and seal or close the bottle or jar. Place in a cool, dark place overnight.

The next day, strain the infused vodka back into its original bottle, seal and use as and when required.

Antibacterial
cardamom, cinnamon, cloves

Antifungal
cardamom, cinnamon, cloves

Antiviral
cinnamon, cloves

Anti-inflammatory
cardamom, cinnamon, cloves

Analgesic
cloves

Spiced Green Tea (Kahwa)

Makes 3 mugfuls

Kahwa is by far my favourite way to enjoy tea and is my hot drink of choice. It's nothing at all like how we have come to expect green tea to taste. Flavoured deeply by an ambrosial combination of warming superspices and honey, it has an unmistakable and most pleasurable taste that words alone cannot describe.

Kahwa originates from the Kashmir province at the foot-hills of the Himalayan mountain range in India, where the people share a common culinary tradition with both Central Asia and India. Hence, it's one of the very few regions in the subcontinent where you'll find the use of green tea regularly.

Evidently, India has lent her indelibly exotic feel to kahwa, with the addition of superspices. This region has some of the coldest winters known to India's over 1 billion inhabitants, and is one of the very few places in the country where you will find snowfall. Inherently, it would be safe to assume that the Kashmiri people may best know how to deal with colds and flu. And they recommend steaming cups full of kahwa, first thing in the morning. It does help to soothe a sore throat and to relieve a cough.

This marvellous recipe was kindly shared with me by my dearest friend, Muz. It is quite possibly the healthiest and most delectable cup of tea to ever pass through my lips.

1 green tea bag
1 cinnamon stick
2 green cardamom pods, lightly crushed
a large pinch of ground ginger
a pinch of saffron
5 tablespoons honey (you can use less, as per your taste)

flaked almonds, to decorate

Place the green tea bag, cinnamon stick, cardamom pods, ground ginger, saffron and honey in a saucepan. Now add 3 mugfuls of cold water to the pan, and bring to the boil. Reduce to a low heat, then cover and simmer gently for 10 minutes.

Remove the pan from the heat and pour the tea into mugs. Decorate each mugful with a generous sprinkle of flaked almonds. Serve.

Cook's Tip
For a light breakfast, Kahwa may be served with Dried Fruit and Nut Balls (see page 189).

One serving = 150%+ RDA antioxidants

Antibacterial
cardamom, cinnamon, ginger, saffron

Antifungal
cardamom, cinnamon, ginger, saffron

Antiviral
cinnamon

Anti-inflammatory
cardamom, cinnamon, ginger, saffron

Indian Christmas Spicy Mulled Wine

Serves 10+

I first fell head-over-heels for mulled wine on a trip to Heidelberg in Germany, where I had it with friends at the local Christmas market. A few sips and my cold and flu symptoms seemed to 'magically' dissipate with the steam rising from my cup. I for one cannot think of a more festive drink. One mouthful and I am away with the fairies in snowy Heidelberg.

My version uses Indian superspices to give the traditional drink additional warmth. Make it in the days running up to Christmas, and serve steaming cupfuls to guests on the wintry nights and watch the cold melt away from them. They will adore you for it.

1.5 litres red wine
125ml orange juice
215g sugar
3 strips of orange rind
2 strips of lemon rind
4cm x 3cm piece of fresh root ginger, peeled
10 green cardamom pods, lightly crushed
5 cloves
2 cinnamon sticks
4 star anise
1 teaspoon coriander seeds

toasted flaked almonds, to decorate

Place all the ingredients, except the almonds, in a saucepan and heat over a low heat until the wine begins to bubble. Keep heating, uncovered, over a very low heat for 20 minutes, so that the mixture is barely simmering. Do not allow the mixture to simmer properly or boil as this will eliminate the alcohol from the wine.

Remove the pan from the heat and let it stand, covered, overnight in a cool place.

Strain into clean wine bottles and seal with corks. Serve immediately or store until required – it should keep for up to 1 month, stored in a cool, dark place.

To serve, reheat gently and pour in cups; decorate with the flaked almonds. When reheating, be careful not to simmer or boil the mulled wine. I usually heat each cupful of wine in the microwave oven for about 1 minute on HIGH.

Antibacterial
cardamom, cinnamon, cloves, coriander, ginger, star anise

Antifungal
cardamom, cinnamon, cloves, coriander, ginger

Antiviral
cinnamon, cloves

Anti-inflammatory
cardamom, cinnamon, cloves, coriander, ginger

Analgesic
cloves

Bedtime Milk Toddy

Makes 2 mugfuls

Sometimes when I can't sleep, I find a warm glass of milk works a treat by sending me into a blissful slumber. Superspices make milk that little bit more appetising and soothing.

550ml semi-skimmed milk
a couple of drops of vanilla extract
1/2 cinnamon stick
2 green cardamom pods, lightly crushed
sugar, to taste

Pour the milk into a saucepan, then add the vanilla extract, cinnamon stick, cardamom pods and sugar. Bring gently to the boil, then simmer gently for 10 minutes.

Remove the pan from the heat and strain the hot milk into mugs. Serve immediately.

One serving =
90%+ RDA
antioxidants

Antibacterial
cardamom,
cinnamon

Antifungal
cardamom,
cinnamon

Antiviral
cinnamon

Anti-inflammatory
cardamom,
cinnamon

"17 spice and medicinal plant extracts were examined for their antimicrobial activity against Arcobacter butzleri, A. Cryaerophilus, and A. Skirrowii. Cinnamon extract showed strong and enhanced antibacterial activity."

University of Pardubice, Czech Republic[8]

Sweets

Indian sweets are widely misunderstood, most likely because in the past we were presented with only a few complex, old-fashioned and sticky concoctions as options for dessert. *Indian Superfood* once again sets out to right a wrong; this time by simplifying classic desserts and then ingeniously interweaving the superfood twist into their very fabric, adapting them to the way we eat today.

Indian Superfood

Black Rice Pudding

Serves 2–3

Intriguingly, in this recipe, during the cooking process, the black rice turns the condensing milk a pretty pink colour, resulting in a pudding that's a matchless combination of a mystifying appearance and sublime taste. It has certainly got to be one of the world's most sophisticated rice puddings. And, if the vogue factor doesn't quite catch you, perhaps the aphrodisiac cardamom just might.

Granting that light coconut milk does contain a little fat, surprisingly its oils also simultaneously raise the body's metabolic rate and, therefore, help in burning body fat.

Just sit back, relax, fasten your seat belt and enjoy with plenty of fresh fruit.

$1/2$ tablespoon black glutinous rice (available from Oriental grocers)
$1/2$ tablespoon basmati rice
350ml semi-skimmed milk
400ml light coconut milk
2 tablespoons sugar
6 green cardamom pods, lightly crushed
20 unsalted pistachio nuts, coarsely chopped

Place all the ingredients, except the pistachio nuts, in a deep, heavy-based saucepan and cook over a medium heat until the milk starts to boil. Reduce to a low heat and cook, uncovered, for 1 hour or until a light custard-like consistency is attained, stirring frequently to avoid sticking.

Remove the pan from the heat. Using a spoon, remove and discard the cardamom pods. Mix through the pistachio nuts, then allow the black rice pudding to cool.

Once cool, refrigerate the pudding until chilled – the rice pudding will continue to thicken whilst chilling.

Serve with fresh fruit.

One serving =
25%+ RDA
antioxidants

Antibacterial
cardamom

Antifungal
cardamom

Anti-inflammatory
cardamom

Indian Devil's Chocolate Pot

Serves 6

If you haven't yet had an opportunity to experience dark chocolate with the distinct and sensual inclusion of cardamom, chilli and coffee, you haven't been in this world for long at all. The light and frothy chocolate 'cappuccino' top, leads into a deep swamp of luxurious, dark and spicy chocolate that commands your unrequited submission.

This is, beyond any reasonable doubt, an utterly 'wicked' dessert recipe, designed with chocoholics in mind. It is, therefore, condemned to the back of this book – chocolate fiends, you have been warned.

On a lighter note, our little 'devils' contain loads of cocoa antioxidants, beneficial for cardiovascular health, and no cream is added. Rich dark chocolate also means we are satisfied with the smaller portions.

170g Bournville dark chocolate, broken into bite-size pieces
1 teaspoon instant coffee powder
1/3 teaspoon green cardamom powder (see Cook's Tip on page 190)
a pinch of chilli powder
2 egg yolks
160ml semi-skimmed milk

Place the chocolate, instant coffee and cardamom and chilli powders in a food processor and blitz until the chocolate resembles fine crumbs. Pour in the egg yolks and blend until combined. Set aside.

Gently heat the milk in a saucepan to boiling point, then pour it into the food processor and blend until smooth.

Pour the chocolate mixture into 6 small shot glasses. Refrigerate for 6 hours before serving.

One serving = 160%+ RDA antioxidants

Antibacterial
cardamom, chilli

Antifungal
cardamom, chilli

Anti-inflammatory
cardamom

Analgesic
chilli

Carrot Cake Kulfi

Serves 3–4

My Carrot Cake Kulfi is India's world-class challenge to the French-led trend in barmy, flavoured ice creams, and is the majestically rich and creamy 'Maharajah of the kulfi world'. I first made it for the Mövenpick Hotel, Istanbul; those people sure know a thing or two about how a good 'ice cream' should taste – and they liked it.

If you can imagine a flourless carrot cake blended into a Swiss ice cream, you will be able to daydream just how good this actually tastes. What I didn't get around to was telling the Mövenpick crowd about how this kulfi soothes a sore throat with its potent cooling and antibacterial properties.

2 carrots, grated
$1/4$ teaspoon green cardamom powder (see Cook's Tip on page 190)
1 tablespoon olive oil
405g can light condensed milk
330ml low-fat Greek yogurt

Place the carrots, green cardamom powder and olive oil in a small saucepan and cook over a low heat for 5-10 minutes, stirring frequently, until the carrots are soft. Remove the pan from the heat and allow the mixture to cool.

Pour the condensed milk into a small bowl and add the cooked carrot mixture. With a hand-held blender, blitz the mixture until the carrots are an almost puréed texture.

Now pour in the yogurt, folding it through the carrot mixture.

Pour this mixture into a wide, shallow freezerproof container. Freeze for about $1^{1}/_{2}$ hours or until slushy and starting to freeze.

Remove the mixture from the freezer. Tip it into a chilled bowl and whisk to remove any ice crystals.

Return the mixture to the container and freeze for another 2 hours or until frozen. Serve in scoops.

One serving =
12%+ RDA
antioxidants

Antibacterial
cardamom

Antifungal
cardamom

Anti-inflammatory
cardamom

Indian Superfood

Passion Fruit and Ginger Kulfi

Serves 3–4

Intensely sweet and sour, this kulfi is seemingly loved by all. Passion fruit adds unabashed refreshment and ginger settles the tummy.

2 passion fruits, cut in half, pulp and seeds scooped out
1 teaspoon ground ginger
330ml low-fat Greek yogurt
405g can light condensed milk

Thoroughly combine all the ingredients in a large bowl.

Pour this mixture into a wide, shallow freezerproof container. Freeze for about 1$\frac{1}{2}$ hours or until slushy and starting to freeze.

Remove the mixture from the freezer. Tip it into a chilled bowl and whisk to remove any ice crystals.

Return the mixture to the container and freeze for another 2 hours or until frozen. Serve in scoops.

One serving = 15%+ RDA antioxidants

Antibacterial ginger

Antifungal ginger

Anti-inflammatory ginger

Peppermint and Seaweed Kulfi

Serves 3–4

This kulfi is all about extreme refreshment; one you can get possibly only by surfing down the side of a snowy mountain and into a glacial stream, or by, more agreeably, hurdling your tongue into this kulfi. It's a combination which, at first, seems peculiar, but on second glance appears to be quite sensible.

2 drops of peppermint oil
1 tablespoon sea salad (available from health-food shops)
330ml low-fat Greek yogurt
405g can light condensed milk

Thoroughly combine all the ingredients in a large bowl. Pour this mixture into a wide, shallow freezerproof container. Freeze for about $1\frac{1}{2}$ hours or until slushy and starting to freeze.

Remove the mixture from the freezer. Tip it into a chilled bowl and whisk to remove any ice crystals.

Return the mixture to the container and freeze for another 2 hours or until frozen. Serve in scoops.

One serving =
7%+ RDA antioxidants

Antibacterial mint

Antifungal mint

" The inhibitory effect of 30 plant oils was evaluated against a strain of Candida. Eucalyptus and peppermint tested to be most active. The substantial antifungal activity shown by these plant oils suggests their potential against infections caused by Candida."

Motilal Nehru National Institute of Technology, Allahabad, India[15]

Dried Fruit and Nut Balls

Serves 4

Inspired by a profound desire to make Indian sweets healthier, here we have the next generation of mithai for India's fitness fanatical X-Factor youth. It is a high-energy-all-day treat that's comparable in taste to classical sweets, whilst simultaneously being pressurised with vitamin C and antioxidants, as well as bereft of added sugars and bad fats.

Unquestionably, my Dried Fruit and Nut Balls are the healthiest remake of Indian sweets, to date. Best of all, they can be ready to eat within a moment's flurry of a food processor blade.

The raw food movement is coming to India. I have a feeling this is the start of something special. You can also try them as part of a breakfast-on-the-run.

75g unsalted cashews
$1/4$ teaspoon ground ginger or ground cinnamon, as per your taste
85g pitted dried dates, chopped
50g dried cranberries
30g dried goji berries
sesame seeds, for coating

Place the cashews and ground ginger or cinnamon in a food processor and blitz until the nuts resemble breadcrumbs.

Add the dried fruits to the food processor and process until the mixture resembles a paste. You may need to add a few drops of cold water to get the right consistency. Start with 15ml cold water, working up to about 50ml, if necessary.

Divide the mixture into 4 equal portions, and, using the palms of your hands, shape each portion into a ball. Roll the balls in the sesame seeds to coat all over. Cover each ball with cling film and chill before serving.

These will keep for up to 3 days in the refrigerator.

One serving =
105%+ RDA
antioxidants

Antibacterial
cinnamon, ginger

Antifungal
cinnamon, ginger

Antiviral
cinnamon

Anti-inflammatory
cinnamon, ginger

Carrot Lamingtons

Makes 18

In India, we have the gajar ka halwa, a wintertime dessert of grated carrots candied with sugar and superspices and typically served smouldering hot. It's even delivered to schoolchildren in tiffin boxes prepared by their doting mothers.

Australia is where you will find cubes of sponge cake dipped in chocolate and coconut – known locally as lamingtons. Having reached iconic levels, they can be found up and down the vast continent of Australia, hidden deep inside children's lunchboxes and savoured as the apex of their lunchtime haute cuisine.

In this recipe, we bring the two unlikely counterparts together. Grated carrots, which are nature's richest source of vitamin A and protect against blindness, are first caramelised with antibacterial superspices and then rolled in antioxidising chocolate and coconut. This is a gluten-free fairyland.

Try them with fresh fruit and ice cream, or by themselves with just a cuppa or, if you really want to, out of a lunchbox at 'school'. You can keep them refrigerated for up to a week.

2 teaspoons ground ginger
2 teaspoons green cardamom powder
   (see Cook's Tip)
50ml olive oil
1kg carrots, grated
250g sugar
150ml double cream
200g dark chocolate, broken into small
   chunks
plenty of desiccated coconut, sprinkled
   onto a wide plate

Sprinkle the ginger and green cardamom powder into a deep saucepan. Pour in the olive oil and cook over a medium heat until the oil is hot. Add the grated carrots and sugar and mix well. Cook until the mixture begins to simmer.

Reduce to a very low simmer and cook until the moisture is evaporated and the mixture starts to stick to the bottom of the saucepan. This process takes no more than 35 minutes and you must remember to stir frequently.

Slowly pour in the cream, stirring all the time, and continue to cook until it is absorbed – this should take no more than 5 minutes. Take the pan off the heat and allow the mixture to cool to room temperature.

Divide the carrot mixture into 18 equal portions, and, using the palms of your hands, roll each portion into a small ball. Place these balls on a small tray or large plate, put them into the freezer and chill for about 1–2 hours or until almost frozen.

Melt the chocolate in a small heatproof bowl placed over a pan of gently simmering hot water, stirring frequently. Remove the carrot balls from the freezer, roll them off the tray carefully, and, using a teaspoon, roll each one into the melted chocolate and then into the desiccated coconut.

Place the chocolate-and-coconut-coated balls onto a wire rack, and repeat the process until finished. Allow them to cool for 10 minutes, then refrigerate for 30 minutes before serving.

Cook's Tip
Green cardamom powder can be acquired by crushing whole green cardamom pods with a pestle and mortar, and discarding the husks. Alternatively, you may blend the whole cardamom pods in a coffee grinder.

One serving =
75%+ RDA
antioxidants

Antibacterial
cardamom, ginger

Antifungal
cardamom, ginger

Anti-inflammatory
cardamom, ginger

Indian Spotted Dick with Goji Berries and Toasted Almonds

Serves 4

Probably one of the cinchiest puddings you'll ever prepare, it's also incredibly suave in appearance and, needless to say, healthy; and therefore delivers effortlessly, with cannons firing on all levels - this one's a knockout alright.

Goji berries contain up to 500 times more vitamin C than oranges and, paired up with saffron's anti-ageing antioxidants, there is little more to want here.

Serve it immediately and warm for the spotted dick feel. If you prefer something that's more Indian in taste, prepare and let it rest in the refrigerator for a few hours. The raisin bread will soak up much of the coconut milk sauce, eventuating in a moist, chilled pudding, very similar in taste to the classic Indian dessert, ras malai.

4 teaspoons sugar
400ml light coconut milk
4 green cardamom pods, lightly crushed
a pinch of saffron
2 tablespoons dried goji berries
4 slices of raisin/fruit bread

a handful of toasted flaked almonds and extra dried goji berries, to decorate

Place the sugar, coconut milk, cardamom pods, saffron and goji berries in a saucepan and bring to the boil. Reduce the heat and simmer rapidly, uncovered, for 8 minutes. Remove the pan from the heat, then remove the cardamom pods using a slotted spoon and discard.

Cut away the crusts from the slices of raisin bread and discard. Lightly toast the bread. Place 1 slice of the toasted raisin bread in each serving bowl and pour some of the warm coconut milk sauce over each slice, dividing it evenly.

Decorate with the flaked almonds and extra goji berries. Serve immediately, or cool and chill before serving.

One serving =
50%+ RDA
antioxidants

Antibacterial
cardamom, saffron

Antifungal
cardamom, saffron

Anti-inflammatory
cardamom, saffron

Indian Ocean Sorbet

Serves 3–4

There isn't any more of a refreshing way to finish an Indian meal off, than with an icy sorbet. With just a mouthful, I find myself daydreaming of sitting on a sandy white beach in the Spice Islands looking out towards a tranquil sea. The sun is bursting full like an overripe mango and gently caressing my face with its loving warmth. A cool breeze is as scintillating as a freshly squeezed lemon. The sorbet melts on my tongue in the same way the mango melts into the sorbet. It sounds too good to be true. But, it isn't all just a dream.

An abundance of fruits means the sorbet counts towards your 5-a-day. And, there's no cooking or straining required. So, sit back, relax and enjoy a slice of paradise.

75g caster sugar
100ml ginger beer
400g frozen mango chunks
2 tablespoons Chai Vodka
    (see page 176)
juice of 4 lemons
1 passion fruit, cut in half, pulp and
    seeds scooped out

In a small bowl, mix together the sugar and ginger beer, stirring until the sugar has dissolved.

Pour the ginger beer-and-sugar mixture into a blender, then add the frozen mango, chai vodka and lemon juice. Blitz until smooth.

Transfer to a shallow, freezerproof container and freeze for a few hours prior to serving (due to the alcohol content, the sorbet won't freeze solid).

Serve in scoops, decorated with the passion fruit pulp and seeds.

One serving =
55%+ RDA
antioxidants

Antibacterial
cardamom,
cinnamon,
cloves, ginger

Antifungal
cardamom,
cinnamon,
cloves, ginger

Antiviral
cinnamon,
cloves, ginger

Anti-inflammatory
cardamom,
cinnamon,
cloves, ginger

Analgesic
cloves

Superfoods Directory

This chapter of the book serves as an invaluable alphabetical directory to all of the superfoods used in the recipes. All the foods listed in it are recognised for their exceptional nutritional value by science or Ayurveda, and quite often by both. It is here that you will find information relating to their health benefits.

A

Acai Berry *(see also* **Berries***)*
This little berry from the Amazon can be found in health-food shops in the form of juice. It contains high levels of the cholesterol-fighting omega-6 and omega-9 fatty acids, and an extraordinary concentration of cancer-fighting antioxidants known as anthocyanins – up to 30 times more than red wine. Acai berries are widely regarded to contain the optimal nutritional value of any fruit.

Apple
Like many other fruits, apples contain vitamin C and a host of antioxidant compounds, in particular quercetin, which is linked with the prevention of cancer and helps protect the brain from neuro-degenerative diseases like Alzheimer's and Parkinson's. Apples also aid with weight loss because they are high in fibre and make for a filling snack. Fibre reduces cholesterol by preventing its re-absorption into the body and, therefore, an apple could help prevent heart disease. Also, biting into an apple can help remove food trapped between the teeth.

Apple Gourd *(see* **Pumpkin***)*

Apricot
Packed full of vitamin A, apricots help protect the eyes, and guard against heart disease. They contain high amounts of beta-carotene, one of nature's most powerful antioxidants, that has been found beneficial in preventing many types of cancer, including that of the prostate and skin.

Arugula (Rocket) *(see* **Leafy Greens***)*

Aubergine
Research has found aubergines to be effective at controlling cholesterol. They are a major source of potassium - the mineral which helps balance salt intake. Interestingly, aubergines contain the highest amount of nicotine found in any edible plant; but this amount, as such, is very negligible.

B

Banana
Bananas are an antioxidising fruit containing alpha-carotene and beta-carotene, both of which are being investigated for their role in cancer prevention. Bananas are loaded with vitamins, minerals, potassium and magnesium that helps protect the circulatory system. Almost a complete meal in themselves, bananas can prevent radical swings in blood sugar levels.

Basil *(see* **page 202***)*

Basmati Rice
This is a super source of nutrition and carbohydrate energy, which helps regulate blood sugar levels, keeping the tummy feeling fuller for longer. For all these reasons, it is considered to be the healthiest white rice. Basmati rice is traditionally grown at the foothills of the Himalayas, and has the world's longest grain amongst various rice crops. It is prized for its delicate and fragrant aroma. In India, it's known as the 'prince of rice'.

Beans *(for* **Soy Beans***, see* **Soy Products***)*
All types of beans, including red kidney beans and the navy variety used to make Heinz Baked Beans are an incredibly rich source of vital nutrients. They provide us with vitamin B1 and minerals including iron, folic acid, zinc and potassium. Beans are a good source of fibre, which helps lower high blood sugar levels and regulate cholesterol levels. Interestingly, 3 tablespoons of beans, including the Heinz variety, count for a maximum of one of five portions of fruit and vegetables that we should aim to eat daily. They are also a low-fat alternative to meat protein. Beans contain the feel-good amino acid, tryptophan, and are linked to a reduction in the risk of heart disease.

Bean Sprouts *(see* **Beans***)*

Beef
Beef is rich in proteins which help the body repair itself and build muscle tissue. It is an important source of vitamin B12, which is crucial for the normal functioning of the brain and nervous system. Beef is a good source of selenium, as well as of zinc and iron, which can reduce the risk of cancer, and are essential for the body's immune function and wound-healing. Beef from grass-fed cattle contains omega-3 fatty acids, similar to those found in oily fish.

Beetroot

Beetroot is an excellent source of folate, manganese, potassium, fibre and vitamin C. It contains betaine, which is bursting full of nitrate that can lower blood pressure rapidly; drinking just 500ml of beetroot juice decreases blood pressure within 1 hour and the effect lasts for up to 24 hours. Researchers have also found that the nitrate contained in beetroot leads to a reduction in oxygen uptake, making exercise less tiring. Betaine found in beetroot also protects against liver disease caused by diabetes and alcohol abuse. Beetroot is linked with a reduction in the risk of cardiovascular diseases.

Bell Pepper (see **Peppers**)

Berries

Berries are bursting with vitamin C, folate, fibre, minerals and antioxidants known as anthocyanins, which protect us from the effects of ageing, bacterial infections, cancer, diabetes and neurological diseases. Research has found that eating berries aids memory power and promotes fat-loss.

Black Glutinous Rice

Black glutinous rice contains selenium which helps regulate blood sugar levels, stimulate the metabolism and reduce the risk of cancer. It contains no gluten and therefore is suited to a gluten-free diet. The reason why it is known as 'glutinous' is because it is sticky when cooked.

Blueberry
see **Berries**

Brinjal
see **Aubergine**

Broccoli

This is the 'king' of disease-fighting vegetables and contains vitamin C, as well as folate which reduces the risk of heart disease. Broccoli has been linked to cancer prevention and heart, stomach, eye, bone and skin health. It also acts as an antibacterial and an antifungal agent, and is rich in lutein that delays the development of macular disease. One serving of broccoli provides an impressive 175% of our daily vitamin K and 200% vitamin C requirements. Broccoli is linked with a decreased risk of aggressive prostate and bowel cancers.

C

Cabbage

A member of the cruciferous group of vegetables, which includes broccoli and cauliflower, cabbage is linked with a reduction of incidences of aggressive prostate and bowel cancers. Cabbage contains phytonutrients known as glucosinolates which eliminate free radicals by stimulating the body's own antioxidant response. Remarkably, red cabbage multitasks by containing not only glucosinolates, but also anthocyanins, which are antioxidants found most commonly in deep coloured berries and grapes; these antioxidants can prevent degenerative neurological diseases such as Alzheimer's. Cabbage is also a first-rate source of vitamin K, C and fibre.

Capsicum (see **Peppers**)

Carrot

Carrots are nature's richest known source of vitamin A, which protects against macular disease (that can lead to blindness), cardiovascular disease, stroke and cancer. The rich colour found in carrots is due to the vast amount of beta-carotene that is contained within them. Once carrots are eaten, the body converts the beta-carotene to vitamin A. They are also rich in soluble fibre, which lowers cholesterol that can block arteries. Carrots contain potassium, which lowers blood pressure, as well as folate and vitamin B6, and the antioxidants alpha-carotene, lutein and zeaxanthin.

Cashew Nut (see **Nuts**)

Cauliflower

Cauliflower is high in dietary fibre, folate and vitamin C. It contains numerous phytochemicals which are beneficial to health, including an anticancer compound that is released when it is chopped or chewed. In addition, it contains substances which improve the liver's ability to detoxify carcinogenic substances. A high intake of cauliflower can reduce the risk of aggressive prostate and bowel cancers.

Cheese

In small amounts, cheese can be beneficial to maintain a healthy body. It is rich in proteins and is a concentrated source of calcium, which is best known for maintaining the strength and density of our bones and can even prevent colon cancer, osteoporosis, migraine and PMS.

Chicken

If you want to build muscle, a diet high in protein is essential, and chicken is an excellent source. It is generally low in fat and is a good source of vitamin B3 and selenium, which are fundamental for all-round health. Chicken also contains the amino acid, tryptophan, which decreases mood swings by effecting neurotransmitters in the brain.

Chickpeas

A vegetarian alternative for meat, chickpeas are one of the best sources of plant protein, and a great source of zinc, which is essential for the body's immune function, wound-healing and regulating the body's metabolic rate. Chickpeas also contain molybdenum, a trace element that helps build and trigger enzymes involved in repairing and making genetic matter.

Chilli (see **page 203**)

Chocolate

In small doses, dark chocolate has beneficial health effects, including providing considerable amounts of antioxidants that help prevent cardiovascular diseases. Cocoa, from which chocolate is made, is rich in polyphenols that are also found in berries, grapes and tea. Eating chocolate releases endorphins in the brain which makes us 'feel good', and is also widely considered to be an aphrodisiac.

Citrus Fruits

Vitamin C is one of the most essential nutrients required by the body and absolutely vital for fighting off cold and flu symptoms. Our bodies, as such, are unable to produce vitamin C, but we can replace it by consuming citrus fruits, which are jam-packed with this crucial vitamin. Vitamin C is also needed to protect our tendons, teeth, gums, bones and blood vessels. In addition, citrus fruits also contain monoterpene, which is a compound that clears the body of carcinogens.

Cocoa (*see* **Chocolate**)

Coconut/Coconut Milk
Coconut contains less sugar and more protein than most fruits, and is relatively high in minerals. Coconut milk, although high in fat, is crammed with nutrients, fibre, vitamin E, folic acid, calcium, copper, selenium, magnesium and manganese. Surprisingly, coconut oil raises the body's metabolic rate and therefore helps us burn more body fat. Monolaurins found in the oil of the coconut have been proven to be very powerful antibacterial, antifungal and antiviral agents. Botanically, coconut is classified as a nut. Coconut-like fossils predating 15 million years have been discovered in India and New Zealand.

Coriander (*see* **page 203**)

Cornmeal (*see also* **Popcorn**)
Gluten-free cornmeal is a rich source of vitamin B1 (thiamine), folate, fibre, phosphorous and manganese. It also contains the antioxidant, zeaxanthin, which helps protect our vision by increasing the concentration of macular pigment in our eyes. For a balanced diet, we should always try to eat the full colour rainbow of foods, and cornmeal is one of our most colourful flours.

Courgette
Courgettes are low in fat and calories. They contain folate, potassium, vitamin A, manganese and small amounts of phytonutrients that have cancer-suppressing qualities.

Crab (*see* **Shellfish**)

Cranberry/Cranberry Juice
(*see also* **Berries**)
Cranberries are abundant in vitamins and minerals, and contain antibacterial agents which actually acidify the urine, reduce E. coli bacteria and are effective in treating kidney and urinary tract infections. They are a source of antioxidants that include the anti-inflammatory quercetin, which is under research for its benefits to the cardiovascular system, immune system and as an anti-cancer agent. Cranberries help prevent metastasis, that is the spread of cancer to other organs or parts of the body.

D

Daikon (*see* **Radish**)

Dill (*see* **page 203**)

E

Eggplant (*see* **Aubergine**)

Eggs
Eggs consist of complete high-quality proteins, essential for the body to repair itself and build muscle tissue. They are rich in B vitamins, selenium and choline, which is a nutrient required for general good health and the development of the brain. Eggs also contain phosphorous that is essential for bone health, and iodine which is required to produce the thyroid hormone and regulate our metabolism. Egg yolks contain the nutrients lutein and zeaxanthin, which help prevent and even reverse macular disease.

Enoki Mushroom
(*see* **Exotic Mushrooms**)

Exotic Mushrooms
Buna shimeji, eryngii, enoki, maitake, oyster, reishi, shiroshimeji, shiitake and zhuling mushrooms contain beta-glucan, which has been found to stimulate the immune system. They have an antiviral and anticancer effect on the body, which is proven by science, and are being researched for the treatment of severe allergies and arthritis. Exotic mushrooms also contain ergothioneine, an antioxidant that contributes to immune support and protects the eyes, skin, liver, kidneys and bone marrow.

F

Fish (White Fish)
(*see also* **Oily Fish** *and* **Shellfish**)
White fish are an excellent low-calorie and low-fat source of protein, which is essential for the body to build and repair itself. They are also rich in selenium which can help prevent the risk of cancer. White fish are a good source of omega-3 fatty acids (but they contain much lower levels than oily fish) that help guard against cardiovascular diseases and aid brain development. Omega-3 can also protect from respiratory infections. The oils in the fish increase activity of white blood cells in the body, which eliminate bacteria and, therefore, fight off infection. Studies have shown that people who eat fish regularly are much less likely to suffer from heart disease, than others who don't. White fish contains considerable amounts of the amino acid tryptophan that regulates our mood by effecting neurotransmitters in the brain and helping us to feel good.

Fruit (*see* **individual fruits**)

G

Garbanzo Bean (*see* **Chickpeas**)

Garlic (*see* **page 204**)

Ginger (*see* **page 204**)

Goji Berry
This legendary berry contains beta-carotene, 18 types of amino acids and polysaccharides known to strengthen the immune system. Goji berries have played a major role in traditional Chinese medicine, where they are said to enhance immune system function, improve eyesight, protect the liver, boost sperm-production, improve complexion and blood circulation. Fascinatingly, per weight, goji berries contain 500 times more vitamin C than oranges!

Grape (*see also* **Wine**)
A good source of vitamin C, grapes contain antioxidants known as flavonoids, including resveratrol and quercetin that are linked to fighting cancer, degenerative nerve diseases and heart disease and prevent blood from clotting. Resveratrol is found primarily in the skin and seeds of grapes.

Grapefruit (see **Citrus Fruits**)

Green Papaya (see **Papaya**)

Green Pea
The humble green pea is nature's multi-vitamin pill, and contains no less than 8 vitamins and 7 minerals, as well as fibre, and as much protein as an egg, by weight. Green peas help protect the heart and bones, and aid general well-being.

Green Tea (see **Tea**)

Honey
Honey is an antibacterial, antifungal, anti-inflammatory and antiviral substance. It contains antioxidants known to lower cholesterol and reduce damage done to the colon by colitis. It is effective in increasing the population of probiotic bacteria in the gut, which help strengthen the immune system, improve digestion and prevent colon cancer. Honey can be taken neat as a cough suppressant. For at least 2,700 years, it has been used to treat a variety of ailments, including wounds and burns.

I

Imli (see **Tamarind, page 205**)

J

Javitri (see **Nutmeg, page 205**)

K

Kale (see also **Cabbage**)
Kale is an earthy and delicious tasting source of beta-carotene, vitamin C, lutein, zeaxanthin, and calcium. It's also an incredibly rich source of vitamin K which helps our blood to clot. Like the more familiar cabbage, kale is part of the cruciferous family and is linked with the prevention of heart disease, cancer, and neurological diseases.

Kumara (see **Sweet Potato**)

Lamb
Whilst generally higher in saturated fats than beef, lamb works wonderfully with Indian spicing, and can be enjoyed in moderation. It is rich in proteins essential for the building and repair of body muscle and tissue, and contains considerable amounts of selenium, zinc, and vitamin B12, which are important for the proper functioning of the brain and nervous system. It's also a worthy resource of tryptophan, which normalises appetite, elevates mood and induces a good night's sleep.

Leafy Greens
A rich source of vitamins A, C, E and K, magnesium, folate and several vital antioxidants, these health-boosting greens are packed full of fibre. One serving of leafy greens contains up to 150% of our daily vitamin A requirements. Vitamin A helps our eyes adapt from bright light to darkness, while insufficient intake can lead to night blindness and poor vision in dim light. Leafy greens help protect the entire cardiovascular system and guard against osteoporosis, heart disease, cancer, and arthritis. The yellow pigmentation found in leafy greens contains lutein and zeaxanthin which protect against the occurrence of blindness.

Lemon (see **Citrus Fruits**)

Lentils
Lentils are one of nature's most amazing superfoods and contain phytochemicals which help prevent cancer, and comprise of antioxidants, folic acid and potassium. They are high in protein, dietary fibre, vitamin B1 and minerals. The reddish hue in lentil pigments wield antioxidant activity up to 50 times stronger than vitamin E. Eating lentils lowers incidences of cardiovascular diseases and reduces cholesterol, whilst improving the flow of blood and oxygen in the body. Lentils increase energy levels and replenish iron stores.

Lime (see **Citrus Fruits**)

Lotus Root
Ancient Indian texts report its use for many illnesses, including diarrhoea, dysentery, fungal infections, piles, ringworm, fever, leprosy and sexually transmitted diseases, such as gonorrhoea and syphilis. Lotus root is also believed to strengthen a weak heart. The flower of the lotus root is sacred to Hindus and is considered to be an example of divine beauty; its unfolding petals mimic the expansion of the soul, and the growth of its pure beauty from the murky waters of its origin, holds a benign spiritual promise.

M

Mackerel (see **Oily Fish**)

Maitake Mushroom
(see **Exotic Mushrooms**)

Mango
The national fruit of India is a super form of nutrition, containing vitamins A, C and E, and fibre, iron, minerals, antioxidants and flavonoids that aid the immune system and reduce the incidence of cancer. Mangoes contain lutein which is employed by our body as an antioxidant to protect our eyesight. Enzymes like magniferin and lactase, which aid digestion, are found in abundance in these exotic fruits. In some parts of South East Asia, it is taken as a supplement for sexual potency. For taste, nothing quite compares to Alphonso, the 'king of mangoes', which can be found in Indian grocers during the summer months.

Milk
Milk is a complete food and a super source of calcium, which is recognised in its role in maintaining the strength and density of bones. It is packed full of vitamins A, B12, D and K, and iodine which regulates thyroid production and helps maintain healthy energy use. Milk is loaded with enzymes that aid digestion. Researchers have found that individuals who follow a calorie-controlled diet and consume low-fat milk and dairy products, are able to lose more body fat than those who don't include dairy products in their diet.

Mooli *(see* **Radish***)*

Mushrooms
   (see **Exotic Mushrooms***)*

Mussels *(see* **Shellfish***)*

N

Nuts
Packed full of proteins, calcium, folate, magnesium, potassium and 'good fats', nuts are a great snack to keep hunger pangs at bay. They contain antioxidants and the mineral selenium, which suppresses the growth of cancer. Nuts contain the amino acid arginine, and omega-3 and omega-6 fatty acids, which work wonders for both the brain and heart. Research has found that nuts reduce cholesterol and dilate blood vessels. Phytosterols, contained in nuts, prevent the accumulation of fats in artery walls and, therefore, further reduce the risk of strokes, angina and heart attack. All nuts, and in particular almonds, are rich in the antioxidant vitamin E and the amino acid arginine which boosts all-round immunity and hampers tumour growth. Walnuts contain the highest amount of the polyphenol-rich antioxidant, ellagic acid, which is known to prevent and fight cancer; they also contain the antioxidant melatonin, which promotes a good night's sleep.

O

Oats
Oat protein is roughly equivalent to that contained in soy. Consuming oats lowers bad cholesterol. They are a rich source of magnesium, potassium, zinc, copper, manganese, selenium, thiamine, pantothenic acid and phytonutrients. They are high in complex carbohydrates and soluble fibre, which means they release their energy slowly and take a long time to digest – an ideal food for anyone trying to lose weight. Oats are recognised by the US FDA (US Food and Drug Administration) for their role in reducing the risk of coronary heart disease.

Oily Fish *(see also* **Fish (White Fish)** *and* **Shellfish***)*
Oily fish is a super source for proteins, which aid the body in its continuous building and the repair of muscle tissues. Mackerel, pilchards, salmon and fresh tuna are all bountiful in omega-3 fatty acids, zinc, selenium and vitamins A, D and B. Over a decade of research has shown that if a person eats one portion of oily fish a week, he or she can decrease the likeliness of dying of a heart attack. Omega-3 can also protect from inflammatory respiratory infections. The oils in the fish increase activity of white cells in the body, which eliminate bacteria and, therefore, fight off infection.

Olive Oil
In modern science, there is much evidence to support the fact that olive oil contributes to a reduction in the risk of coronary heart disease. Olive oil lowers bad cholesterol levels and increases good cholesterol. Interestingly, it contains some of the most powerful natural polyphenols known to man, which contribute to its slightly bitter taste and have an antioxidant, anti-inflammatory and anti-blood clotting action. Individuals who use olive oil in place of other fats, have much lower rates of heart disease, atherosclerosis, diabetes, colon cancer and asthma. Adding olive oil into our diet means that we can easily pour some of the goodness of the 'Mediterranean diet' into our lives. The prophet of Islam, Muhammad, recommended its use in the following terms, "Consume olive oil and anoint it upon your bodies since it is of the blessed tree". He also stated that it cures seventy diseases.

Onion
An essential kitchen ingredient, the humble onion aids the liver in eliminating toxins and carcinogens and creates 'killer cells' in the blood that fend off tumours and infections. Onions reduce the risk of blood clots, atherosclerosis (hardening of the arteries) and help combat neurological diseases such as Alzheimer's. Evidence suggests that onions provide effective protection against the common cold, heart disease and osteoporosis. They contain antibacterial, antifungal, anti-inflammatory and anti-cancer properties, as well as the antioxidising agent quercetin. The regular consumption of onions has, like garlic, proven to lower high cholesterol and blood pressure levels and thus resulting in improved heart health. It is said that ancient Egyptians believed onions could bring the dead back to life, and thus worshipped them.[4]

Orange *(see* **Citrus Fruits***)*

Oyster *(see* **Shellfish***)*

P

Paneer *(see* **Cheese***)*

Papaya
Papayas are a bountiful source of antioxidant nutrients including carotenes, vitamin C, vitamin K, flavonoids, B vitamins, folate and pantothenic acid, and the minerals, potassium and magnesium; and fibre. Papaya is rich in enzymes that aid digestion and help combat a multitude of health problems including allergies, auto-immune disorder, AIDS and cancer. The ripe fruits help treat ringworm, and the green fruits, high blood pressure. Papaya is considered to be an aphrodisiac. Papaya seeds are anti-inflammatory and analgesic and, in Ayurveda, are used to treat fungal infections and stomach aches. They can also be dried and then crushed and used as an alternative to black pepper.

Passion Fruit
Passion fruits are endowed with a mild sedative property and contain plentiful vitamin A, vitamin C, minerals and alkaloids, which lower blood pressure. Passion fruit contains, weight-for-weight, as much potassium as a banana; and is under research for its potential anti-cancer properties.

Peppers
Peppers are packed with two extremely powerful antioxidants – vitamin A and C – which work as a duo to effectively eliminate free radicals that can cause damage to the body. Just 1 medium pepper can provide us with over 450% of our daily requirement of vitamin C. Peppers are an extremely rich source of some of the best nutrients, and contain

vitamin B6, folic acid and cancer-busting lycopene. They can alleviate some of the symptoms associated with asthma, cataracts, diabetes and joint pain.

Pilchard (see **Oily Fish**)

Pistachio Nut (see **Nuts**)

Pomegranate
Pomegranates are a good source of vitamins A, C and E. They contain polyphenols, which help the body rid itself of cancer-causing agents; tannins, which regulate blood pressure and stimulate the immune system; and anti-inflammatory anthocyanins. Pomegranates also slow the oxidation of bad cholesterol. Interestingly, pomegranate juice contains much higher levels of antioxidants than most other fruit juices, red wine or even green tea. Pomegranates are being investigated for their role in cancer prevention.

Popcorn (see also **Cornmeal**)
Popcorn is a snack food which contains more antioxidising polyphenols and fibre than most other convenience foods. Polyphenols are linked with a lower risk of heart disease and cancers. Popcorn can be prepared quite easily using little or no fat and is a source of B vitamins and protein. It has more proteins than any other cereal grain and contains as much iron as spinach and eggs.

Potato
Potatoes are a carbohydrate powerhouse and a source of vitamins B6 and C, and they contain manganese, potassium, fibre and phytonutrients that act as antioxidants against free radicals which can cause damage to the body. Potatoes also contain lectins which are proteins known to inhibit tumour growth. The humble potato may be in for a reputation overhaul as people become aware that its antioxidants may compare with, and even rival, those found in other fruits and vegetables.

Prawn (see **Shellfish**)

Pumpkin
Pumpkins are rich in vitamins A and C and the antioxidant beta-carotene, which gives them the bright colour they're known for. Pumpkins are being investigated for their role in cancer

prevention; the phytonutrients from pumpkin have the ability to prevent cell mutations, which can lead to cancer. Pumpkins are high in fibre and low in calories, and are a great source of important minerals that include iron, potassium and magnesium. They are also said to be beneficial in ridding the body of intestinal worms.

Pumpkin Seed
An excellent source of iron, zinc, essential fatty acids, potassium and magnesium. Pumpkin seeds promote prostate health, since components within them disrupt the triggering of the multiplication of prostate cells. They are beneficial for bone strength and have proven favourable when compared to non-steroidal anti-inflammatory drugs used to treat symptoms in diseases such as arthritis. They also contain phytosterols, which improve the body's immune system and reduce levels of harmful cholesterol.

Puy Lentil (see **Lentils**)

Quinoa
Once held sacred by the Incas and referred to as 'mother of all grains', quinoa was suppressed by Spanish colonialists during their conquest of South America, as 'food for Indians'. Quinoa has been an important food for more than 6,000 years, and is a complete protein source as it contains all 9 essential amino acids normally found in meat, in particular lysine, which is essential for growth and repair of tissue. It contains more protein than any other grain and therefore will keep you feeling fuller for longer - great news if you're trying to control your weight. It is a good source of manganese and magnesium which help relax blood vessels; therefore, if you are prone to migraines, adding quinoa to your diet can be a good idea. It is gluten-free and a great source of fibre, and for all these reasons is being considered as a possible crop in NASA'S controlled ecological life support system for long-duration manned space flights.

Radish
A root vegetable abundant with antioxidants, vitamin C and minerals, radishes contain active enzymes which aid the digestion of food. They can be used to remedy a variety of health conditions, including arthritis, cancer, coughs, gastric discomfort, liver problems, constipation and intestinal parasites.

Raisin (see **Grape**)

Red Lentil (see **Lentils**)

Rice (see **Basmati Rice** and **Black Glutinous Rice**)

Rocket (see **Leafy Greens**)

Salmon (see **Oily Fish**)

Samphire
An abundant source of vitamin C, samphire also aids the body's digestive processes. It is used in herbal medicine as a diuretic. There is research underway for the role of samphire in tackling obesity. Fascinatingly, there is no need to add salt when eating samphire, as it comes ready salted by Mother Nature. Samphire is available from good fishmongers during the summer months.

Scallops (see **Shellfish**)

Sea Vegetables/Sea Salad
Known in the Orient as the 'secret elixir' to long life, sea vegetables are bursting with goodness, including beta-carotene, vitamin B12, fibre, chlorophyll and fatty acids. They offer the most immense range of minerals of any food, comprising of just about all of the minerals found in the ocean – the same minerals which are found in our blood. Sea vegetables are also nature's best source of iodine, which is crucial for thyroid health and a healthy metabolism; in fact, seaweed extract can be found in many weight-loss supplements. It is suggested that sea vegetables possess curative properties for arthritis,

cancer, common cold, flu, worm infestations and tuberculosis.

Sesame Seed/Oil
Sesame seeds are rich in vitamin E, calcium, copper, manganese, magnesium, iron and zinc. In addition to these nutrients, they contain the substances sesamin and sesamolin which help to lower cholesterol and high blood pressure. Sesame seeds are also a source of cancer-preventing lignans. The women of Babylon would eat halva, a mixture of sesame seeds and honey, to enhance their health and beauty. In the Indian kitchen, sesame oil is used primarily in the south, where it is known locally as 'til oil'. The oil is also used in lamps kept for worship in Hindu temples. In early Indian legends, tales are told in which sesame seeds represent immortality.

Shallot (see Onion)

Shellfish
Oysters, mussels, scallops, prawns and crabs are all rich in zinc, which is essential for the immune function, wound-healing and stabilising blood sugar levels. Oysters contain the highest natural source of zinc of any food. Shellfish are also loaded with selenium, which stimulates the metabolism and helps in preventing cancer. All shellfish, except for prawns, contain omega-3 fatty acids, which guard against cardiovascular diseases and feed the brain with essential nutrients. Shellfish contain low-calorie and low-fat proteins that are essential for the body to build and repair itself.

Shiitake Mushroom
(see Exotic Mushrooms)

Soy Products
Soy products, including soy beans, soy milk and tofu, are undisputed superfoods and researched the world over for their remarkable nutritional properties. They are a good source of omega-3 fatty acids, including tryptophan, which is known to enhance our mood, and molybdenum, a trace element that helps build and trigger enzymes involved in repairing and making genetic matter. Soy is a complete protein, and is rich in fibre and isoflavones (a type of phytoestrogen that is considered to be useful in the prevention of cancer). The US FDA (US Food and Drug Administration) granted official approval for health claims that soy products reduce cholesterol; and recently, the American Heart Foundation ruled soy products such as tofu, soy butter and soy nuts to be beneficial to cardiovascular health. Soy products have been appreciated in the East for thousands of years. Their frequent use in the Far Eastern diet can perhaps explain the highest life expectancy in this region, amongst all the other parts of the world.

Spelt Flour
Spelt dates back to the time of the Romans, and is a superb source of vitamin B2, manganese, niacin, thiamine and copper. This particular combination of nutrients found in spelt make it especially beneficial for those of us who suffer from diabetes and migraines. It is wheat-free and, because its proteins are easier to digest, it's often tolerated by those with allergies. However, a word of warning – spelt is very closely 'related' to wheat, so if you have wheat intolerance, proceed with caution.

Spinach (see Leafy Greens)

Split Pea (see Lentils)

Spring Onion (see Onion)

Strawberry (see Berries)

Sultana (see Grape)

Swede (see Turnip)

Sweet Potato
Sweet potatoes are brimming with vitamin A and substantial amounts of vitamin C and manganese; just one serving provides us with over 350% of our daily vitamin A requirements. They are a good source of antioxidant and anti-inflammatory compounds linked with a reduced risk of cancer. Sweet potatoes help keep the tummy feeling fuller for longer by stabilising blood sugar levels and lowering insulin-resistance in individuals who suffer from diabetes.

T

Tamarind (see page 205)

Tea
Tea is rich in polyphenols, which prevent carcinogenic cells from multiplying and protect against cardiovascular disease – between 25 and 30% of the tea leaf alone consists entirely of flavonoids. Interestingly, consumption of tea, and in particular green tea, raises the metabolic rate, speeds up fat-oxidation and stimulates the body's thermo-genesis process – the rate at which the body burns calories. Green tea can also help boost the immune system. Health infusions made from tea have been taken for over 4,700 years.

Tofu (see Soy Products)

Tomato
Tomatoes are packed with legendarily high levels of vitamins A, C and K. Eating tomatoes, in particular cooked and processed forms such as tomato purée, benefits us enormously, as the body digests their processed nutrients more easily. Tomatoes contain nature's most prevalent source of lycopene, one of the most powerful antioxidants known to mankind. Lycopene has been found beneficial in preventing many types of cancer, including that of the prostate and skin. A recent study broadcast on the BBC found that consuming tomatoes reduces the risk of sunburn, and the obvious signs of ageing due to it, by up to one-third. Tomatoes contain lutein, which is used by the body as an antioxidant that protects the retina from free radical damage. They also contain high levels of collagen, which helps strengthen tendons and slow degenerative diseases. Additionally, tomatoes are a dexterous source of potassium, niacin, vitamin B6 and folate, which are identified with lowering high cholesterol levels and the risk of heart disease. Consuming tomatoes, like many other antioxidant-rich foods, can reduce the prevalence of inflammatory diseases such as asthma and bronchitis.

Indian Superfood

Tuna *(see* **Oily Fish***)*

Turnip
Part of the cruciferous group of vegetables, which includes broccoli and cauliflower, turnips are linked with a reduction of incidences of cancer. Low in calories, they are a superb source of vitamin C, fibre, folic acid, manganese, pantothenic acid and copper. They are also a good supply of thiamine, potassium, niacin and magnesium. Although they are a starchy vegetable, turnips contain only one-third of the amount of calories that potatoes do. Turnip juice contains up to twice the amount of vitamin C that orange juice does.

U

Ulli *(see* **Onion***)*

V

Venison
Venison is a red meat that's very low in saturated fats and a brilliant source of proteins. In addition, it contains all of the vitamins, minerals and nutrients found in lamb, with markedly less fat and calories (similar to that of chicken). It's also a very good source of vitamin B12, riboflavin, niacin and vitamin B6. Vitamins B12 and B6 are linked with a reduction in the risk of heart disease; vitamin B12 has also proven to protect against colon cancer.

Vinegar
Vinegar has myriad remedies and treatments attributed to it. It reduces cholesterol and blood sugar levels; even small amounts of vinegar taken with meals can reduce the release of glucose into the blood from carbohydrate-rich foods. It is used in traditional medicine as an antibacterial, digestive aid and as an ointment for skin rashes and bruising. Many trials have also proven that vinegar helps us to feel satiated and, therefore, consume less food.

Walnut *(see* **Nuts***)*

Wholemeal Flour
Wholemeal flour is a rich source of manganese, fibre, tryptophan, magnesium and B vitamins. Magnesium is involved in regulating glucose and insulin levels, and therefore the risk of contracting type-2 diabetes is also greatly reduced. People that regularly consume wholegrain products such as wholemeal flour are less likely to be overweight or suffer from heart disease.

Wine *(see also* **Grape***)*
Wine consists of a bounty of flavonoids, polyphenols and the antioxidant compound resveratrol, which promotes cardiovascular health by reducing harmful blood clots and, therefore, protecting the heart from free radical damage. This may explain why the French, although consuming a diet rich in saturated fats, have a much lower rate of heart disease, than individuals in most other Western countries; this statistic is quite often referred to as the 'French Paradox'. Wine slows the development of neurological degenerative disorders like Alzheimer's and Parkinson's disease. Moderate consumption also lowers bad cholesterol levels. However, excessive consumption of wine would negate any potential health benefits. Wine is also an antibacterial.

Wolfberry *(see* **Goji Berry***)*

Xardal *(see* **Mustard Seed, page 204***)*

Yogurt
Yogurt is a complete protein, considered on par with both meat and eggs. It's a superb source of calcium, iodine, potassium and vitamins A, B and D. Calcium is essential for strong bones, and aids the healthy functioning of nerves and muscles. Iodine is crucial for the thyroid gland to function properly and regulate our metabolism. Yogurt plays a role in colon health and the proper functioning of the immune system. It balances pH levels in the stomach, aiding digestion and faster absorption of nutrients into the bloodstream. Acidophilus bacteria contained in yogurt can protect the lining of the stomach and intestines by coating the surface and, therefore, preventing the formation of ulcers. Researchers have found that individuals following a calorie-controlled diet, whilst consuming low-fat and unsweetened yogurt, were able to lose more body fat than those who didn't include it in their diet.

Zhuling Mushroom
  (see **Exotic Mushrooms***)*

Zucchini *(see* **Courgette***)*

Superspices Directory

It is in this chapter that I share with you the precious knowledge of the superspices, in the form of an alphabetical directory. The superspices included within it are recognised for their medicinal benefits by Ayurveda and, quite often, by science too.

A

Ajwain
Taste: Similar to thyme, only stronger and therefore less subtle.
Medical Uses: Antibacterial, antifungal, anti-inflammatory and antioxidant; asthma, bronchitis, common cold, nausea, migraine and vomiting. Used as a digestive aid and as a hangover remedy. [4]
Additional Information: Ajwain can be used in the preparation of masala chai. Also known as bishop's weed and carom seed. Often confused with caraway.

B

Basil
Taste: Strong and characteristic, not comparable to any other herb/spice.
Medical Uses: Antioxidant, antibacterial, antiviral and anti-inflammatory properties. Phytochemicals derived from basil have been found to interrupt a variety of diseases, including cancer, atherosclerosis, myocardial infarction, diabetes, allergy, asthma, arthritis, Crohn's disease, osteoporosis, psoriasis, septic shock and AIDS. [1] [5]
Additional Information: Known to millions of followers of the Hindu faith as the 'sacred basil leaf'; and for this reverence it is not used much as a culinary herb in India. Basil is sacred to the Hindu god Vishnu, symbolising his

wife, Lakshmi. It is known to the Greeks simply as 'king' because of its royal fragrance. There are many types of basil. The centre of diversity for this herb is Africa, however, it was first cultivated in India.

Bishop's Weed (see **Ajwain**)

Black Cardamom
Taste: Strong smoky flavour, acquired by drying the spice over open flames.
Medical Uses: Antibacterial, antifungal, antioxidant; bronchitis, common cold, cough, congestion of lungs, fever, infection of teeth and gums and inflammatory conditions. Black cardamom is also used as a digestive aid, and as an aphrodisiac. [6]
Additional Information: Used in Indian cuisine to intensify and enhance the taste of other ingredients.

Black Pepper (see **Pepper**)

C

Caraway
Taste: Aromatic and warm.
Medical Uses: Analgesic, antioxidant, appetite suppressant; asthma, colic, digestive disorders and intestinal worms. Caraway is being evaluated for its possible antioxidant and cancer-fighting effects.
Additional Information: Used in Europe since the Roman times. Its present day use is mainly in Central and Eastern European cuisines. Known to Indian cuisine as 'vilayti zeera' or foreign cumin.

Cardamom
Taste: Aromatic, sweet and slightly bitter; sweeter after roasting.
Medical Uses: Antibacterial, antifungal, anti-inflammatory, antioxidant; asthma, blood pressure, bronchitis, common cold,

congestion of lungs, cough, fever, infection of teeth and gums and inflammatory conditions. It is used as a digestive aid and also acts as an aphrodisiac. Cardamom is being investigated for its potential role in cancer prevention and alleviating the symptoms associated with epilepsy and hypertension. [4] [6]
Additional Information: Cardamom is the third most expensive spice after saffron and vanilla. India is the world's largest producer, however, most of it is used domestically. Interestingly, cardamom is used in Scandinavia for baking.

Carom Seed (see **Ajwain**)

Cassia (see also **Cinnamon**)
Taste: Aromatic, sweet and warm, with just a touch of bitterness.
Medical Uses: Antioxidant, anti-inflammatory and antibacterial, which can prohibit the growth of certain types of bacteria, when used in cooking. It is antifungal and antiviral, and can help in treating the common cold and flu. It is an effective digestive aid, and is used to treat gastrointestinal problems, diarrhoea, stomach upsets and vomiting. It can also help reduce blood sugar levels. Cassia is being investigated for its potential role in cancer prevention.
Additional Information: Often confused with cinnamon, however cassia bark is thicker. Indian cuisine does not distinguish between the two; they were first imported to India from China and were simply known as 'Chinese wood'. Mentioned several times in the Bible, and used by the ancient Egyptians as part of the mummification process for the Pharaohs' bodies.

Cayenne Pepper (see **Chilli**)

Chilli

Taste: Generally, chilli is 'hot', with a fresh and fruity aroma. However, the intensity of the 'heat' varies immensely, depending on the variety of the chilli.

Medical Uses: Antibacterial, antifungal, antioxidant; effective against bronchitis and rhinitis (by thinning and clearing mucus from stuffed noses or congested lungs), eliminates certain parasites in the gastrointestinal tract, analgesic with proven treatment for arthritis, skin and muscle pain. Phytochemicals derived from chilli have been found to interrupt a variety of diseases, including cancer, atherosclerosis, myocardial infarction, diabetes, allergy, asthma, arthritis, Crohn's disease, osteoporosis, psoriasis, septic shock and AIDS. Chillies are being studied for their potential role in preventing gastric ulcers. [1] [7]

Additional Information: Chillies have been a part of mankind's diet in the Americas since at least 7500 B.C. The Spanish brought them to Europe, and they spread onwards to India and the rest of the world. Presently, India is the world's largest producer of chilli, and it is in India where they are also used to ward off the 'evil eye' and 'evil spirits'.

Cinnamon *(see also* **Cassia***)*

Taste: Sweet, pleasant and uplifting.

Medical Uses: Antioxidant, anti-inflammatory, and antibacterial, which can prohibit the growth of certain types of bacteria when used in cooking. It is antifungal and antiviral, and can help in treating the common cold and flu. It is an effective digestive aid, and is used to treat gastrointestinal problems, diarrhoea, stomach upsets and vomiting. It can also help reduce blood sugar levels. Cinnamon is being investigated for its potential role in cancer prevention. [4] [8] [9]

Additional Information: First discovered by Western traders, in Sri Lanka. Cinnamon is mentioned in the Old Testament several times, and was very popular in Europe from the 16th to the 18th century.

Cloves

Taste: Instantly recognisable, strong and intense fragrance.

Medical Uses: Antibacterial, antiviral, anti-inflammatory, antifungal, analgesic, antioxidant; cold sores, genital herpes and insect repellent. Anaesthetic, used in dentistry. Considered an aphrodisiac.

Can be used as a digestive aid effective for flatulence, nausea and vomiting, particularly during pregnancy. Phytochemicals derived from cloves have been found to interrupt a variety of diseases, including cancer, atherosclerosis, myocardial infarction, diabetes, allergy, asthma, arthritis, Crohn's disease, osteoporosis, psoriasis, septic shock and AIDS. [1] [4] [5] [10] [11]

Additional Information: Cloves are a spice that date back to antiquity and, because of their exceptional aromatic strength, are held in high esteem the world over. In India, cloves are most commonly used in rich meat dishes and sweets. In England, they are used for pickling and preserving meats and, most famously, are an important ingredient in Worcestershire Sauce. Cloves are native to the Indonesian Islands.

Coriander

Taste: Pleasant aroma that is fresh, tangy and citrus-like.

Medical Uses: Antibacterial, antifungal, anti-inflammatory and antioxidant; anxiety, cystitis and other urinary tract infections, diarrhoea and insomnia. It is used as a digestive aid and is an effective diuretic, sedative and muscle relaxant. Coriander seed is being investigated for its potential role in cancer prevention. [4] [12]

Additional Information: Archaeological findings seem to indicate that coriander has been around since the early Bronze Age. It was found in the tomb of Tutankhamen, is mentioned in the Bible, and the Greeks cultivated it since at least the second millennium B.C. The Romans introduced it to Britain, where it was used to preserve meat. During the European Medieval era, it was popular due to its ability to 'mask' the unpleasant aroma of spoiled meat. Even today, coriander seed is an important ingredient in many sausage products. In India, fresh coriander is used in generous amounts to season most savoury dishes. It is also the most commonly used garnish ingredient.

Cumin Seed

Taste: Strongly aromatic and nutty, and even more so when roasted.

Medical Uses: Anti-inflammatory; common cold and colic. It is an antibacterial and antifungal, and acts as a digestive aid effective for flatulence, and as a stimulant that temporarily increases

alertness. Phytochemicals derived from cumin have been found to interrupt a variety of diseases, including cancer, atherosclerosis, myocardial infarction, diabetes, allergy, asthma, arthritis, Crohn's disease, osteoporosis, psoriasis, septic shock and AIDS. Cumin is being evaluated for its antioxidant effects, and its potential role in preventing gastric ulcers. [1] [4] [7] [13]

Additional Information: Originates from Western Asia, where it has been cultivated since Biblical times. Cumin is mentioned in both the Old and New Testament. It is an essential ingredient for making the Indian spice mixture garam masala.

Dill

Taste: Very sweet and aromatic.

Medical Uses: Antibacterial, antifungal, anti-inflammatory and antioxidant; colic, and therefore extremely popular in gripe water, used to treat mild bowel disorders, flatulence and stomach upsets. Dill is also being investigated for its potential role in the prevention of tuberculosis and leprosy. [4] [14]

Additional Information: Dill that is used in Europe is not the same as that found in India; the Indian variety is less fragrant. Dill is mentioned in both the Talmud and the Bible.

Elaichi *(see* **Cardamom***)*

Fennel Seed

Taste: Sweet and aromatic, similar to anise seed.

Medical Uses: Antibacterial, analgesic, antifungal, anti-inflammatory, antioxidant; asthma, rhinitis, allergies; digestive aid effective in treating stomach upsets, and helpful in lowering blood pressure. It also acts as an appetite suppressant. Studies have found fennel seed to be a powerful pain-reliever. Phytochemicals derived from fennel interrupt a variety of diseases, including cancer, atherosclerosis, myocardial infarction, diabetes, allergy, asthma, arthritis, Crohn's disease, osteoporosis, psoriasis, septic shock and AIDS. [1] [4]

Additional Information: Originates from the Mediterranean and is known to the Greeks for three millennia. The popularity of fennel seeds spread during the middle ages when they were grown in monasteries. They are typically used in Indian cuisine for preparation of pickles.

Fenugreek

Taste: The seed has very little aroma and is bitter to taste; the leaves are aromatic and earthy.

Medical Uses: Antibacterial, analgesic, antifungal, anti-inflammatory, antioxidant, anti-pyretic (reduces high temperature during fever); bronchitis, digestive disorders, infections, inflammation, high blood cholesterol, skin irritations, sore throat and ulcers. Most commonly used as a milk-producing agent for nursing mothers to increase inadequate milk supply. Used in India as a hair conditioner, by crushing the seeds and mixing into yogurt and then applying directly to the hair. Fenugreek is being investigated for its potential role in cancer prevention. [4]

Additional Information: The earliest instance of fenugreek has been found in Iraq, dating back to around 4,000 B.C. Seeds were also found in the tomb of Tutankhamen.

G

Garlic

Taste: Pungent and intense, becoming deep and mellow after cooking.

Medical Uses: Garlic helps prevent heart disease, including hardening of the arteries, high cholesterol and high blood pressure. It is an antioxidant, antibacterial, anti-inflammatory, antifungal and antiviral, and can help improve the immune system and protect against diabetes and cancer. Garlic destroys infection-causing viruses, helps combat neurological diseases such as Alzheimer's and produces more "natural killer" cells in the blood to fight tumours and infections. Phytochemicals derived from garlic have been found to interrupt a variety of diseases, including cancer, atherosclerosis, myocardial infarction, diabetes, allergy, asthma,

arthritis, Crohn's disease, osteoporosis, psoriasis, septic shock and AIDS. [1] [4] [5]

Additional Information: Garlic has been used both as food and medicine for millennia, since the time the pyramids were being built. It was considered a powerful health tonic by ancient Greek and Roman soldiers. In Europe, many cultures have used it for protection and white magic.

Ginger

Taste: Invigorating, fresh, sharp, with a touch of citrus.

Medical Uses: Antibacterial, antifungal and anti-inflammatory, and is used as a digestive aid and protects against digestive infections; arthritic pain, common cold, cramps, griping pains, headaches, motion sickness, nausea, respiratory infections, stomach upsets and toothache. Ginger can also help lower cholesterol and thin the blood and, thus, can enhance blood circulation. Phytochemicals derived from ginger have been found to interrupt a variety of diseases, including cancer, atherosclerosis, myocardial infarction, diabetes, allergy, asthma, arthritis, Crohn's disease, osteoporosis, psoriasis, septic shock and AIDS. Ginger is very high in antioxidants that fight various diseases, and is being investigated for its potential role in preventing gastric ulcers. [1] [4] [6] [7]

Additional Information: First cultivated in China, from where it spread west to India and the rest of the world. Popular in Europe during the Roman Empire, however use declined after the fall of the Empire. Re-introduced to Europe by Marco Polo. Queen Elizabeth I is credited for the invention of the Gingerbread Man.

H

Haldi *(see* **Turmeric***)*

I

Imli *(see* **Tamarind***)*

Indian Saffron *(see* **Turmeric***)*

J

Javitri *(see* **Nutmeg***)*

Jeera *(see* **Cumin***)*

K

Kali Elaichi *(see* **Black Cardamom***)*

Kalownji *(see* **Nigella Seed***)*

L

Lal Mirch *(see* **Chilli***)*

M

Mace *(see* **Nutmeg***)*

Methi *(see* **Fenugreek***)*

Mint

Taste: Pure and refreshing.

Medical Uses: Antibacterial, antifungal, antioxidant; common cold, chest pains and headache. It soothes the digestive tract and reduces the severity and length of stomach upsets. Mint is being researched for its potential anticancer properties. [15]

Additional Information: Spearmint is the most commonly used mint in India and Europe. In Indian cuisine, mint is used mainly for the preparation of chutneys and sauces. Peppermint originates from England.

Mirch *(see* **Chilli***)*

Mustard Seed

Taste: Pungent and bitter; nutty aroma after roasting.

Medical Uses: Antibacterial, antifungal, anti-inflammatory, antioxidant and digestive aid. Mustard seeds are part of the cruciferous family and contain a concentrated source of cancer-fighting compounds, found also in cabbage, and are being studied for their potential anticancer properties. [4]

Additional Information: Mustard seeds are recounted in ancient Indian Sanskrit writings since at least 5,000 B.C. Pope

John XXII was particularly fond of mustard and created a position in the Vatican for a 'mustard maker to the Pope'. They are also mentioned in the New Testament in which the heaven is compared to a single grain of mustard.

N

Nigella Seed
Taste: Mild, peppery and strawberry-like aroma.
Medical Uses: Antibacterial, anti-inflammatory, antifungal, analgesic; asthma, allergies, bowel problems, fungal skin infections, rheumatism, respiratory disorders. It is beneficial to stomach and intestinal health and provides support to circulatory and immune systems, and to the kidney and liver. It promotes general and overall wellbeing, and is an antioxidant. Nigella seed is being investigated for its potential role in cancer prevention and treatment. [2] [16] [17]
Additional Information: In Islam, it is regarded as one of the greatest forms of healing medicine available, and Muhammad once stated that the black seed can heal every disease.

Nutmeg
Taste: Strongly aromatic and warm.
Medical Uses: Antibacterial, antifungal, antioxidant, antiviral; blood pressure, diarrhoea, flatulence, nausea and vomiting. Nutmeg is well-documented in Ayurveda for its capacity to treat diarrhoea. It is under research for its potential role in fighting leukaemia. [10]
Additional Information: Native to the Indonesian Islands and introduced to Europe by Arab traders in the 11th Century, where it was used to flavour beer. In Indian cuisine, it is added to flavour delicate meat dishes.

O

Onion (see **page 198**)

P

Paprika
Taste: Sweet, warm and spicy.
Medical Uses: see Chilli.
Additional Information: Known to the Indian cuisine as 'degi mirch'. Paprika is made by grinding dried sweet peppers, and is used mainly to give meat dishes a deep red colour.

Pepper
Taste: Various types available; all derived from the same plant, but each having a distinct flavour and aroma. White pepper is the strongest in aroma, black pepper has a mature flavour, whereas, red/pink peppercorns are slightly sweeter in taste. Green peppercorns are the most aromatic of the peppers.
Medical Uses: Antibacterial, antioxidant; improves circulation, relieves constipation, stimulates digestion and can be used to stop minor cuts from bleeding. Black pepper is being investigated for its potential role in preventing diabetes, cardiovascular diseases and cancer. [10] [18]
Additional Information: Undoubtedly, the most commonly used spice the world over. Pepper is native to South India and is known since antiquity. It was brought to the West when Alexander the Great warred upon Central Asia and India, in the 4th Century B.C.

Q

Qasia (see **Cassia**)

R

Rai (see **Nigella Seed**)

S

Saffron
Taste: Very sweet, bitter and intense, hay-like aroma.
Medical Uses: Antibacterial, antifungal, anti-inflammatory; baby colic, blood disorders, common cold, coughs, asthma, gout, insomnia, respiratory infections and stomach upsets. It contains antioxidants which can delay the effects of ageing. Saffron extract has been known to suppress cancer, delay tumour growth, and prevent cancer mutation. It also acts as an aphrodisiac and anti-depressant. [4]
Additional Information: Saffron is the world's most expensive spice, and was first documented in a 7th Century B.C. Assyrian botanical reference. Further documentation of saffron's use in ancient civilizations, for the treatment of some 90 illnesses, has been uncovered as well. Alexander the Great used saffron in infusions for the treatment of battle wounds. Cleopatra used saffron in her baths so that love-making would be more pleasurable. Buddhist monks adopted a saffron-coloured robe after the death of Buddha. It was used by ancient civilizations in the Mediterranean, Egypt and Gaza in their perfumes, ointments, medicine and divine offerings. In Iraq, saffron-based pigments have been found in 50,000-year-old depictions of prehistoric beasts.

Saunf (see **Fennel Seed**)

Star Anise
Taste: Very much like anise seeds – only more intense.
Medical Uses: Antibacterial, antioxidant; rheumatism. Star anise acts as a digestive aid. It is also being investigated for its potential role in cancer prevention.
Additional Information: Native to China, where it is widely used as an ingredient for making the popular Chinese five spice powder.

T

Tamarind
Taste: Sour, tart and fruity.
Medical Uses: Antibacterial, anti-flatulent, antioxidant, antiseptic; coolant, digestive aid, laxative and effective at regulating cholesterol levels. In South India, it is prepared as a soup to treat the common cold; the steaming hot soup has a flushing effect and, when taken, causes the nose and eyes to water and, thus, clearing nasal blockage. Studies have indicated that tamarind incorporated into a meal substantially increases the

bioavailability of aspirin and ibuprofen. Tamarind is being studied for its potential role in cancer prevention.

Additional Information: Originates from East Africa. Used in Indian meat dishes and chutneys. Although technically a fruit, it's used like a superspice to flavour and enhance recipes.

Turmeric

Taste: Astringent and bitter.

Medical Uses: Anti-inflammatory, antioxidant; Alzheimer's disease, allergies, atherosclerosis, arthritis, asthma, chronic inflammatory lung diseases, cold sores, depression, diabetes, gastric ulcers, genital herpes, heart disease, irritable bowel syndrome, joint pains, multiple sclerosis, Parainfluenza virus II, stomach problems, thyroiditis, uveitis, systemic lupus erythromatosis, and myasthenia gravis. It is an antibacterial, antifungal, antiviral and antiseptic, and therefore used to treat burns and cuts. Turmeric is being investigated for its possible benefit in treating Alzheimer's disease, cancer, diabetes, and liver disorders. It is also used as a digestive aid. Phytochemicals derived from turmeric have been found to interrupt a variety of diseases, including cancer, atherosclerosis, myocardial infarction, diabetes, allergy, asthma, arthritis, Crohn's disease, osteoporosis, psoriasis, septic shock and AIDS. The active agent in turmeric is a polyphenol known as curcumin which is also responsible for the colour of turmeric. [1] [5] [7] [19] [20] [21] [22] [23] [24]

Additional Information: Turmeric has been used in India for at least 2500 years. It is the most important spice used in Ayurvedic medicine, and is relentlessly under the microscope of Western science.

U

Ulli *(see* **Onion, page 198***)*

V

Vanilla

Taste: Very sweet and aromatic, and instantly recognisable.

Medicinal Uses: Antioxidant, aphrodisiac and stimulant (considered addictive).

Additional Information: Native to Central America. Both the Aztecs and the Mayas used it to flavour chocolate drinks. Interestingly, vanilla was used by the Mughal rulers in India to flavour the Indian ice cream, kulfi, which was kept frozen using ice from the Himalayas. Vanilla has remained popular in Europe since the 17th century.

W

White Pepper *(see* **Pepper***)*

X

Xardal *(see* **Mustard Seed***)*

Y

Yavan *(see* **Ajwain***)*

Z

Zafraan *(see* **Saffron***)*

Zeera *(see* **Cumin***)*

References

[1] Phytochemicals derived from spices such as turmeric, chilli, cloves, ginger, cumin, anise, fennel, basil and garlic have been found to interrupt a variety of diseases, including cancer, atherosclerosis, myocardial infarction, diabetes, allergies, asthma, arthritis, Crohn's disease, osteoporosis, psoriasis, septic shock and AIDS. Therefore providing "reasoning for seasoning". **Bharat B. Aggarwal, Ph.D. Ransom Horne, Jr., Professor of Cancer Research, Professor of Cancer Medicine (Biochemistry) and Chief, Cytokine Research Laboratory, Department of Experimental Therapeutics, The University of Texas: MD Anderson Cancer Center, Houston, US.**

[2] Nigella and its oil have traditionally been used for the treatment of rheumatism and other inflammatory diseases. Thymoquinone (TQ) has been proposed to be one of the major active components contained within nigella contributing to the effectiveness in treating inflammatory diseases. In laboratory tests, TQ extracted from nigella has proven as a very potent drug in treating inflammatory diseases. The pharmacological properties of nigella oil support the traditional use of nigella and its derived products as a treatment for rheumatism and related inflammatory diseases. **Peter Houghton, Emeritus Professor in Pharmacognosy, Department of Pharmacy, King's College London.**

[3] Information published by Nutrient Data Laboratory, Agricultural Research Service, US Department of Agriculture (USDA) – 2007 and ORAC Values. Sourced from **www.usda.gov** and **www.oracvalues.com**

[4] In traditional medical systems, the ability of spices to heal various physical, mental and emotional problems has widely been reported. With this view, analysis was performed on 21 spices. It was found that asafoetida, bishop's weed, black mustard, cardamom, cinnamon, coriander, clove, curry leaf, cumin, dill, fennel, fenugreek, garlic, ginger, onion and saffron contained considerable antibacterial, anti-inflammatory and antifungal properties. **U.P. Singh, Department of Mycology and Plant Pathology, Institute of Agricultural Sciences, Banaras Hindu University, India.**

[5] The antimicrobial effects of spices and herbs from 18 plant species were examined on a food borne pathogen, Vibrio parahaemolyticus. Basil, cloves, garlic and turmeric exhibited antibacterial activities. These results suggest that the spices and herbs can be practical for protecting seafood from the risk of contamination by V. Parahaemolyticus. **Dr. Yutaka Yano, Seafood Safety Section, National Research Institute of Fisheries Science, Yokohama, Japan.**

[6] Essential oils of cardamom and ginger were tested for antibacterial effects towards E. Coli, Staphylococcus aureus, Bacillus cereus and Listeria monocytogenes. Essential oil of cardamom could inhibit growth of all the tested bacteria. Essential oil of ginger had the highest efficiency against the three positive strains of bacteria (S. Aureus, B. Cereus, L. Monocytogenes). **Krittika Norajit, School of Bioresources and Technology, King Mongkut's University of Technology Thonburi, Bangkok, Thailand.**

[7] Under laboratory conditions, 25 plants were tested for their bactericidal activity against Helicobacter pylori which is strongly linked to the development of gastric ulcers and stomach cancer. Among the plants that killed H. Pylori, turmeric was the most efficient, followed by cumin, ginger and chilli. **O'Mahony, R. et al, World J Gastroenterol. 2005; 11(47):7499-507. Centre for Infectious Diseases and International Health, Royal Free and University College London Medical School.**

[8] 17 spice and medicinal plant extracts were examined for their antimicrobial activity against Arcobacter butzleri, A. Cryaerophilus, and A. Skirrowii. Cinnamon extract showed strong and enhanced antibacterial activity. **Libor Červenka, Department of Analytical Chemistry, Faculty of Chemical Technology, University of Pardubice, Czech Republic.**

[9] A few essential oils were tested against food poisoning, spoilage fungi, plant and animal pathogens. Cinnamon oil showed the strongest antifungal activity. **Ana Simic, Institute of Botany, Faculty of Biology, University of Belgrade, Serbia and Montenegro.**

[10] The oils of black pepper, clove and nutmeg were assessed for antibacterial activity against 25 genera of bacteria. These included animal and plant pathogens, food poisoning and spoilage bacteria. The volatile oils exhibited considerable inhibitory effects against all the organisms under test while major components demonstrated various degrees of growth inhibition. **Dr. Mike Smith, Aromatic and Medicinal Plant Group, Scottish Agricultural College.**

[11] The extracts of 12 plants selected on the basis of the folk-medicine reports were examined for their antibacterial effects against eight pathogenic bacteria. Clove extract proved to be the most effective against the bacteria tested. **Prof. M. Larhsin, University Cadi Ayyad, Laboratory of Medicinal Plants and Phytochemistry, Department of Biology, Faculty of Sciences Semlalia, Marrakech, Morocco.**

[12] The clinical applications of benzodiazepines, such as diazepam, as anti-anxiety drugs are limited by their unwanted side effects. Therefore, the development of new pharmacological agents is well justified. Among medicinal plants, coriander has been recommended for relief of anxiety in traditional Iranian folk medicine. Under laboratory test conditions, coriander extract has proven to have an anti-anxiety effect and may have potential sedative and muscle relaxant effects. **M Emamghoreishi, Department of Pharmacology, Medical School, Shiraz University of Medical Sciences, Iran.**

[13] The essential oil extracted from cumin seeds has been proven to be very effective against all tested bacteria. Cumin oil is equally or more effective when compared with standard antibiotics. **Prof. Gurdip Singh, Emeritus Scientist (CSIR), Department of Chemistry DDU Gorakhpur University, India.**

[14] Under test conditions, dill extract exhibited antibacterial activity against a panel of rapidly growing mycobacteria known to cause tuberculosis and leprosy. **Professor Simon Gibbons, Department of Pharmaceutical and Biological Chemistry, Centre for Pharmacognosy and Phytotherapy, The School of Pharmacy, University of London.**

Indian Superfood

[15] The inhibitory effect of 30 plant oils was evaluated against a strain of Candida which is highly resistant to the antifungal drug fluconazole. Eucalyptus and peppermint tested to be most active. The substantial antifungal activity shown by these plant oils suggests their potential against infections caused by Candida.

Dr. Vishnu Agarwal, Motilal Nehru National Institute of Technology, Division of Biotechnology, Department of Applied Mechanics, Allahabad, India.

[16] The essential oil of nigella has tested under stringent laboratory conditions as a potent analgesic and anti-inflammatory drug.

Dr. Hajhashemi, Department of Pharmacology, School of Pharmacy and Pharmaceutical Sciences, Isfahan University of Medical Sciences, Iran.

[17] The antifungal activity of nigella seed extract and thymoquinone, a phytochemical compound derived from it was tested against eight species of dermatophytes (fungi that commonly cause skin disease in humans and animals). Nigella and thymoquinone inhibited fungal growth, denoting the potentiality of nigella as a source of antidermatophyte drugs and supporting its use in folk medicine for the treatment of fungal skin infections.

Salih Aljabre, Department of Dermatology, College of Medicine, King Faisal University, Dammam, Saudi Arabia.

[18] Piper nigrum (black pepper) finds an extensive application in antibacterial preparations belonging to the Ayurvedic system of medicine. The petroleum ether extract of the berries was isolated. Under laboratory conditions, all of the isolated compounds were active against Bacillus subtilis, Bacillus sphaericus, Staphylococcus aureus, Klebsiella aerogenes and Chromobacterium violaceum strains.

Kumar P, Reddy SV, Srinivas PV, Praveen B, Kishore KH, Raju BC, Murthy US, Rao JM, National Products Lab, Indian Institute of Chemical Technology, Hyderabad, India.

[19] In severe asthma and in chronic obstructive pulmonary disease (COPD) patients, oxidative stress is a major predicament. Curcumin is a polyphenol present in the spice turmeric, which can directly scavenge free radicals such as superoxide anion and nitric oxide. Polyphenols also down-regulate expression of pro-inflammatory mediators, matrix metalloproteinase's, adhesion molecules and growth factor receptor genes, and they up regulate HDAC2 in the lung. Thus, curcumin may be a potential antioxidant and anti-inflammatory therapeutic agent against chronic inflammatory lung diseases.

Dr. Irfan Rahman, Ph. D. Department of Environmental Medicine, Lung Biology and Disease Program, University of Rochester Medical Center, New York, US.

[20] Curcumin is a predominant compound derived from turmeric, it shows antibacterial and anti-inflammatory activity and is an antineoplastic that inhibits and combats the development of abnormal mass growth in cells.

Jia-You Fang, Pharmaceutics Laboratory, Graduate Institute of Natural Products, Chang Gung University, Taiwan.

[21] Turmeric has been shown to exhibit antioxidant, anti-inflammatory, antiviral, antibacterial, antifungal, and anticancer activities and thus has a potential against various malignant diseases, diabetes, allergies, arthritis, Alzheimer's disease, and other chronic illnesses. Considering the recent scientific bandwagon that multi-targeted therapy is better than mono-targeted therapy for most diseases, turmeric can be considered an ideal "Spice for Life".

Bharat B. Aggarwal, Ph.D. Ransom Horne, Jr., Professor of Cancer Research, Professor of Cancer Medicine (Biochemistry) and Chief, Cytokine Research Laboratory, Department of Experimental Therapeutics, The University of Texas: MD Anderson Cancer Center, Houston, US.

[22] Recently we assessed the effects of turmeric extract on irritable bowel syndrome symptomology in otherwise healthy adults. 500 volunteers were screened for IBS. 207 suitable volunteers were randomised. One or two tablets of turmeric extract were taken daily for 8 weeks and the volunteers monitored. During the assessment, IBS prevalence decreased significantly in both groups between screening and baseline (41% and 57%), with a further significant drop of 53% and 60% between baseline and after treatment, in the one- and two-tablet groups respectively. A post-study analysis revealed abdominal pain/discomfort score reduced significantly by 22% and 25% in the one- and two- tablet groups respectively, the difference tending toward significance. Approximately two thirds of all subjects reported an improvement in symptoms after treatment, and there was a favourable shift in self-reported bowel pattern. There were no significant differences between groups. CONCLUSIONS: Turmeric may help reduce IBS symptomology.

Dr. Rafe Bundy, Hugh Sinclair Unit of Human Nutrition, School of Food Biosciences, The University of Reading.

[23] Under laboratory conditions, curcumin extracted from turmeric inhibited the herpes simplex virus which can lead to cold sores and genital herpes.

Steven J Triezenberg, Director, Van Andel Education Institute, Michigan, US.

[24] Curcumin is an orange-yellow component of turmeric, a spice often found in most Indian curries. Traditionally known for its anti-inflammatory effects, curcumin has been shown in the last two decades to be a potent immunomodulatory agent that can modulate the activation of T cells, B cells, macrophages, neutrophils, natural killer cells, and dendritic cells. Curcumin can also down-regulate the expression of various pro-inflammatory cytokines including TNF, IL-1, IL-2, IL-6, IL-8, IL-12, and chemokines, most likely through inactivation of the transcription factor NF-kappaB. Interestingly, however, curcumin at low doses can also enhance antibody responses. This suggests that curcumin's reported beneficial effects in arthritis, allergy, asthma, atherosclerosis, heart disease, Alzheimer's disease, diabetes, and cancer may be due in part to its ability to modulate the immune system. Together, these findings warrant further consideration of curcumin as a therapy for immune disorders.

Bharat B. Aggarwal, Ph.D. Ransom Horne, Jr., Professor of Cancer Research, Professor of Cancer Medicine (Biochemistry) and Chief, Cytokine Research Laboratory, Department of Experimental Therapeutics, The University of Texas: MD Anderson Cancer Center, Houston, US.

Index

Black, **bold** entries refer to Directory listings for superfood ingredients and superspices. *Italic* entries refer to specific mentions within the text.

A

B

C

Indian Superfood

Acknowledgements

It was in 2005 when I first realised my true path would be found by indulging myself in a love of food and writing. In 2007, the concept of *Indian Superfood* was conceived and merged with an ambition to write, and wow, what a ride it's been ever since. On the way, I have met many people that have helped me on this path. And, these are the people I wish to thank now. For listening to me unconditionally and for the countless blessings I have received, I'd like to thank Waheguru Ji. For believing in me, I'd like to thank Dad, Jas, Nit, Siyar, Harjoth, Jasamaran, Balsiran, Auntie Zehra, Sarah, Masood, Manjit, Rinzi, Wajid, Kamaljit Singh, John Singh Johal, Deborah Sass, Ted Cohen, Ishtiaq Khan, Mark Stephenson, Tizer Bailey, Dame Vivienne Westwood, Andreas Kronthaler, Meera Syal MBE, Ching-He Huang, Katie Rice, Musty Aziz, Alison Kay, Wendy Golledge, Joanna Knight, Laura Jones, Claire Garnham, Fiona Macrae, Andrew Hough, Anna Magee, Himadree Bora, Rebecca Smith, Saad Bashir, Claire Sutton, Dan McKeown, Patrick Davies, Vivek Singh, Shane Safi, Cathy Glass, HE Reena Pandey Ambassador of India, Alex Wenman, Mark Diacono, Justin Dealey, Coral Kelly, Rebecca Pike, Chris Evans, Heather Holden-Brown, Anne Sheasby, Leanne Yendell, Vicky Bhogal, Pinky Lilani OBE, Zoe Chamberlain, Iqbal Ahmed, Richard Mylan, Angela Chan, Steve Johnston. Anjum Anand, for inspiring me through her originality, sheer hard work and lip-smacking food. To Bill Granger, Charlotte Rollin and the team at Bill's for their inspiration and enthusiasm which egged me on and, of course, for 'ordering' me to find an editor, and that special person being Muzaffar Shafi, who quite literally 'fell out of the sky'; I don't know where I'd be now without your help. You made it happen.

To Serkan, for taking me to that bar on the Bosphorus where my life would take a turn; to Roger, for giving me the confidence to go up and introduce myself to Lorraine Sinclair, the chef who I had just read about in Time Out Istanbul, and who in turn introduced me to Richard P. Applebaum at the Mövenpick Hotel. Thank you all for my big break. Thank you, Istanbul. Thank you Gulf Air for sponsoring my endeavours. To my agent Andrew Lownie, for being my rock and guiding light since 2005, when I first decided to follow my dream. Jon Croft, Meg Avent, Matt Inwood, Claire Siggery, Andrea O'Connor and everyone else at Absolute Press for making it a reality. My humble gratitude goes out to Lara Holmes and Aya Nishimura, who understood my concept and brought it to life with their gorgeous food and photographs.

Huge thanks to PR whizz Elizabeth of Mar and to my personal PR guru, Jon Kirk, who helped shape who I am today, as well as egging me on to run down a street outside of the Charlotte Street Hotel to accost Sanjeev Bhaskar OBE who in turn so kindly gave me the time of day that made all the hard-work even more worthwhile.

To the scientific experts who have worked tirelessly for decades to bring us priceless knowledge. Your medical researches truly shadow my work with their supremacy. Without you, *Indian Superfood* could never even have been dreamed. These people and institutions include, Prof. Bharat B. Aggarwal, Ana Simic, Dr. Hajhashemi, Dr. Irfan Rahman, Dr. Mike Smith, Dr. Rafe Bundy, Dr. Vishnu Agarwal, Dr. Yutaka Yano, Kumar P., Jia-You Fang, Kishore KH, Krittika Norajit, Libor Červenka, M. Emamghoreishi, Murthy US, Prof. Gurdip Singh, Prof. M. Larhsin, Prof. Peter Houghton, Praveen B., Prof. Simon Gibbons, Raju BC, Rao JM, Reddy SV, R. O'Mahony, Srinivas PV, Steven J. Triezenberg, U.P. Singh; King's College London, Royal Free and University College London Medical School, University of London, The University of Reading, Scottish Agricultural College, University of Michigan, The University of Texas, University of Rochester, Van Andel Education Institute, Gorakhpur University, Banaras Hindu University, Motilal Nehru National Institute of Technology, National Products Lab – Indian Institute of Chemical Technology, University of Belgrade, Serbia and Montenegro, University of Pardubice, Isfahan University of Medical Sciences, Shiraz University of Medical Sciences, University Cadi Ayyad, Chang Gung University, King Mongkut's University of Technology Thonburi and National Research Institute of Fisheries Science.

And finally, last but not least, thank you Mum, for inspiring me with your food and for never ever giving up on me. Without your unconditional support and contribution of endless man-hours to the cause, my dream would have remained just a dream. Thank you, thank you and thank you all again for helping me reach the end of the amazing rainbow that's *Indian Superfood*.